Any official changes to the publications can be found online along with the digital versions.
https://www.marines.mil/News/Publications/MCPEL/

ISBN: 9781790638086

CD&I (C 116)

Change 1
to
MCDP 1-0
MARINE CORPS OPERATIONS

26 July 2017

1. Replace pages 2-11 and 2-12 with attached pages 2-11 and 2-12. This change removes an erroneous paragraph discussing specific MEBs.

2. Replace appendix C, pages C-1 through C-6 with attached appendix C, pages C-1 through C-12. This change corrects an outdated discussion of tactical tasks and replaces it with an expanded and accurate discussion of tactical tasks. It also groups tactical tasks into enemy-oriented tasks, terrain-oriented tasks, friendly-oriented tasks, and population-oriented tasks.

3. File this transmittal sheet in the front of this publication.

Reviewed and approved this date.

ROBERT B. NELLER
General, United States Marine Corps
Commandant of the Marine Corps

Publication Control Number 142 000014 01

DISTRIBUTION STATEMENT A: Approved for public release; distribution is unlimited.

This Page Intentionally left blank

DEPARTMENT OF THE NAVY
HEADQUARTERS UNITED STATES MARINE CORPS
WASHINGTON, D.C. 20380-1775

9 August 2011

FOREWORD

First published in September 2001, Marine Corps Doctrinal Publication (MCDP) 1-0, *Marine Corps Operations*, provided a bridge between the maneuver warfare philosophy articulated in our first nine MCDPs and the tactics, techniques, and procedures contained in our warfighting and reference publications. It focused on describing the role of the Marine Corps component in providing, sustaining, and deploying Marine Corps Forces at the operational level of war and on how the largest of our Marine air-ground task forces (MAGTFs), the Marine expeditionary force, conducted operations at the tactical level. Developed just prior to, and published shortly after, the momentous events of 11 September 2001, the original edition reflected the language and operational constructs prevalent within joint doctrine at that time. Key among them were the notions of "war" versus "military operations other than war," as well as the unstated, but imbedded, belief that the ability to defeat a conventional adversary granted the ability to succeed against "lesser" foes.

Since then, Marines have successfully conducted a wide variety of expeditionary missions. These missions have included the projection of a landing force from amphibious ships in the Indian Ocean more than 400 miles inland into Afghanistan; a mechanized attack from Kuwait to Baghdad, followed by prolonged counterinsurgency operations to pacify major portions of Iraq; and numerous foreign humanitarian assistance and crisis response operations worldwide. Critical to the success of these missions was the role played by forward-postured, sea-based forces and resources that were employed singly or with others and surged from dispersed global locations. Crisis response has long been the stock-in-trade of—indeed the rationale for—forward-deployed, sea-based Marines; however, Marines have also become a force of choice for various engagement activities employed by the geographic combatant commanders to build partnerships and proactively shape what is now called the *operational environment*.

The diversity of operations, the expanded application of Marine Corps capabilities, and the changing lexicon all illustrate how our collective American understanding of the security era, our national strategy, our organizations, and our employment of military power have evolved during nearly ten years of conflict. Accordingly, this edition, which supersedes its predecessor, reflects that evolution. This publication records changes to Marine Corps organization and force posture. It discusses the use of smaller MAGTFs and other, nonstandard formations that are increasingly employed with our joint and multinational partners—especially those in the Navy and special operations forces—and how we plan, execute, and assess our expanded activities across the range of military operations. It provides concise descriptions of the various operations Marines may conduct and elaborates on the various tactical operations that Marine Corps commanders may integrate, in varying degrees, to successfully accomplish assigned missions.

Marine Corps commanders and staffs at all levels should read, study, and be thoroughly conversant with the content of MCDP 1-0. The notion that "words matter," is embedded throughout this publication, which defines key terms to ensure Marines speak a common operational language. Inasmuch as MCDP 1-0 illustrates how the flexibility and rapid deployability of our task-organized, combined arms forces apply across the range of military operations, joint and multinational force commanders and their staffs can also use this publication to better understand Marine Corps capabilities and considerations for their employment.

This publication supersedes MCDP 1-0, *Marine Corps Operations*, dated 27 September 2001.

JAMES F. AMOS
General, United States Marine Corps
Commandant of the Marine Corps

Publication Control Number: 142 000014 00

DISTRIBUTION STATEMENT A: Approved for public release; distribution is unlimited.

MCDP 1-0, Marine Corps Operations

TABLE OF CONTENTS

Chapter 1—The Marine Corps in National Defense

Expeditionary Force in Readiness 1-1
Maneuver Warfare Philosophy and Mission Command 1-3
Enduring Marine Corps Principles. 1-4
Instruments of National Power and the Range of Military Operations 1-5
    Military Engagement, Security Cooperation, and Deterrence 1-5
    Crisis Response and Limited Contingency Operations. 1-5
    Major Operations and Campaigns. 1-6
Levels of War. 1-6
The National Security Structure and Strategic Direction. 1-7
    The President and the Secretary of Defense 1-8
    The Chairman of the Joint Chiefs of Staff. 1-9
    The Joint Chiefs of Staff 1-9
    The Combatant Commanders and United States Ambassadors. 1-10
Unified Action 1-10
    Joint Phasing Model for Operations 1-11
    Multinational Operations, Alliances, and Coalitions 1-12
Roles and Functions of the Marine Corps 1-13
    United States Code, Title 10, *Armed Forces*. 1-14
    Department of Defense Directive 5100.1, *Functions
        of the Department of Defense and Its Major Components*. 1-14
    Marine Corps Manual. 1-15
Key Marine Corps Tasks 1-15
The Commandant of the Marine Corps 1-17

Organization and Structure of the Marine Corps 1-18
    Headquarters, Marine Corps. 1-18
    Marine Corps Operating Forces 1-19
    Supporting Establishment. 1-21

Chapter 2—Marine Corps Forces and Expeditionary Operations

Marine Corps Components 2-1
    Role and Responsibilities to the Commandant 2-2
    Role and Responsibilities to the Joint Force Commander 2-3
Joint Operations Conducted Through Service Component Commanders 2-4
Joint Operations Conducted Through Functional Component Commanders . . . 2-4
Marine Corps Component Commander
as a Functional Component Commander 2-6
Marine Air-Ground Task Forces 2-6
    Elements of a MAGTF 2-6
    Types of MAGTFs. 2-9
Other Task-Organized Marine Corps Forces. 2-15
United States Marine Corps Forces, Special Operations Command. 2-16
United States Marine Corps Forces, Cyber Command 2-17
Marine Corps Core Competencies 2-18
Power Projection 2-20
Amphibious Operations 2-23
    Types of Amphibious Operations 2-23
    Operational Environments of Amphibious Operations 2-24
    Amphibious Operation Command Relationships 2-26
    Phases of Amphibious Operations 2-29
Maritime Prepositioning Force Operations. 2-30
Sustained Operations Ashore 2-31
    Enabling Force 2-31
    Decisive Force 2-32

Exploitation Force 2-32
Sustaining Force 2-32
Command and Control of Marine Corps
Tactical Air During Sustained Operations Ashore 2-32

Chapter 3—Conducting Expeditionary Operations

Planning 3-1
Planning Tenets 3-1
The Marine Corps Planning Process 3-2
    Problem Framing... 3-2
    Course of Action Development................................. 3-4
    Course of Action War Game 3-4
    Course of Action Comparison and Decision 3-5
    Orders Development 3-5
    Transition... 3-5
Planning Considerations... 3-5
    Operational Environment 3-6
    Battlespace.. 3-6
    Battlespace Framework 3-10
    Battlespace Considerations 3-12
    Maneuver Control and Fire Support Coordination Measures 3-13
    Centers of Gravity and Critical Vulnerabilities 3-13
    Commander's Intent 3-15
    Commander's Guidance 3-15
    Lines of Operations.. 3-18
    Commander's Critical Information Requirements 3-18
    Information Operations 3-19
    Cyberspace Operations....................................... 3-21
Execution 3-22
    Command and Control....................................... 3-23
    Information Management 3-23

Assessment 3-24
    Planning for Assessment 3-24
    Assessment Cell 3-25
    Measures of Performance and Measures of Effectiveness 3-25
    Assessment Considerations 3-25
Tactical Tenets 3-26
    Achieving a Decision 3-27
    Gaining Advantage 3-27
    Tempo 3-30
    Adapting 3-31
    Exploiting Success and Finishing 3-32

Chapter 4—Military Engagement, Security Cooperation, and Deterrence

Nation Assistance 4-4
    Humanitarian and Civic Assistance 4-4
    Support to Foreign Internal Defense 4-4
    Security Assistance 4-5
Maritime Security Operations 4-5
Combating Terrorism 4-5
    Antiterrorism 4-5
    Counterterrorism 4-5
Show of Force Operations 4-6
Arms Control 4-6
Sanctions Enforcement/Maritime Interception Operations 4-6
Protection of Shipping 4-7
Freedom of Navigation and Overflight 4-7
Defense Support to Public Diplomacy 4-7
Exclusion Zones Enforcement 4-8
Department of Defense Support to Counterdrug Operations 4-8
Support to Insurgency 4-8

Chapter 5—Crisis Response and Limited Contingency Operations

Consequence Management..5-3

Foreign Humanitarian Assistance..................................5-4

Noncombatant Evacuation Operations..............................5-5

Strikes and Raids..5-6

Embassy Defense...5-6

Recovery Operations...5-7

Defense Support of Civil Authorities.............................5-7

Peace Operations..5-8
    Peacekeeping..5-8
    Peace Enforcement.......................................5-8
    Peacemaking..5-9
    Peace Building..5-9
    Conflict Prevention.....................................5-9

Chapter 6—Major Operations and Campaigns

Counterinsurgency...6-3

Defensive Operations..6-3

Offensive Operations..6-4

Other Tactical Operations......................................6-4

Reconnaissance and Security Operations..........................6-4

Stability Operations...6-4

Sustainment Operations..6-5

Chapter 7—Counterinsurgency Operations

Contemporary Imperatives of Counterinsurgency....................7-2
    Manage Information and Expectations........................7-2
    Use the Appropriate Level of Force..........................7-3
    Learn and Adapt..7-4
    Attack the Network..7-5
    Empower at the Lowest Levels Through Mission Command........7-5

Support the Host Nation.......................................7-5
Establish Genuine Partnerships 7-6
Successful and Unsuccessful Counterinsurgency Practices 7-6

Chapter 8—Defensive Operations

Organization of the Defense 8-2
Deep Area...8-2
Close Area 8-3
Rear Area 8-4
Types of Defensive Operations....................................8-4
Mobile Defense 8-5
Area Defense 8-7
Retrograde 8-8
Defensive Methods 8-11
Battle Position 8-12
Strong Point..8-12
Perimeter 8-12
Linear...8-12
Reverse Slope 8-12
Sector...8-13

Chapter 9—Offensive Operations

Organization of the Offense 9-2
Deep Operations..9-3
Close Operations 9-3
Rear Operations 9-4
Type of Offensive Operations.....................................9-4
Movement to Contact 9-5
Attack...9-5
Exploitation..9-7
Pursuit 9-8

Forms of Maneuver 9-9
    Frontal Attack 9-10
    Flanking Attack... 9-10
    Envelopment.. 9-11
    Turning Movement.. 9-13
    Infiltration.. 9-14
    Penetration 9-16

Chapter 10—Other Tactical Operations

Passage of Lines.. 10-1
Linkup 10-3
Relief in Place 10-3
Obstacle Crossing... 10-4
    Breach... 10-5
    River Crossing 10-5
Breakout From Encirclement..................................... 10-6

Chapter 11—Reconnaissance and Security Operations

Reconnaissance Assets of the MAGTF 11-2
    Command Element.. 11-2
    Ground Combat Element 11-3
    Aviation Combat Element.................................. 11-4
    Logistics Combat Element 11-6
National and Theater Assets....................................... 11-6
Reconnaissance Planning... 11-6
Types of Reconnaissance Missions 11-7
    Route Reconnaissance 11-7
    Area Reconnaissance 11-7
    Zone Reconnaissance 11-8
    Force-Oriented Reconnaissance............................ 11-8
Reconnaissance Pull and Reconnaissance Push...................... 11-8
Counterreconnaissance.. 11-10

Security Operations..11-11
    Screening Force 11-12
    Guarding Force..11-13
    Covering Force..11-13

Chapter 12—Stability Operations

Initial Response..12-3
Transformation 12-3
Fostering Stability..12-3
Functions..12-3
    Security..12-4
    Foreign Humanitarian Assistance..........................12-4
    Economic Stabilization and Infrastructure...................12-5
    Rule of Law 12-5
    Governance and Participation 12-5

Chapter 13—Sustainment Operations

Levels of Logistic Planning 13-2
    Strategic Logistics 13-2
    Operational Logistics....................................13-3
    Tactical Logistics 13-4
Logistic Functions..13-4
Logistics in Joint and Multinational Operations.........................13-4
Strategic Logistic Support...13-5
    Strategic Mobility.......................................13-5
    United States Transportation Command....................13-6
    Department of Transportation 13-6
    Defense Logistics Agency 13-6
Operational Logistic Support 13-7
    Marine Corps Component 13-7
    Organization of MAGTF Logistics 13-7
    Reconstitution..13-8

Command and Control 13-9
Logistic Support to MAGTF Operations 13-9
    Maritime Prepositioning Forces 13-10
    Aviation Logistics Support Ship 13-10
    Norway Geoprepositioning Program.......................... 13-10
    War Reserve Materiel Support.............................. 13-10
Other Support to MAGTF Operations 13-11
    Marine Corps Combat Development Command................... 13-11
    Marine Corps Systems Command.............................. 13-11
    Marine Corps Logistics Command 13-12
    Marine Corps Installations Command 13-13
    Department of the Navy Agencies........................... 13-13
    Naval Logistics Integration 13-14

Appendices

A   Principles of Joint Operations A-1
B   Warfighting Functions B-1
C   Tactical Tasks C-1

Glossary

References

CHAPTER 1

The Marine Corps in National Defense

> *"The Marine Corps is America's Expeditionary Force in Readiness—a balanced air-ground-logistics team. We are forward-deployed and forward-engaged: shaping, training, deterring, and responding to all manner of crises and contingencies. We create options and decision space for our Nation's leaders. Alert and ready, we respond to today's crisis, with today's force . . . TODAY. Responsive and scalable, we team with other services, allies and interagency partners. We enable and participate in joint and combined operations of any magnitude. A middleweight force, we are light enough to get there quickly, but heavy enough to carry the day upon arrival, and capable of operating independent of local infrastructure. We operate throughout the spectrum of threats—irregular, hybrid, conventional—or the shady areas where they overlap. Marines are ready to respond whenever the Nation calls . . . wherever the President may direct."*
>
> —General James F. Amos
> *Commandant's Planning Guidance*

EXPEDITIONARY FORCE IN READINESS

The Marine Corps has long provided the Nation with a force adept at rapidly and effectively solving complex, multifaceted, and seemingly intractable security challenges—so much so that "Send in the Marines" connotes both a demand for action and a presumption of success. While the general public may not be conversant with all the Marine Corps is or does, they display an intuitive understanding that whenever and wherever crises arise, the Marines stand ready to get there fast and do whatever needs to be done.

Like all members of the joint team, the Marine Corps conducts expeditions—military operations by an armed force to accomplish a specific objective in a foreign country. Each Service contributes complementary capabilities to any expedition. The Navy, Air Force, and Army are optimized to dominate the sea, air, and land, respectively. Generally, the greater the capability and capacity required to dominate those portions of the sea, air, or land necessary to accomplishing the overall objective of the expedition, the longer it will take to deploy the associated forces. Simply put, there is a tradeoff between size and speed whenever an expedition is put in motion.

While the Marine Corps may operate on and from the sea, in and from the air, and on the land, it is not optimized to dominate any of them. Rather, the Marine Corps is optimized to be *expeditionary*—a strategically mobile *middleweight force* that can fill the gaps created by the size/speed tradeoff. Usually task-organized and employed as Marine air-ground task forces (MAGTFs),

Marine Corps forces are light enough to leverage various combinations of amphibious shipping, maritime prepositioning, and intertheater airlift to quickly get to the scene of action, yet heavy enough to either accomplish the mission or provide a stopgap pending the arrival of additional forces, whose arrival/employment Marine Corps forces may facilitate.

A key aspect of *being* expeditionary is providing, in partnership with the Navy, the ability to bridge the difficult seam between operations on land and sea. Although Marines are often thought of exclusively as an amphibious *assault* force, World War II was the only time in US history that the Marine Corps was organized, trained, and equipped primarily for that one mission. Both before and after that period, the Marine Corps has focused on being able to respond rapidly and effectively to crises. Within that context, the amphibious capabilities provided by the Navy-Marine Corps team—especially those that are forward postured—have long played a critical role across a range of military operations. They assure littoral access and enable the introduction of capabilities provided by the other Services, other government agencies, nongovernmental organizations, US allies, or other international partners.

Since the end of the Cold War, our amphibious forces have employed with increased frequency to conduct diverse operations, such as foreign humanitarian assistance, noncombatant evacuations, and the suppression of piracy. Additionally, sea-based forces are increasingly prized by the geographic combatant commanders to conduct engagement activities that address mutual security concerns while respecting partner-nation sovereignty.

Many of the crisis response operations that Marine Corps forces conduct involve what have historically been known as "small wars," from minor interventions to protect US citizens, friends, or interests to punitive expeditions or longer-duration counterinsurgency operations. Marines have a long track record of success—from recent actions in al Anbar Province back to the suppression of the slave trade and piracy in the Barbary Wars in the early 19th century—in solving complex problems for which purely military solutions would not suffice. The fundamental causes of such conflicts are often a complicated combination of security, economic, political, and social issues. In other cases, Marine Corps forces have responded to contingencies or major operations involving combat against conventional forces, such as Operation Desert Storm. Still others have involved various blends of conventional and irregular conflict, such as Operation Iraqi Freedom. Regardless of the nature of the conflict—conventional, irregular, or a hybrid of the two—expeditions that require larger forces/longer duration may require capabilities or capacities not resident in a middleweight force. The ability to rapidly aggregate additional Marine Corps capabilities—often provided by the

United States Marine Corps Forces Reserve—as well as the ability to integrate capabilities provided by the US Army or multinational partners are essential enablers for the conduct of sustained operations ashore.

MANEUVER WARFARE PHILOSOPHY AND MISSION COMMAND

Marines operate in the spirit of, and are guided by, the philosophy of maneuver warfare articulated in the nine Marine Corps doctrinal publications (MCDPs), which predate this publication—MCDP 1, *Warfighting*; MCDP 1-1, *Strategy*; MCDP 1-2, *Campaigning*; MCDP 1-3, *Tactics*; MCDP 2, *Intelligence*; MCDP 3, *Expeditionary Operations*; MCDP 4, *Logistics*; MCDP 5, *Planning*; and MCDP 6, *Command and Control*. These publications constitute overarching and enduring doctrine that should not be confused with more numerous, frequently revised, subordinate Marine Corps warfighting publications (MCWPs) and Marine Corps reference publications (MCRPs), which address evolving tactics, techniques, and procedures. The MCDPs provide an overarching philosophy of warfighting with the expectation that readers will consider, discuss, and creatively apply the ideas contained therein. They do not prescribe specific techniques or procedures; instead, they provide ideas and values that require a high degree of professional competence and judgment in their application. While these ideas and values are expressed within the context of warfighting, they are pertinent and applicable not only across the range of military operations, but also in how the Corps organizes, trains, and equips Marines for conducting operations.

This philosophy recognizes that war is ultimately a violent clash of human wills with an enduring nature characterized by friction, uncertainty, disorder, and complexity. Success in fluid environments demands leaders and organizations that can understand the nature of a given situation and adapt to it faster than their opponents. There are several ways we can increase speed. First, we can emphasize simplicity in all we do. Second, we can employ mission tactics and commander's intent to decentralize execution of operations. Mission tactics is the assignment of a task to a subordinate without specifying how it must be accomplished, while the accompanying commander's intent provides the overall purpose behind the task. Joint doctrine describes this as mission command. By conveying the higher purpose, seniors give their subordinates the authority—and responsibility—to adapt their methods for achieving the task as the situation unfolds. This approach permits a faster decision cycle than the enemy's, allowing Marines to exploit the advantages of speed, focus, tempo, shock, and surprise. A third way to become faster is through experience, gained through training, planning, or actual operations, which promotes implicit and lateral communication within the organization. Finally, a commander can generate speed by positioning himself at the point of friction.

The human dimension of war is the most critical element; boldness, creativity, intelligence, and the warrior spirit are prime attributes. The warrior spirit includes not only tactical and technical proficiency, but also adherence to the highest standards of personal and professional integrity. In doing so, Marines, individually and collectively, "keep our honor clean."

Marines conduct all military operations in accordance with all applicable laws, regulations, and polices. In particular, Marines comply with the law of war, whether operating alone or with joint or multinational forces. Marines also do their best to prevent violations of the law of war and report all violations to their superiors. The Marine Corps' warfighting philosophy of maneuver warfare is rooted in the long-standing principles of war. These original nine principles are part of the twelve principles of joint operations, which are discussed in detail in appendix A.

ENDURING MARINE CORPS PRINCIPLES

The Marine Corps' core values are *honor*, *courage*, and *commitment*. From these values come the principles that help to further define the cultural identity and beliefs of Marines in the most basic terms—

- *Every Marine is a rifleman.* Every Marine, regardless of military occupational specialty, is first and foremost a rifleman.

- *The Marine Corps is an expeditionary naval force.* Marines are "soldiers of the sea," an integral part of the Naval Service—lean, versatile, flexible, and ready. Marines are organized, trained, and equipped to conduct naval campaigns on and from naval platforms or to fight in protracted campaigns ashore.

- *The Marine Corps is a combined arms organization.* In 1952, Congress directed the integration of Marine air and ground forces. The Marine Corps codified this directive in December 1963 with Marine Corps Order 3120.3, *The Organization of Marine Air-Ground Task Forces*, which formalized the MAGTF construct. The MAGTFs have unique and incomparable warfighting capabilities. They contain organic air, ground, and logistic elements under a single command element, making them integrated and self-sustaining.

- *Marines will be ready and forward deployed.* The intent of Congress that the Marine Corps serve as the Nation's "force in readiness" reflected a recognized national need for a force capable of rapid response to emerging crises. To meet this need, Marines routinely forward deploy around the globe with operational forces ready to deploy on short notice.

- *Marines are agile and adaptable.* The Marine Corps derives its agility from its expeditionary mindset, flexible structure, and ability to operate either from the sea or in sustained operations ashore. Marines can adapt quickly across an extraordinary range of military operations with the organizational design and training to transition seamlessly between these operations, providing the necessary capability to operate effectively.
- *Marines take care of their own.* The Marine Corps is the steward of the Nation's most important resource—its sons and daughters. The Corps makes Marines, imbues them with its core values, and offers them the opportunity to serve a cause greater than themselves. Marines live up their motto: *Semper Fidelis*, or "always faithful." Marines are faithful to those who fall and care for wounded Marines and their families.

INSTRUMENTS OF NATIONAL POWER AND THE RANGE OF MILITARY OPERATIONS

There are four instruments of national power—diplomatic, informational, military, and ecomonic (commonly referred to as DIME). These instruments are employed in various combinations to achieve national strategic objectives in various situations from peace to war. National leaders can use the military instrument of national power at home and abroad in a wide variety of military activities, tasks, missions, and military operations that vary in purpose, scale, risk, and combat intensity. Commonly characterized as operations, they are grouped in three areas that compose the range of military operations.

Military Engagement, Security Cooperation, and Deterrence

Military engagement, security cooperation, and deterrence are ongoing activities that establish, shape, maintain, and refine relations with other nations. They encompass the actions that military capabilities may employ in cooperation with or in support of other government agencies, intergovernmental organizations, nongovernmental organizations, and other countries to mitigate the sources of conflict, address common security interests, and deter conflict. These activities generally occur continuously in all geographic regions regardless of other ongoing crises, contingencies, major operations, or campaigns.

Crisis Response and Limited Contingency Operations

Crisis response and limited contingency operations are episodic operations conducted to alleviate or mitigate the impact of an incident or situation involving a threat to a nation, its territories, citizens, military forces, possessions, or vital interests. These situations develop rapidly and create conditions of such diplomatic, economic, humanitarian, political, or military importance that they warrant the commitment of military forces and resources to achieve national objectives. The level of complexity, duration, resources, and degree of cooperation with or support for other organizations and countries depends on the circumstances. Many of the missions associated with crisis response and limited contingency operations, such as foreign humanitarian assistance, may not require combat. Others, as evidenced by Operation Restore Hope in Somalia (1992–1993), can be undertaken primarily as a peaceful mission, but require combat operations to protect US forces, aid workers, or the local citizenry.

Major Operations and Campaigns

Major operations and campaigns are extended-duration, large-scale operations that usually involve combat. They typically involve multiple phases, such as Operations Desert Shield, Desert Storm, and Iraqi Freedom, wherein the military instrument of national power predominates in some or all phases. Some specific crisis-response or limited contingency operations may not involve large-scale combat, but could be considered major operations or campaigns depending on their scale and duration, such as the relief efforts after the tsunami in Indonesia or the earthquake relief in Haiti in 2010. Some major operations and campaigns may contribute to a larger endeavor. Operation Enduring Freedom, for example, is linked to the global counterterrorism campaign.

LEVELS OF WAR

The three levels of war—strategic, operational, and tactical—help clarify the links between national strategic objectives and tactical actions. The strategic level is that level of war at which a nation, often as a member of a group of nations, determines national or multinational strategic objectives and guidance and develops and uses national resources to achieve these objectives. Strategy involves establishing goals, assigning forces, providing assets, and imposing conditions on the use of force. Strategy derives from political and policy objectives and is the sole authoritative basis for military operations.

The strategic level of war involves the art of *winning wars* and *maintaining the peace*. The operational level links the tactical employment of forces to national and military strategic objectives through the planning and conduct of operations. It encompasses the art of campaigning, which includes deciding when, where, and under what conditions to engage the enemy in battle. The operational level of war is the art and science of *winning campaigns*.

The tactical level focuses on planning and executing battles, engagements, and activities to achieve military objectives assigned to tactical units or task forces. Tactics are the concepts and methods used to accomplish a particular mission. In war, tactics focus on applying combat power to defeat an enemy force. The tactical level of war involves the art and science of *winning engagements and battles* to achieve the objectives of the campaign.

The distinctions between the levels of war are rarely clear and normally overlap in planning and execution, while the levels of command are more clearly defined. Commanders may operate at multiple levels of war simultaneously. Small unit leaders may conduct tactical actions that align with the commander's intent and have operational and strategic consequences.

THE NATIONAL SECURITY STRUCTURE AND STRATEGIC DIRECTION

The national security structure provides the strategic direction that guides employment of the military instrument of national power as part of a global strategy. Continuing assessments of the current and future strategic environment inform the national strategy, goals, and objectives. National strategic direction provides strategic context for the employment of the instruments of national power.

The national security structure is established in public law. Title 50, *National Security Act of 1947*, United States Code unified the defense establishment and assigned roles and functions among major Department of Defense agencies, including the Joint Chiefs of Staff, Military Services, and combatant commands. The *Goldwater-Nichols Department of Defense Reorganization Act of 1986* (United States Code, Title 10, sec. 151–155) further refined the organization and division of responsibilities within the Department of Defense and features the following:

- The operational chain of command is clearly established from the President through the Secretary of Defense to the combatant commanders.
- Service Chiefs (Chief of Staff of the Army, Commandant of the Marine Corps [hereafter referred to as the Commandant], Chief of Naval Operations, and Chief of Staff of the Air Force) are responsible for organizing, training, and equipping Service forces. While the Service Chiefs are members of the Joint Chiefs of Staff, the combatant commanders are responsible for the planning and execution of joint operations.
- Chairman of the Joint Chiefs of Staff (hereafter referred to as the Chairman) is the *principal* military advisor to the President, National Security Council,

and the Secretary of Defense. While he outranks all other officers of the Armed Forces, he does not exercise military command over the combatant commanders, Joint Chiefs of Staff, or any of the Armed Forces.

- The Joint Staff is under the exclusive direction of the Chairman. It is organized along conventional staff lines to support the Chairman and the other members of the Joint Chiefs of Staff in performing their duties. The Joint Staff does not function as an overall Armed Forces general staff and has no executive authority.

The President and the Secretary of Defense

The President and the Secretary of Defense, or their duly deputized alternates or successors, exercise authority over the Armed Forces through combatant commanders and through the Secretaries of the Military Departments and the Service Chiefs for those forces not assigned to the combatant commanders. The President and the Secretary of Defense translate policy into national strategic military objectives.

In general, the President frames strategic context by defining national interests and goals in documents, such as the *National Security Strategy of the United States of America* presidential policy directives, executive orders, and other strategic documents, with additional guidance and refinement from the National Security Council/Homeland Security Council. The *National Strategy for Homeland Security*, also signed by the President, provides national direction to secure the homeland through a comprehensive framework for organizing the efforts of federal, state, local, and private organizations whose primary functions are often unrelated to national security.

The President also signs the *Unified Command Plan* and the *Guidance for Employment of the Force*, which are both developed by the Office of the Secretary of Defense. The *Unified Command Plan* establishes combatant command missions, responsibilities, and force structure, while the *Guidance for Employment of the Force* provides the written policy guidance and priorities to the Chairman and combatant commanders for reviewing and preparing operation plans and theater campaign plans.

The *National Defense Strategy of the United States of America* is published by the Secretary of Defense and outlines how Department of Defense will support objectives, providing a framework for other Department of Defense policy and planning guidance, such as contingency planning, force development, and intelligence.

The Chairman of the Joint Chiefs of Staff

In accordance with United States Code, Title 10, *Armed Forces* (1956), sec. 151 and 153, the Chairman assists the President and the Secretary of Defense in providing strategic direction of the Armed Forces. His responsibilities include—

- Presiding over the Joint Chiefs of Staff.
- Acting as the spokesman for the combatant commanders.
- Preparing military strategy, assessments, and strategic plans.
- Providing for the preparation and review of operation plans.
- Providing military guidance to the Services for the preparation of their detailed plans.

The Chairman periodically publishes *The National Military Strategy of the United States of America*, which is prepared in consultation with the Office of the Secretary of Defense, the Service Chiefs, and the combatant commanders. The *National Military Strategy* describes the strategic environment and articulates the National military objectives. Additionally, the Chairman publishes the *Joint Strategic Capabilities Plan*, which provides guidance to combatant commanders, directors, and the Chief of the National Guard Bureau, to accomplish tasks and missions based on near-term military capabilities. The *Joint Strategic Capabilities Plan* implements campaign, campaign support, contingency, and posture planning guidance reflected in the *Guidance for Employment of the Force*.

The Joint Chiefs of Staff

The Joint Chiefs of Staff are the Chairman, the Vice Chairman, and the four Service Chiefs. The Chairman is the principal military advisor to the President, the National Security Council, the Homeland Security Council, and the Secretary of Defense. The other members of the Joint Chiefs of Staff are military advisers to the President, the National Security Council, and the Secretary of Defense. A member of the Joint Chiefs of Staff (other than the Chairman) may submit to the Chairman an opinion in disagreement with or in addition to the advice presented by the Chairman to the President, the National Security Council, the Homeland Security Council, or the Secretary of Defense. In their capacity as military advisers, the members of the Joint Chiefs of Staff, individually or collectively, provide advice to the President, the National Security Council, the Homeland Security Council, or the Secretary of Defense on a particular matter when those entities request such advice.

The Combatant Commanders and United States Ambassadors

The combatant commanders exercise combatant command (command authority) over assigned forces and are responsible to the President and the Secretary of Defense for the preparedness of their command for, and the performance of, assigned missions. There are geographic combatant commanders who have responsibility for an area of responsibility and functional combatant commanders whose responsibilities are assigned in the *Unified Command Plan*.

The six geographic combatant commanders are—

- Commander, United States Pacific Command (USPACOM).
- Commander, United States Central Command (USCENTCOM).
- Commander, United States European Command (USEUCOM).
- Commander, United States Africa Command (USAFRICOM).
- Commander, United States Southern Command (USSOUTHCOM).
- Commander, United States Northern Command (USNORTHCOM).

The three functional combatant commanders are—

- Commander, United States Special Operations Command (USSOCOM).
- Commander, United States Strategic Command (USSTRATCOM).
- Commander, United States Transportation Command (USTRANSCOM).

In a foreign country, the US ambassador is responsible to the President for directing, coordinating, and supervising all US Government elements in the host nation, except those under the command of a combatant commander. Geographic combatant commanders are responsible for coordinating with US ambassadors in their geographic area of responsibility across the range of military operations and for negotiating memoranda of agreement with the chiefs of mission in designated countries to support military operations.

UNIFIED ACTION

Unified action in military usage is a broad term referring to the synchronization, coordination, and/or integration of the activities of governmental and nongovernmental entities with military operations to achieve unity of effort. (Joint Publication [JP] 1-02, *Department of Defense Dictionary of Military and Associated Terms*) The geographic combatant commanders are the vital link between those who determine national security policy and strategy and the

Service components that conduct military operations within the geographic combatant commanders' areas of responsibility. Directives flow from the President and Secretary of Defense, through the Chairman, to the geographic combatant commanders. The geographic combatant commanders plan and conduct the operations that achieve national, alliance, or coalition strategic objectives. They provide guidance and direction through strategic estimates, command strategies, theater campaign plans, contingency plans, operation plans, and operation orders for the employment of military force, which may occur in cooperation with other government agencies, intergovernmental organizations, nongovernmental organizations, multinational forces, and elements of the private sector.

Joint Phasing Model for Operations

The geographic combatant commanders commonly employ security cooperation in their theater campaign plans, contingency plans, and operation plans as the means to translate strategic objectives into tactical actions. To assist in formulating such plans, joint doctrine (see JP 5-0, *Joint Operation Planning*) provides the following "phasing model," which describes a continuum of operations:

- *Phase 0: Shape.* This phase involves those ongoing and routine joint, interagency, and multinational activities conducted to assure or solidify friendly relationships and alliances and/or deter potential adversaries.
- *Phase 1: Deter.* This phase focuses on deterring specific opponents by demonstrating the capability and resolve to apply force in pursuit of US interests. These actions will likely build upon phase 0 activities and may include a show of force or initiatives that would facilitate deployment, employment, and sustainment of additional forces within the region.
- *Phase 2: Seize initiative.* Hostilities commence during this phase. The joint force applies combat power to delay, impede, halt, or dislodge the adversary as well as to gain access to theater infrastructure and enhance friendly freedom of action. Concurrently, the joint force provides assistance to relieve conditions that precipitated the crisis in order to promote stability.
- *Phase 3: Dominate.* The focus during this phase is on the exploitation, pursuit, and destruction of the enemy in order to break the opponent's will for organized resistance. Stability operations occur as needed to facilitate transition to the next phase.
- *Phase 4: Stabilize.* The priority during this phase is on stabilizing operations, reconstitution of infrastructure, and restoration of services.

The joint force may have to perform limited local governance and to coordinate activities of multinational and interagency organizations and nongovernmental organizations. This phase concludes with the transfer of regional authority to a legitimate civil entity.

- *Phase 5: Enable civil authority.* The joint force will enable the legitimate civil authority and its provision of essential services to the populace. This action includes coordinating joint force activities with those of multinational, nongovernmental, and interagency organizations and promoting a favorable attitude among the population toward US and host nation objectives.

While these numbered phases reflect a likely sequence, activities from one phase will normally overlap with other phases and may occur simultaneously. Commanders may omit some phases or expand others based on mission needs.

The significance of this phasing construct is that it describes the applicability of military capabilities broader than simply defeating an adversary's military forces. It gives greater visibility to sustaining continuous forward operations, working with numerous and diverse partner organizations, responding quickly to a variety of emergencies, conducting wide ranging and often simultaneous activities, effectively dealing with changing operational situations, and quickly transitioning from one mission to the next.

Multinational Operations, Alliances, and Coalitions

Although the United States may act unilaterally when the situation requires, it pursues its national interests through alliances and coalitions when possible. Alliances and coalitions can provide larger and more capable forces, share the costs of the operation, and enhance the legitimacy of the operation in world and US public opinion. Multinational operations are usually conducted within the structure of an alliance or coalition. Alliances normally have established agreements for long term objectives and have developed contingency plans and some standardized equipment and procedures to ease interoperability. The North Atlantic Treaty Organization is an example of a standing military alliance. Coalitions are normally established for shorter periods or for specific multinational operations and normally do not have established procedures or standardized equipment. The multinational force formed for Operations Desert Shield and Desert Storm and disbanded after the war is an example of a coalition.

However organized, multinational operations normally involve complex cultural issues, interoperability challenges, conflicting national command and control procedures, intelligence sharing, and other support problems.

Even long-established alliances, to some degree, share in these challenges. Since unity of command can be difficult to achieve in multinational operations, commanders concentrate on obtaining unity of effort among the participating national forces. Consensus-building and cross-cultural competence are key elements to unity of effort within multinational operations.

Multinational operations' command and control processes normally involve either parallel or lead nation command and control structures. Parallel command requires coordinated political and senior military leadership to make decisions and transmit their decisions through existing chains of command to their deployed forces. Though this method is the simplest to establish, it limits tempo. Lead nation command and control requires one nation (usually the one providing the preponderance of forces or capabilities) to provide the multinational force commander and uses that nation's command and control system. Other nations' forces are then assigned as subordinate forces. Normally, this structure requires some integration of national staffs.

Multinational commanders must be prepared to accommodate differences in operational and tactical capabilities by nations within the combined force. The commander must clearly articulate his intentions, guidance, and plans to avoid confusion that might occur due to differences in language, culture, doctrine, and terminology. Detailed planning, wargaming, exchange of standing operating procedures and liaison officers, and rehearsals help overcome procedural difficulties among nations. Finally, the commander should ensure the missions assigned to nations within the multinational force reflect the specific capabilities and limitations of each national contingent. Mission success should not be jeopardized because of unrealistic expectations of the capabilities or political will of member forces. Similarly, one of the biggest dangers to multinational operations is mission creep—member nations could be placed in an untenable situation due to either their limited capabilities or their political caveats.

ROLES AND FUNCTIONS OF THE MARINE CORPS

Roles are the broad and enduring purposes Congress established by law for the Services and for USSOCOM. *Functions* are specific responsibilities assigned to the Services by the President and Secretary of Defense to enable the Services to fulfill their legally established roles. Various laws, directives, and manuals establish the roles and functions of the Marine Corps and describe its general composition and responsibilities. The key sources are United States Code, Title 10; Department of Defense Directive 5100.1, *Functions of the Department of Defense and Its Major Components* (1987, updated in 2002 and 2010); and *Marine Corps Manual* (1980 with changes in 1982, 1984, and 1986).

United States Code, Title 10, *Armed Forces*

United States Code, Title 10, chap. 507, sect. 5063 and chap. 1006, sec. 10173 detail the composition and functions of the Marine Corps. It directs that the Marine Corps—

- Shall be organized to include not less than three combat divisions, three aircraft wings, and other organic land combat forces, aviation, and services.
- Shall be organized, trained, and equipped to provide Fleet Marine Forces of combined arms, together with supporting aviation forces, for service with the fleet in the seizure and defense of advanced naval bases and for the conduct of such land operations as may be essential to the prosecution of a naval campaign.
- Shall provide detachments and organizations for service on armed vessels of the Navy, provide security detachments for the protection of naval property at naval stations and bases, and perform such other duties as the President may direct. These additional duties may not detract from or interfere with the operations for which the Marine Corps is primarily organized.
- Shall develop, in coordination with the Army and Air Force, those phases of amphibious operations that pertain to the tactics, techniques, and equipment used by landing forces.
- Shall maintain the Marine Corps Reserve for the purpose of providing trained units and qualified individuals to be available for active duty in the Marine Corps in time of war or national emergency and at such other times as the national security may require.
- Is responsible, in accordance with integrated joint mobilization plans, for the expansion of the peacetime components of the Marine Corps to meet the needs of war.

Department of Defense Directive 5100.1, *Functions of the Department of Defense and Its Major Components*

Pursuant to United States Code, Title 10, sect. 5063, the Marine Corps, within the Department of the Navy, shall develop concepts, doctrine, tactics, techniques, and procedures; organize, train, equip, and provide forces, normally employed as combined arms air-ground task forces, to serve as expeditionary forces in readiness; and perform the following specific functions:

- Seize and defend advanced naval bases or lodgments to facilitate subsequent joint operations.
- Provide close air support for ground forces.

- Conduct land and air operations essential to the prosecution of a naval campaign or as directed.
- Conduct complex expeditionary operations in the urban littorals and other challenging environments.
- Conduct amphibious operations, including engagement, crisis response, and power projection operations, to assure access. The Marine Corps has primary responsibility for the development of amphibious doctrine, tactics, techniques, and equipment.
- Conduct security and stability operations and assist with the initial establishment of a military government, pending transfer of this responsibility to other authority.
- Provide security detachments and units for service on armed vessels of the Navy, provide protection of naval property at naval stations and bases, provide security at designated US embassies and consulates, and perform other such duties as the President or the Secretary of Defense may direct. These additional duties may not detract from or interfere with the operations for which the Marine Corps is primarily organized.

Marine Corps Manual

The *Marine Corps Manual* adds two more functions. The Marine Corps shall—

- Provide Marine Corps officer and enlisted personnel in support of the Department of State security program overseas. (See also United States Code, Title 10, sec. 5983.)
- Organize Marine Corps aviation, as a collateral function, to participate as an integral component of naval aviation in the execution of such other Navy functions as the fleet commanders may direct.

KEY MARINE CORPS TASKS

In 2010, the Marine Corps conducted a formal review of the security environment, strategic direction, public law, and departmental policy and guidance to refine the organization, posture, and capabilities necessary to ensure the Marine Corps can fulfill its role as the Nation's expeditionary force in readiness. The national strategy documents describe a geostrategic context that has dramatically changed in the last two decades, increasing the importance of the global commons and shifting strategic focus to the littoral regions. Future adversaries are likely to employ both conventional and irregular capabilities in a hybrid form of conflict. Increased challenges to access and reductions to forward basing and strategic transportation complicate the deployment, employment, and sustainment of US forces overseas. Furthermore, these documents note that 21st-century security challenges cannot be solved by any single nation or by military action alone. They call for the expansion of engagement activities that leverage all elements of national power, to promote the international partnerships necessary to collectively address common security concerns.

This context demands a ready force that fills the void between special operations forces and heavy ground formations—a force that can leverage its expeditionary character to respond not only to crises, but also to proactively influence regional conditions. As a result, this formal review identified the following five interrelated tasks that Marine Corps forces must be able to perform:

- *Conduct military engagement.* The ability of the Marine Corps to conduct military engagement is essential to building partner capability and capacity, forging relationships across cultural barriers, and promoting diplomatic access. Sea-based military engagement also facilitates interaction while treading lightly on the sovereignty of the partner-nations. Forward posture is critical to providing effective engagement and ensuring rapid response to crises.
- *Respond rapidly to crisis.* Whether natural or manmade, crisis response operations alleviate or mitigate the impact of an incident or situation. In addition to those forward-postured forces, a high state of expeditionary readiness is essential to rapidly projecting additional Marine Corps capabilities in response to a crisis.
- *Project power.* The Marine Corps forces leverage and contribute to a larger, "whole-of-government" system of projecting "smart" power across the range of military operations. Smart power is the ability to selectively apply soft and hard power in combinations appropriate to a given situation to achieve national objectives. Soft power is the use of persuasive means, such as cultural affinity, diplomacy, economic interaction, and foreign assistance, to establish legitimacy and influence or attract others to align their policies, interests, or objectives with one's own. Hard power is the use of military/economic coercion to influence the behavior of others. Power projection includes joint assured access operations from the sea, as enabled by littoral maneuver.
- *Conduct littoral maneuver.* Naval forces are uniquely capable of transitioning ready-to-fight combat forces from the sea to the shore in order to achieve a position of advantage over the enemy. Littoral maneuver may be used to deny adversaries sanctuary, destroy critical enemy capabilities,

recover personnel or sensitive equipment, safeguard weapons of mass destruction or associated materials, seize lodgments for the introduction of additional joint or multinational forces, or cause an adversary to disperse his forces.

- *Counter irregular threats.* These operations involve military force, usually in combination with the other elements of power, in the affairs of another state whose government is unstable, inadequate, or unsatisfactory. Military measures may not, by themselves, restore peace and order because the fundamental causes of unrest may be economic, political, or social. Often these operations occur in response to crises under austere conditions. They are the modern manifestation of our "small wars" legacy.

Note

These tasks are nested under the missions identified in naval strategy and concept documents. The maritime strategy notes that naval forces perform many missions, but that six comprise our core cababilities. *Naval Operations Concept 2010* elaborates on these missions in a sequence designed to describe how globally-dispersed naval forces conducting an array of steady state actitivities designed to prevent war will, when required, come together to prevail in crisis response or combat operations. Forward presence enables building partner capacity while facilitating our ability to perform all other missions. Maritime security involves partnering with others to promote safety, economic security, and homeland defense in depth. Humanitarian assistance and disaster response applies naval power to mitigate suffering. Sea control and power projection are the application of naval power in fulfillment of our warfighting responsibilities. The ability of naval forces to perform all of these missions contributes to an expanded form of deterrence.

THE COMMANDANT OF THE MARINE CORPS

The Commandant has two vital functions—as a member of the Joint Chiefs of Staff and as Marine Corps Service Chief (see United States Code, Title 10, sect. 5043). His duties as a member of the Joint Chiefs of Staff take precedence over all other duties.

As a member of the Joint Chiefs of Staff, the Commandant may submit his advice or opinion to the Chairman when it is in disagreement with, or provides additional insight to, the Chairman's point of view. When the Chairman submits his advice or opinion to the President, the National Security Council, the Homeland Security Council, and the Secretary of Defense, he is obligated to submit any additional input from the Commandant or other members of the Joint Chiefs of Staff. When the Commandant is acting in his capacity as a military adviser, he may provide advice to the President, the National Security Council, the Homeland Security Council, and the Secretary of Defense when his opinion is requested.

The Commandant may make recommendations to Congress relating to Department of Defense providing he has informed the Secretary of Defense prior to the meeting with Congress. The Commandant will attend the regularly scheduled meetings of the Joint Chiefs of Staff. As long as his independence as a member of the Joint Chiefs of Staff is not impaired, the Commandant will keep the Secretary of the Navy informed of military advice given by the other members of the Joint Chiefs of Staff on matters that impact the Department of the Navy.

As the Service Chief, the Commandant is subject to the authority, direction, and control of the Secretary of the Navy. He is directly responsible for the administration, discipline, internal organization, training, requirements, efficiency, and readiness of the Marine Corps. He is also responsible for the Marine Corps materiel support system and accountable for the total performance of the Marine Corps.

ORGANIZATION AND STRUCTURE OF THE MARINE CORPS

The organization of the Marine Corps consists of Headquarters, Marine Corps, the Marine Corps operating forces, and the supporting establishment. Collectively, they form the Marine Corps total force.

Headquarters, Marine Corps

The Commandant presides over the daily activities of Headquarters, Marine Corps, which provides staff assistance to the Commandant by—

- Preparing the Marine Corps for employment through recruiting, organizing, supplying, equipping (including research and development), training, servicing, mobilizing, demobilizing, administering, and maintaining the Marine Corps.

- Investigating and reporting on the efficiency of the Marine Corps and its preparation to support military operations by combatant commanders.
- Preparing detailed instructions for the execution of approved plans and supervising the execution of those plans and instructions.
- Coordinating the actions of organizations of the Marine Corps.
- Performing other duties, not otherwise assigned by law, as may be prescribed by the Secretary of the Navy or the Commandant.

Marine Corps Operating Forces

The Marine Corps operating forces consist of Marine Corps forces assigned to combatant commanders or retained under the control of the Commandant, the Marine Corps Reserve under the control of the Commandant, security forces under the control of designated fleet commanders, and special activity forces under the control of the Secretary of State.

Marine Corps Forces

Marine Corps forces consist of combat, combat support, and combat service support units that are normally task-organized as MAGTFs. The content of this publication focuses primarily on expeditionary operations by Marine Corps forces and those elements of the Marine Corps Reserve activated to augment or reinforce them.

Within the Secretary of Defense memorandum, *Global Force Management Implement Guidance,* the Forces for Unified Commands section assigns designated Marine Corps operating forces to three combatant commanders—Commander, United States Pacific Command; Commander, USSOCOM; and Commander, United States Strategic Command, who exercise combatant command (command authority) through Commander, United States Marine Corps Forces, Pacific (MARFORPAC); Commander, United States Marine Corps Forces, Special Operations Command (MARSOC); and Commander, United States Marine Corps Forces, Strategic Command, respectively.

The remaining Marine Corps forces are under Service control, which the Commandant exercises through the Commander, United States Marine Corps Forces Command (MARFORCOM). In that capacity Commander, MARFORCOM provides forces to the combatant commanders when tasked through the Global Force Management process.

Whether assigned to a combatant commander or retained under Service control, Marine Corps forces are apportioned to the geographic combatant commanders to plan for contingencies and are provided to these unified combatant commands when directed by the Secretary of Defense through the

Global Force Management Process. Whether assigned, attached, transiting through, or training in a geographic combatant commander's area of responsibility, a Marine Corps component commander commands those forces. He is responsible for—

- Training and preparing Marine Corps forces for operational commitment commensurate with the strategic situation and the combatant commander's requirements.
- Advising the combatant commander on the proper employment of Marine Corps forces, participating in associated planning, and accomplishing such operational missions as may be assigned.
- Providing Service administration, discipline, intelligence, and operational support for assigned forces.
- Identifying requirements for support from the Marine Corps supporting establishment.
- Performing such other duties as may be directed.

Marine Corps Reserve

The Marine Corps Reserve consists of the Ready Reserve, the Retired Reserve, and the Standby Reserve.

The Ready Reserve's personnel are liable for active duty in time of war or national emergency as proclaimed by the President, declared by Congress, or when otherwise authorized by law. Included in the Ready Reserve are the Selected Reserve and the Individual Ready Reserve:

- The Selected Reserve consists of Marine Corps Forces Reserve units and personnel assigned to individual mobilization augmention billets who are required to participate in inactive duty training periods and annual training. Also classified as Selected Reserves are those Active Reservists who serve on full time active duty to support the training and administration of the reserves. These units at the regiment/group level and below are deployable formations that generally mirror their Active Component counterparts in structure, capability, and operational readiness. (Headquarters above the regiment/group level perform administrative duties.) With the exception of a few unique capabilities that are typically employed during major operations and campaigns, Reserve Component units are indistinguishable from those of the Active Component with regard to the range of missions they are capable of performing. They can augment or reinforce MAGTFs primarily composed of Active Component units or task-organize into MAGTFs composed entirely of Reserve Component units.

- The Individual Ready Reserve generally consists of Marines who have recently served in the active forces or Selected Marine Corps Reserve and have a period of obligated service remaining on their contract. Members of the Delayed Entry Program also belong to the Individual Ready Reserve. The Retired Reserve includes reservists who are retired under various laws and regulations. Retired Reserves may be mobilized under conditions similar to those for Standby Reserve mobilization.

The Standby Reserve is composed of Marines not in the Ready or Retired Reserve who are subject to recall to active duty in time of war or a national emergency as declared by Congress.

Security Forces

The Marine Corps Security Force Regiment provides armed antiterrorism and physical security trained forces to designated naval installations, vessels, or units. Fleet antiterrorism security team companies provide fleet commanders with forward-deployed fleet antiterrorism security team platoons for responsive, short-term security augmentation of installations, ships, or vital naval and national assets when force protection conditions exceed the capabilities of the permanent security forces. Marine Corps Security Force companies operate under the operational control of the designated Navy commanding officer and under the administrative control of the Commandant through Commander, MARFORCOM.

Special Activity Forces

Special activity forces provide security and services or perform other special duties for agencies other than the Department of the Navy. Assignment of the missions of these forces and the personnel to them are specified by the supported agency and approved by the Commandant. For example, detachments from the Marine Corps Embassy Security Group guard foreign service posts throughout the world. Marines belonging to these security guard detachments provide internal security services to selected Department of State embassies, consulates, and legations. They prevent the compromise of classified material and equipment and protect United States citizens and government property. Marine security guard detachments operate under the operational control of the Secretary of State and under the administrative control of the Commandant.

Supporting Establishment

The supporting establishment assists in the training, sustainment, equipping, and embarkation of deploying forces. The supporting establishment includes—

- Marine Corps bases.
- Marine Corps air stations.

- Individual training installations.
- Special supporting activities.

The supporting establishment is vital to the success of the Marine Corps. Bases and stations of the supporting establishment manage the training areas, ranges, and the modeling and simulation facilities necessary to prepare Marines and their units for operations. These posts serve as training, staging, and marshalling areas for deploying units and are the foundation for a responsive replacement, supply, and equipment pipeline into the area of operations.

The Marines, Sailors, and civilians of the supporting establishment are true partners with the Marine Corps operating forces in accomplishing the mission. Bases and stations of the supporting establishment also provide facilities and support to the families of deployed Marines, allowing Marines to concentrate fully on their demanding missions without undue concern for the welfare of their families.

CHAPTER 2

Marine Corps Forces and Expeditionary Operations

> *"We are by our nature 'expeditionary.' This means several things. It means a high state of readiness; we can go at a moment's notice. It means our organization, our equipment, our structure are designed to allow us to deploy very efficiently . . . It's a mind-set, too, about being ready to go, about being ready to be deployed, and about flexibility. We can easily and quickly move from fighting to humanitarian operations."*
>
> General Tony Zinni
> Battle Ready

MARINE CORPS COMPONENTS

Marine Corps forces normally conduct operations as part of a joint force, which consists of significant elements, assigned or attached, from two or more Military Departments operating under a single commander. As noted in JP 1, *Doctrine for the Armed Forces of the United States*, and JP 3-0, *Joint Operations*, joint forces are established at three levels—unified combatant commands, subordinate unified commands, or joint task forces. While the terms combatant commander and geographic combatant commander are used in reference to the commanders of unified combatant commands, the broader term of joint force commander is applicable at all three levels.

A joint force commander may organize his forces and conduct operations through Service components, functional components, or a combination of the two. While each joint force commander defines the authority and responsibilities of the Service and functional component commanders, he must also consider Service-specific administrative and logistic responsibilities. In accordance with joint doctrine, a joint force commander should allow Service tactical and operational assets to function generally as they were designed, trained, and equipped. Regardless of the level of the joint force or how a joint force commander organizes his force, if Marine Corps forces are assigned, there is always a Marine Corps Service component. There are two levels of Marine Corps components—a Marine Corps component under a unified command and a Marine Corps component under a subordinate unified command or a joint task force. The Marine Corps component commander deals directly with the joint force commander in matters affecting Marine Corps forces (see fig. 2-1 on page 2-2).

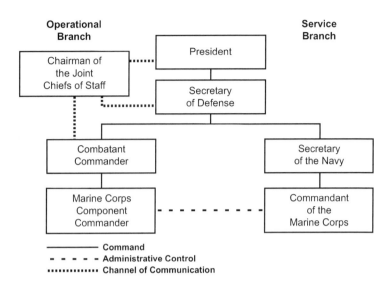

Figure 2-1. Chains of Command and Command Relationships.

Role and Responsibilities to the Commandant

Each Marine Corps component commander is responsible for and accountable to the Commandant for the internal discipline, training, and administration of his forces. Component commander responsibilities specifically include—

- Internal discipline and administration.
- Training in Marine Corps doctrine, tactics, techniques, and procedures.
- Sustainment functions normal to the command, except as otherwise directed by higher authority.
- Service intelligence matters and oversight of intelligence activities according to current laws, policies, and directives.

While the Marine Corps component commander responds to the joint force commander in the operational chain of command, his component is equipped, staffed, and supported by the Commandant through the Service chain of command. The Commandant's relationship with the Marine Corps component commander is through the Service chain—not the operational chain. Unless otherwise directed by the combatant commander, the Marine Corps component commander communicates through the combatant command on those matters over which the combatant commander exercises combatant command (command authority) or directive authority. On Service-specific matters, such as personnel, administration, and unit training, the Marine Corps component commander normally communicates directly with the Commandant. For example, the component commander may provide input to the Commandant regarding the organization, training, and equipping of Marine Corps forces in order to support the combatant commander's operational requirements. When communicating with the Commandant, the component commander informs the combatant commander as that officer directs.

Role and Responsibilities to the Joint Force Commander

A joint force commander conducts a campaign through a series of related operations. He conducts his campaign by assigning component commanders missions that accomplish strategic and operational objectives. The orientation of the Marine Corps component commander is *normally* at the operational level of war, advising the joint force commander regarding the employment of Marine Corps forces. Commanders of MAGTFs or other task-organized forces are *normally* focused at the tactical level as shown in figure 2-2. Naturally, there is some overlap. The Marine Corps component commander is normally responsible to set the conditions for Marine Corps tactical operations. These operations include military actions executed by the MAGTF, which may include other assigned or attached Marine Corps forces and assigned or attached forces from other Services and nations.

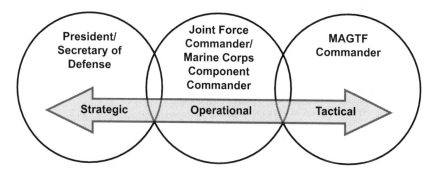

Figure 2-2. Commander's Level of War Orientation.

JOINT OPERATIONS CONDUCTED THROUGH SERVICE COMPONENT COMMANDERS

A joint force commander may conduct operations through the Service component commanders, which has advantages, including clear and uncomplicated command lines. This relationship is appropriate when stability, continuity, economy, ease of long-range planning, and scope of operations dictate preserving the organizational integrity of Service forces. These conditions apply when most of the required functions in a particular domain are unique to a single-Service force or when Service force capabilities or responsibilities do not significantly overlap. In addition, Service component commands provide administrative and logistic support for their forces in a joint operation.

When the joint force commander conducts joint operations through Service component commanders, the Marine Corps component commander and the other Service component commanders have command—operational control and administrative control—of their assigned Service forces. The joint force commander may also establish a support relationship (supporting/supported) between Service components to facilitate operations. Support—which can be general, mutual, direct, or close—is a command authority. A superior commander establishes a support relationship between subordinate commanders and determines when one should aid, protect, complement, or sustain the other.

JOINT OPERATIONS CONDUCTED THROUGH FUNCTIONAL COMPONENT COMMANDERS

A joint force commander may conduct operations through functional components or employ them primarily to coordinate selected functions. Functional components may be established across the range of military operations to perform operational missions of short or extended duration. They can be appropriate when forces from two or more Military Departments must operate in the same domain or when there is a need to accomplish a distinct aspect of the assigned mission. The most common functional components the joint force commander may establish include the joint force maritime component commander, joint force land component commander, joint force air component commander, and the joint force special operations component commander. Functional components are components of a joint force and do not have the authorities and responsibilities of a joint force. Regardless of how the joint force commander organizes his assigned or attached forces, the Marine Corps component provides administrative and logistic support for the assigned or attached Marine Corps forces as in figure 2-3.

When the joint force commander centralizes direction and control of certain functions or types of joint operations under functional component commanders, he must establish the command relationships. The joint force commander must designate the military capability made available for tasking by the functional component commander and the appropriate command relationships the functional component commander will exercise. The functional component commander will normally exercise operational control over forces from his own Service and tactical control over forces from other Services made available for tasking. For example, an Army officer designated as a joint force land component commander would normally execute operational control over assigned Army forces and tactical control of Marine Corps forces made available.

The Marine Corps component commander *advises* functional component commanders on the most effective use of Marine Corps forces or capabilities made available. The Marine Corps forces or capabilities made available by the joint force commander respond to the functional component commander for operational matters based on the existing command relationship. Joint doctrine provides specific guidance regarding how this is accomplished with respect to Marine Corps tactical aviation. All Marine Corps forces receive administrative and logistic support from the Marine Corps component commander.

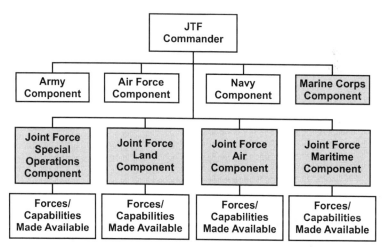

Figure 2-3. Joint Task Force Organized by Function.

MARINE CORPS COMPONENT COMMANDER AS A FUNCTIONAL COMPONENT COMMANDER

Forward-deployed naval forces, including Marine Corps forces, are usually the first conventional forces to arrive in an austere theater or area of operations during expeditionary operations. The Marine Corps component commander's inherent capability to command and control Marine Corps forces and attached or assigned forces of other Services or nations allows him to serve as a functional component commander. Such assignments may be for limited contingencies or for some phases of a major operation or campaign, depending upon the size, scope, nature of the mission, and the functional area assigned. See MCWP 3-40.8, *Componency*, for additional information.

MARINE AIR-GROUND TASK FORCES

Marine Corps component commanders normally task-organize for operations by forming MAGTFs—balanced, air-ground, combined arms formations under a single commander. Due to the operational flexibility inherent in its construct, the MAGTF is the principal organization for all Marine Corps missions across the range of military operations. Expeditionary by nature, MAGTFs vary in size and capability according to their assigned or likely missions and are specifically equipped for rapid deployment by air or sea.

Elements of a MAGTF

All MAGTFs consist of four core elements—a command element, a ground combat element (GCE), an aviation combat element (ACE), and a logistics combat element (LCE), as illustrated in figure 2-4. Although MAGTFs differ in size and capabilities, standard procedures exist for organizing any MAGTF and for planning and executing its operations.

As a modular organization, the MAGTF is tailorable to its mission through task organization. This building block approach also makes reorganization a matter of routine. In addition to its Marine Corps units, a MAGTF may have attached forces from other Services and nations, such as naval construction battalions or infantry/armor brigades.

A key feature of the MAGTF is its expandability. Crisis response may require a larger force than what can initially be brought to bear. Being able to expand the original force—rather than replacing it with a larger one—promotes continuity of operations. The MAGTF's modular structure facilitates rapid expansion into a larger force as a situation demands by simply adding forces as needed to the core units of each existing element.

Command Element

The command element is the MAGTF headquarters. As with all other MAGTF elements, the command element task-organizes to provide the command and control capabilities necessary for effective planning, execution, and assessment of operations.

Additionally, the command element can exercise command and control within a joint force from the sea or ashore and act as a joint task force headquarters core element. A command element may include additional command and control and intelligence capabilities from national and theater assets, force reconnaissance assets, signals intelligence capabilities from the radio battalion, and a force fires coordination center. A command element can employ additional major subordinate commands, such as the force artillery headquarters, naval construction regiments, or Army maneuver or engineering units.

Ground Combat Element

The GCE task-organizes to conduct ground operations in support of the MAGTF's mission. It usually forms around an infantry organization reinforced with artillery, reconnaissance, light armored reconnaissance, assault amphibian, tank, and engineer forces. The GCE can vary in size and composition—from a rifle platoon to one or more divisions. It is the only MAGTF element that can seize and occupy terrain.

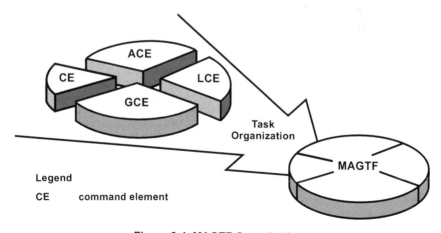

Figure 2-4. MAGTF Organization.

Aviation Combat Element

The ACE task-organizes to conduct air operations, project combat power, and contribute to battlespace dominance in support of the MAGTF's mission by performing some or all of the following six functions of Marine aviation:

- Antiair warfare.
- Assault support.
- Electronic warfare.
- Offensive air support.
- Air reconnaissance.
- Control of aircraft and missiles.

The ACE consists of an aviation headquarters with air control agencies, aircraft squadrons or groups, and logistic units. It can vary in size and composition from a small aviation detachment of specifically required aircraft to one or more Marine aircraft wings. The ACE may operate from ships or from austere expeditionary locations ashore and can readily transition between them without loss of capability. It exercises command and control throughout the battlespace.

Logistics Combat Element

The LCE task-organizes to provide all functions of tactical logistics necessary to support the continued readiness and sustainability of the MAGTF. The LCE performs some or all six functions of tactical logistics:

- Supply.
- Maintenance.
- Transportation.
- Health services.
- General engineering.
- Other services, which include legal, exchange, food, disbursing, postal, billeting, religious, mortuary, and morale and recreation services.

See MCWP 4-1, *Logistics Operations*, for a detailed discussion.

The LCE may vary in size and composition from a support detachment up to one or more logistic groups. The LCE operates from sea bases or from expeditionary bases established ashore. It may be the main effort of the MAGTF during foreign humanitarian assistance missions or selected phases of maritime prepositioning operations.

Types of MAGTFs

There are five types of MAGTFs—Marine expeditionary forces (MEFs), Marine expeditionary forces (Forward) (MEFs[Fwd]), Marine expeditionary brigades (MEBs), Marine expeditionary units (MEUs), and special purpose Marine air-ground task forces (SPMAGTFs), as illustrated in figure 2-5 on page 2-10.

Marine Expeditionary Force

The MEFs are the principal warfighting organizations of the Marine Corps, capable of conducting and sustaining expeditionary operations in any geographic environment. In addition to their warfighting role, MEFs routinely task-organize subordinate units into smaller MAGTFs or other formations to support the geographic combatant commander's ongoing engagement and episodic crisis response requirements. The three standing MEFs vary somewhat in size, with the largest being approximately 40,000 Marines and Sailors. Normally commanded by a lieutenant general, each includes—

- A command element of one MEF headquarters group.
- A GCE of one Marine division (MARDIV).
- An ACE of one Marine aircraft wing (MAW).
- An LCE of one Marine logistics group (MLG).

There are three standing MEFs:

- I MEF, based in southern California and Arizona, under Commander, MARFORPAC. The major subordinate commands within I MEF are the 1st MARDIV, 3d MAW, and 1st MLG.
- II MEF, based in North and South Carolina, under Commander, MARFORCOM. The major subordinate commands within II MEF are the 2d MARDIV, 2d MAW, and 2d MLG.
- III MEF, based in Okinawa, mainland Japan, Hawaii, and Guam, under Commander, MARFORPAC. The major subordinate commands within III MEF are the 3d MARDIV, 1st MAW, and 3d MLG.

A deployed MEF, in addition to its normally assigned units, may command units from other MEFs, the Marine Corps Forces Reserve, other Services and nations, and USSOCOM. When augmented with forces from other MEFs, a deployed MEF can have multiple GCEs, such as I MEF during Operation Desert Storm, which had both 1st and 2d MARDIVs as well as a US Army armored brigade. Augmenting aviation units from other Marine sources normally operate within a single ACE. Additional Marine Corps, Navy, and Army logistic units may

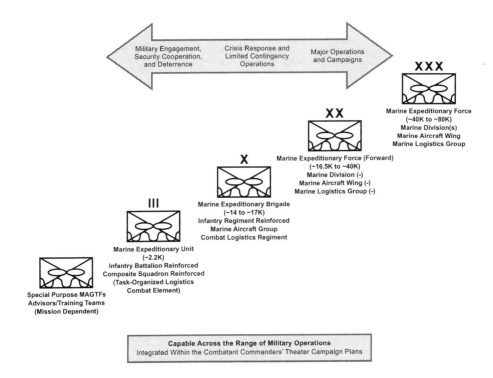

Figure 2-5. Types of MAGTF Organizations.

augment an LCE, as happened during Operation Desert Storm. Allied or coalition units may attach to a MEF, as the United Kingdom's 3 Commando Brigade did during Operation Iraqi Freedom. Given the foregoing, MEFs have grown to more than 90,000 Marines, Sailors, and Soldiers.

A MEF typically deploys by echelon with 60 days of sustainment, which can be extended through external support from other Services or a host nation. The MEF commander and his staff can form the nucleus for a joint task force, combined task force, or functional component headquarters.

Marine Expeditionary Force (Forward)

A MEF (Fwd) is normally the lead echelon of a MEF or, for some contingencies, it can be a stand alone MAGTF capable of sustained expeditionary operations. A MEF (Fwd) is normally smaller than a MEF and larger than a MEB. For example, a MEF (Fwd) commanded by a Marine major general deployed on a rotational basis to execute combat operations in Operations Iraqi Freedom and Enduring Freedom. The GCE of the MEF (Fwd) normally consists of a division (-) or multiple regiments.

Marine Expeditionary Brigade

Mid-sized MAGTFs, MEBs conduct major security cooperation operations, respond to larger crises or contingencies, or participate in major operations and campaigns—such as MEB-Afghanistan. They provide the "building blocks" for forcible entry and other power projection operations, providing the landing forces for amphibious assault and the fly-in echelons that "marry-up" with equipment and supplies delivered by maritime prepositioning ships. During Operation Desert Shield, for example, two MEBs deployed via amphibious ships while Marines and Sailors from two other MEBs traveled to Saudi Arabia by intertheater airlift to fall in on equipment and 30 days of supplies delivered via maritime prepositioning ships. Normally commanded by brigadier generals, MEBs number approximately 16,000 Marines and Sailors once their subordinate units are assigned. A MEB normally consists of—

- A command element that may include additional assets, such as command and control, reconnaissance, signals intelligence capabilities from the radio battalion, and engineering capabilities from the naval construction regiments.
- A GCE composed of an infantry regiment reinforced with artillery, reconnaissance, engineer, light armored reconnaissance units, assault amphibian units, and other attachments as required.
- An ACE composed of a combat assault transport helicopter/tilt-rotor aircraft, utility and attack helicopters, vertical/short takeoff and landing fixed-wing attack aircraft, fighter/attack aircraft, electronic warfare aircraft, unmanned aircraft systems, air refuelers/transport aircraft, and requisite aviation logistic and command and control capabilities.
- An LCE task-organized around a combat logistics regiment. This element normally has engineering; supply; services; transportation; medical; maintenance capabilities; and landing support for beach, port, and airfield delivery operations.

The MEB command elements maintain close coordination and conduct operational planning with key joint and Service headquarters, and are capable of rapidly assuming control of forces for missions across the range of military operations.

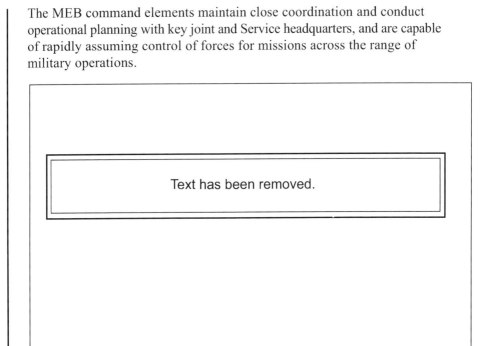

Like the larger MEFs, MEBs may assimilate units from other Services or nations and grow beyond their notional size. The MEBs are the smallest MAGTFs capable of performing all six functions of Marine aviation. A MEB can conduct the full range of expeditionary operations and may serve as the lead echelon of the MEF. The MEB command element can also serve as the nucleus of a joint or multinational task force headquarters.

Marine Expeditionary Unit

The MEUs, embarked aboard Navy amphibious ready groups (ARGs), form ARG/MEUs. The ARG/MEUs provide continuous, forward naval presence in key regions to conduct steady-state security cooperation, military engagement, and deterrence, as well as immediate response to episodic crises and contingencies. The ARG/MEUs may also be called upon to support major operations and campaigns in a variety of ways, such as enabling the introduction of other forces, acting as the lead echelon for expansion to a larger formation, or providing the geographic combatant commander an inherently mobile and flexible sea-based reserve. A MEU is commanded by a colonel. When embarked aboard an ARG, which is commanded by a Navy captain, a support relationship is normally established between them. A MEU normally consists of—

- A command element that may include additional command and control or signals intelligence assets.
- A GCE formed around an infantry battalion landing team reinforced with artillery, reconnaissance, engineer, tanks, light armored reconnaissance units, assault amphibian units, and other attachments, as required.
- An ACE composed of a combat assault transport helicopter/tilt-rotor squadron, utility and attack helicopters, vertical/short takeoff and landing fixed-wing attack aircraft, electronic warfare aircraft, unmanned aircraft systems, shore-based air refuelers/transport aircraft, and other detachments, as required.
- An LCE task-organized around a MEU combat logistics battalion, consisting of engineering, supply, services, transportation, landing support, medical, and maintenance capabilities.

There are seven standing MEU command elements. Six of them are in a rotation cycle that provides continuous forward presence with two ARG/MEUs in key regions. The seventh is permanently forward-deployed in United States Pacific Command. The seven MEU command elements are—

- 11th, 13th, and 15th MEU Command Elements, under Commander, MARFORPAC, which rotationally deploy with subordinate elements provided from I MEF.
- 22d, 24th, and 26th MEU Command Elements, under Commander, MARFORCOM, which rotationally deploy with subordinate elements provided from II MEF.
- 31st MEU Command Elements, under Commander, MARFORPAC, is part of the forward-deployed naval force in the Pacific. It periodically cruises with subordinate elements provided from III MEF. These elements include units that are permanently assigned and others temporarily provided to III MEF from the other MEFs through the unit deployment program.

The major subordinate elements are normally assigned to rotational MEU command elements several months prior to deployment to undergo, in concert with the ARG, an extensive training and certification process. They usually deploy for six to seven months, carrying enough supplies for the MEU to conduct operations ashore for fifteen days, beyond which they are normally sustained through the integrated naval logistics system. The forward-deployed naval force ARG/MEU has a somewhat shorter work-up and deployment cycle. While forward, ARG/MEUs frequently conduct multiple, simultaneous missions distributed over a wide geographic area. In 2010, a single ARG/MEU concurrently conducted foreign humanitarian assistance operations in Pakistan, strike operations in Afghanistan, and counterpiracy operations in the Gulf of Aden. In other cases, ARG/MEUs may aggregate to conduct larger operations, as they did in 2001 to open a lodgment for the introduction of additional forces during Operation Enduring Freedom. Upon return from deployment, ARG/MEUs remain in a stand-by status for 30 to 60 days, prepared for immediate redeployment in response to crisis, as happened following the 2010 earthquake in Haiti.

Special Purpose MAGTF

When situations arise for which a MEU or other unit is either inappropriate or unavailable, a SPMAGTF is formed. A SPMAGTF may be of any size—but normally no larger than a MEU—with tailored capabilities required to accomplish a particular mission. It may be task-organized from nondeployed Marine Corps forces or formed on a contingency basis from a portion of a deployed MAGTF. Regimental-level headquarters often assume the role as a SPMAGTF command element and may conduct training in anticipated mission skills prior to establishment. A SPMAGTF may deploy using commercial shipping or aircraft, intertheater airlift, amphibious shipping, or organic Marine aviation.

Frequently, SPMAGTFs have conducted sea-based security cooperation activities, such as Unitas, Southern Partnership Station and Africa Partnership Station. Others have been formed to provide sea-based foreign humanitarian assistance or military support to civil authorities or participate in freedom of navigation operations.

An important type of SPMAGTF is an alert contingency MAGTF. Each of the MEFs usually maintain an alert contingency MAGTF as an on-call, rapid crisis response force. A MEF commander may prescribe that an alert contingency MAGTF be ready to initiate deployment to any location worldwide within a certain number of days or hours, depending on the indications and warnings associated with an emerging crisis. Because it may need to deploy so rapidly, readiness is paramount. Equipment and supplies intended for use as part of an alert contingency MAGTF are identified and, where appropriate, staged for immediate embarkation. The alert contingency MAGTF usually airlifts to a secure airfield and carries its initial sustainment. Deployment by air necessitates that the size and weight of an alert contingency MAGTF be kept to an absolute minimum. An alert contingency MAGTF may employ independently or in conjunction with amphibious, maritime prepositioning, or other expeditionary forces. The rapid deployment of the II MEF alert contingency MAGTF following the 23 October 1983 terrorist bombing of the Marine Corps barracks in Lebanon is an example of expeditionary agility by a SPMAGTF.

OTHER TASK-ORGANIZED MARINE CORPS FORCES

On occasion, Marine Corps forces may task-organize to conduct operations outside of the MAGTF construct. These occasions usually occur when specific Marine Corps capabilities are required, singly or in concert with those provided by the other Services and USSOCOM, to conduct operations that are narrow in purpose, scope, or duration or to provide a joint force commander, another component, or civil authorities complementary capabilities or additional capacity.

Marine Corps fighter/attack squadrons, for example, are regularly assigned to carrier air groups in order to provide the additional capacity necessary to support rotational deployment of the Navy's aircraft carriers. Similarly, Marine Corps fighter/attack squadrons and detachments of electronic warfare aircraft operated from bases in the Mediterranean in support of allied air operations in the Balkans during the 1990s.

Other examples include the use of Marine rifle companies in 2003 to support the effort by US Army special forces to counter the Abu Sayyaf insurgency in the remote villages of the Philippines by providing security for Navy medical assistance teams. Given the geographic combatant commanders' growing requirements for similar engagement and protection activities, Marine Corps capabilities may employ from a variety of Navy and Military Sealift Command ships to conduct diverse security cooperation, foreign humanitarian assistance, and maritime security missions or to provide increased protection when those ships are transiting high-threat areas.

The Chemical Biological Incident Response Force (CBIRF) provides a scalable response capability for MAGTF operations and may provide direct support to the geographic combatant commanders. For example, CBIRF responded to the 2001 anthrax incident in the US Capitol. Whether capabilities are drawn from MAGTF assets or separate commands, task-organizing Marine Corps forces in nonstandard ways for employment in concert with a variety of partners requires the close involvement of the Marine Corps component commanders. They play a key role in identifying geographic combatant commander and other component commander requirements—especially those of their Navy and special operations counterparts—and developing innovative ways to meet them. The ability to plan, execute, support, sustain, and command and control Marine Corps capabilities task-organized with other components, including the ability to employ Marines from a wider variety of Navy ships, may be essential to meeting geographic combatant commander requirements.

UNITED STATES MARINE CORPS FORCES, SPECIAL OPERATIONS COMMAND

Established February 2006, MARSOC is the Marine Corps component of USSOCOM and is headquartered at Camp Lejeune, NC. The MARSOC recruits, organizes, trains, equips, educates, sustains, and, when directed by the Commander, USSOCOM, deploys task-organized, scalable expeditionary Marine Corps special operations forces in support of combatant commanders and other agencies.

The Commander, MARSOC is responsible for identifying Marine special operations-unique requirements; developing Marine special operations forces doctrine, tactics, techniques, and procedures; and executing assigned missions in accordance with designated conditions and standards. A Marine Corps major general commands MARSOC with a supporting staff compatible in all functional areas with USSOCOM and Headquarters, Marine Corps. The subordinate units of MARSOC are—

- The Marine Special Operations Regiment, consisting of three Marine special operations battalions.
- The Marine Special Operations Support Group, including the Marine Special Operations Intelligence Battalion.
- The Marine Special Operations School.

The Marine Special Operations Regiment trains and deploys task-organized and scalable expeditionary forces to execute special operations activities as directed by Commander, MARSOC. These activities include training, advising, and assisting partner nation and other identified foreign forces, including naval and maritime military and paramilitary forces, enabling them to support their governments' security and stability, enhance their tactical capabilities, counter subversion, and reduce the risk of violence from internal and external adversaries. The three Marine special operations battalions within the Marine Special Operations Regiment train, deploy, and employ task-organized expeditionary Marine special operations forces for worldwide missions as directed by Commander, MARSOC. The 1st Marine Special Operations Battalion is located at Camp Pendleton, CA. The 2d and 3d Marine Special Operations

Battalions are located at Camp Lejeune, NC. Each battalion is composed of four Marine special operations companies and is task-organized with personnel uniquely skilled in special equipment support, intelligence, and fire support. A Marine special operations company is capable of deploying as a task-organized expeditionary special operations force capable of conducting foreign internal defense missions, counterinsurgency operations, special reconnaissance, direct action, and other assigned missions. The Marine special operations battalion staff is capable of deploying as the nucleus of a special operations task force headquarters to provide command and control to operational special operations force elements.

The Marine Special Operations Support Group provides specified support capabilities for worldwide special operations missions as directed by Commander, MARSOC. The Marine Special Operations Support Group provides tailored combat support and combat service support detachments capable of combined arms planning and coordination, multipurpose canine support, special operations communications support, logistic support, and all-source intelligence fusion for deployments and operations as directed by Commander, MARSOC.

The Marine Special Operations Intelligence Battalion within the Marine Special Operations Support Group consists of a headquarters company and three operational companies, one of which is located at Camp Pendleton. The battalion provides mission-specific, integrated intelligence capabilities in support of special operations forces through the deployment of task-organized support teams providing organic all-source, fused intelligence collection; analysis; production; and dissemination.

The Marine Special Operations School, located at Camp Lejeune, screens, assesses, selects, educates, and trains personnel for assignment as Marine special operations forces. The Special Operations Training Branch coordinates and conducts courses of instruction that produce trained and qualified Marine special operations forces. Other Marine Special Operations School branches provide survival, evasion, resistance, and escape instruction and intensive foreign language instruction in MARSOC core languages.

UNITED STATES MARINE CORPS FORCES, CYBER COMMAND

Established October 2009, United States Marine Corps Forces, Cyber Command (MARFORCYBER) is the Marine Corps component of United States Cyber Command (USCYBERCOM). Based at Fort George G. Meade, MD, MARFORCYBER, in support of USCYBERCOM, plans, coordinates, integrates, synchronizes, and directs defensive cyberspace operations. When directed, it executes offensive cyberspace operations to enable freedom of action across the physical domains and the information environment and deny the same to adversaries.

Secretary of Defense memorandum, *Establishment of a Subordinate Unified US Cyber Command Under US Strategic Command for Military Cyberspace Operations*, dated 23 June 2009, directed MARFORCYBER, at initial operating capability, to plan, coordinate, and establish an operational Service component. The MARFORCYBER directs the operations and defense of the Marine Corps Enterprise Network; provides available offensive cyberspace capabilities to USCYBERCOM; and, when directed, plans and forms a joint cyberspace task force and directs joint cyberspace attack teams. At full operating capability, MARFORCYBER will have a fully functioning operational staff that can plan, integrate, synchronize, and execute cyberspace operations within the Marine Corps and across the combatant commands in support of US Government national security interests. A Marine Corps lieutenant general commands MARFORCYBER, with a supporting staff compatible in all functional areas with both USCYBERCOM and Headquarters, Marine Corps.

The Marine Corps Network Operations and Security Center and Company L, Marine Cryptologic Security Battalion are assigned under the operational control of the Commander, MARFORCYBER. The Marine Corps Network Operations and Security Center provides global network operations and computer network defense of Marine Corps Enterprise Network to facilitate information exchange in support of Marine Corps and joint forces operating worldwide. The Marine Corps Network Operations and Security Center concurrently provides technical leadership for Service-wide initiatives that use the enterprise capabilities delivered by the Marine Corps Enterprise Network. Company L, Marine Cryptologic Support Battalion, directed by MARFORCYBER, conducts computer network operations in support of national cyberspace operations. The Marine Corps Information Operations Center is part of Headquarters, Marine Corps, Plans, Policies, and Operations and provides support to MARFORCYBER.

MARINE CORPS CORE COMPETENCIES

The Marine Corps is a naval, expeditionary force in readiness. An expedition is a military operation conducted by an armed force to accomplish a specific objective in a foreign country. (JP 1-02) Expeditionary operations encompass the entire range of military operations, from foreign humanitarian assistance to forcible entry in support of major operations and campaigns. The defining characteristic of expeditionary operations is the projection of force into a foreign setting.

Marines, individually and collectively, possess and demonstrate an expeditionary mindset—an expeditionary culture—devoted to readiness and the mental agility and adaptability to accommodate changing conditions and accomplish rapidly changing missions with the forces and capabilities at hand.

This mindset and culture is embodied in the Marine Corps core competencies, which answers the question, "What does the Marine Corps do?" *The Marine Corps Vision and Strategy 2025* describes the six core competencies of the Marine Corps—

- *Conducts persistent forward naval engagement and is always prepared to respond as the Nation's force in readiness.* The Marine Corps is devoted to an expeditionary way of life. Marines understand that true readiness means much more than being deployable. It requires a force that is deployed with its Navy shipmates and engaged in the littorals, shaping the operational environment and contributing to the prevention of conflict. This agile force can react rapidly across the range of military operations and must prevail, even thrive, in the uncertainty and chaos of emerging crises.

- *Employs integrated combined arms across the range of military operations and can operate as part of a joint or multinational force.* The MAGTFs blend the art and science of executing combined arms operations from air, land, and sea. Marine Corps employment and integration of air- and ground-based capabilities reflect an innovative approach to warfighting. History has shown this approach is effective in missions that range from security cooperation to major operations. The MAGTFs task-organize for each mission and can employ independently or as part of a joint or multinational force.

- *Provides forces and specialized detachments for service aboard naval ships, on stations, and for operations ashore.* The Marine Corps and the Navy share a common heritage. Marines have served aboard Navy ships as marksmen, as embarked MAGTFs, as naval aviators, and as specialized detachments afloat. This heritage is reflected in Marine Corps doctrine and in the design of equipment and weapon systems. Modernization programs for the future are being designed to allow Marine Corps forces to seamlessly deploy, project power, and fight from naval vessels, austere expeditionary bases, or both. Its close association with the Navy continues today, along with a growing interaction with the Coast Guard. The new maritime strategy articulates a renewed emphasis on integrated naval capabilities and capacities.

- *Conducts joint forcible entry operations from the sea and develops amphibious landing force capabilities and doctrine.* When access to critical regions or allies is denied or in jeopardy, forward-deployed, rapidly employable Marine Corps forces are trained and ready to execute amphibious operations to overcome enemy defenses. Together, the Navy and Marine Corps provide the Nation with its primary capability to swiftly project and sustain combat power ashore in the face of armed opposition. The Marine Corps leverages available joint and naval capabilities, projects sustainable combat power ashore, and secures entry for follow-on forces. Sea-based MAGTFs provide the Nation with expeditionary forces to conduct initial operations independent of local infrastructure or in undeveloped, austere areas. This capability enables the accomplishment of amphibious joint forcible entry operations as well as various missions across the range of military operations. These strategic capabilities require focused amphibious resources and doctrine.

- *Conducts complex expeditionary operations in the urban littorals and other challenging environments.* The ability of the Marine Corps to conduct expeditionary operations, such as irregular warfare, against emerging threats in complex environments is well documented. These operations include counterinsurgency; counterterrorism; train, advise, and assist activities; and stability tasks. The complexity of these missions has increased due to the presence of large numbers of noncombatants, urbanization in the littorals, and the dynamics of the information environment. Marines are specifically trained and broadly educated to understand and achieve operational objectives among diverse cultures and populations, to thrive in chaotic environments, and to recognize and respond creatively to demanding situations.

- *Leads joint and multinational operations and enables interagency activities.* The complex nature of existing security challenges demands capabilities that harness the strengths of all the instruments of national power. Marines are well qualified to enable the introduction of follow-on forces and facilitate the integration of military and interagency efforts. This interoperability mandates the establishment of enduring relationships and the orchestration of diverse capabilities, organizations, and cultural awareness across all aspects of an operation.

POWER PROJECTION

During the Cold War, the United States maintained significant military forces positioned overseas in close proximity to likely employment areas. Since the end of the Cold War, most US military forces are now based in the United States and deploy overseas, rotationally or episodically, to meet operational requirements. The Nation's global network of bases now includes a much smaller number of main operating bases complemented by a system of more temporary forward operating sites and cooperative security locations. Overall, however, US operations overseas are increasingly challenged by diplomatic, geographic, and military changes to access, necessitating a renewed emphasis on power projection capabilities.

Power projection is the ability of a nation to apply all or some of its elements of national power—political, economic, informational, or military—to rapidly and effectively deploy and sustain forces in and from multiple dispersed locations to respond to crises, to contribute to deterrence, and to enhance regional stability. The United States has two broad military means—normally employed in combination—for projecting power overseas: air power and sea power. Air power provides a means to deliver fires, personnel (to include airborne and airmobile forces), and limited materiel very quickly. It is less effective, however, in delivering equipment and supplies in the volume necessary to sustain military operations. Sea power provides a means to deliver fires, personnel (to include amphibious forces), and resources with somewhat less immediacy than air power, but in much greater weight and volume. The preponderance of joint force materiel—vehicles, equipment, ammunition, and supplies—is delivered by sea. While air power can project a light force quickly, it is soon outpaced by and cannot compete with sea power in the projection and sustainment of forces.

Given the weight and volume advantages of seaborne transportation, sea power is the most useful means of projecting military power overseas for the range of military operations. It does so through two basic means—*naval maneuver* and *naval movement.*

Naval maneuver may be conducted from strategic distances. It involves fighting on and from the sea and projecting and sustaining ready-to-fight combat forces. It can also involve strikes on a hostile or potentially hostile shore. Littoral maneuver is a critical subset of naval maneuver. *Littoral maneuver* is the ability to transition ready-to-fight combat forces from the sea to the shore in order to achieve a position of advantage over the enemy. It may be employed directly against an objective, including inland objectives, to accomplish the mission singly; to seize infrastructure or lodgments that enable the arrival of follow-on forces; or to pose a continuous coastal threat that causes an adversary to dissipate his forces. Amphibious capabilities provide the means to conduct littoral maneuver. While designed primarily for combat, such capabilities have wide applicability across the range of military operations. Since 1990, US naval forces have conducted more than 100 amphibious operations with 79 of them involving foreign humanitarian assistance, disaster relief, noncombatant evacuations, or similar crisis response events conducted in austere and uncertain environments. Collectively, naval maneuver capabilities provide the ability to conduct operational maneuver from the sea. Modern littoral maneuver capabilities provide the ability to conduct ship-to-objective maneuver, eliminating an operational pause at the shoreline. See figure 2-6.

Naval movement involves military sealift and merchant vessels transporting vehicles, equipment, and supplies in volume over strategic distances for offload at a port or via expeditionary means, such as using roll-on/roll-off discharge facilities, causeway ferries, and/or causeway piers as part of joint logistics over the shore. Naval movement is normally employed in concert with the movement of personnel by intertheater airlift. Maritime prepositioning forces (MPFs) exemplify the combination of naval movement and intertheater airlift. This approach merges the weight and volume advantages of sealift with the speed of airlift. However, unlike naval maneuver, which projects units in a ready-to-fight condition, naval movement and intertheater airlift depend on a secure

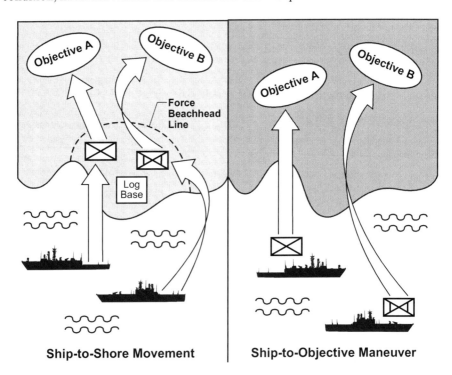

Figure 2-6. Ship-to-Shore Movement and Subsequent Maneuver Ashore Versus Ship-to-Objective Maneuver.

infrastructure ashore to deliver disaggregated elements. These elements undergo a process of reception, staging, onward movement, and integration before units can employ. Therefore, naval movement and intertheater airlift may require amphibious or airborne forces to seize existing infrastructure intact or secure a lodgment for the establishment of expeditionary facilities.

Both naval maneuver and naval movement may be enabled by naval forward presence, which includes sea-based Marines. The day-to-day operations of these deployed naval forces indirectly assures joint access by gaining familiarity with forward operating areas while fostering the international relationships that may alleviate diplomatic impediments to access. More directly, they also provide the means to overcome geographic and, when necessary, military challenges to access.

The Marine Corps conducts power projection primarily through amphibious operations, MPF operations, or a combination of the two.

AMPHIBIOUS OPERATIONS

Amphibious operations require a high degree of training and specialized equipment to succeed. Marine Corps forces organize, train, and equip to operate from amphibious ships, which are designed to project combat power. Under United States Code, Title 10 the Marine Corps has primary responsibility for developing landing force doctrine; tactics, techniques, and procedures; and equipment that are of common interest to the Army and the Marine Corps. Furthermore, the doctrine and tactics, techniques, and procedures are meant to be dynamic and evolutionary, adaptable to new technology, threats, and requirements. The primary reference for amphibious operations is JP 3-02, *Joint Doctrine for Amphibious Operations*.

Types of Amphibious Operations

There are five types of amphibious operations, following in the order of likelihood:

- *Amphibious support to other operations.* This type of support contributes to conflict prevention or crisis mitigation. It may include activities, such as security cooperation, foreign humanitarian assistance, civil support, noncombatant evacuations operations, peace operations, recovery operations, and disaster relief.
- *Amphibious raid.* Amphibious raids involve a swift incursion into or a temporary occupation of an objective followed by a planned withdrawal.

- *Amphibious assault.* Amphibious assault involves the establishment of a landing force on a hostile or potentially hostile shore.
- *Amphibious withdrawal.* Amphibious withdrawal involves the extraction of forces by sea in ships or craft from a hostile or potentially hostile shore.
- *Amphibious demonstration.* Amphibious demonstrations involve a show of force conducted to deceive the enemy with the expectation of deluding the enemy into a course of action (COA) unfavorable to him.

The types of amphibious operations apply to a variety of missions across the range of military operations. For example, a withdrawal could involve the evacuation of nonstate actors within the context of peace operations, as with the removal of the Palestine Liberation Organization from Lebanon (1982). Alternatively, a withdrawal could involve the evacuation of friendly forces within the context of a major war, as at Hungnam, Korea (1950). A demonstration could involve a show of force in support of United Nations' sanctions, as during Operation Restore Democracy (1998), or could be integral to the scheme of maneuver for a large-scale offensive action, as during Operation Desert Storm (1991).

Amphibious operations occur for the purposes of—

- Supporting operations that deter war, resolve conflict, promote peace and stability, and support civil authorities in response to crises, such as the 1999 peace operations in Macedonia or the 2006 disaster relief in the Philippines.
- Achieving operational or campaign objectives in one swift stroke, such as the rescue of American civilians in Grenada or the 1991 evacuation of the US embassy in Somalia.
- Initiating a campaign or major operation, such as the 1942 landing on Guadalcanal, which began the campaign to neutralize the enemy base at Rabaul in the Southwest Pacific, or the 1944 Normandy landings, which established a lodgment for the Allied campaign across Western Europe.
- Supporting an ongoing campaign, such as the 1950 turning movement through Inchon or the 2001 seizure of a lodgment for the introduction of additional joint forces during Operation Enduring Freedom.

Operational Environments of Amphibious Operations

In general, amphibious operations will likely be planned and executed based on one of three operational environments—permissive, uncertain, or hostile.

Permissive Environment

In a permissive environment, host country military and law enforcement agencies have the control, intent, and capability to assist operations that a unit intends to conduct. Forward-postured naval forces routinely conduct a variety of amphibious operations in permissive environments, such as sea-based security cooperation and disaster response. When conducting operations in a permissive environment, personnel and equipment going ashore may be considered a landing force, but are not normally referred to as such due to the cooperative nature of their missions. They are likely to organize by function or location of employment into one or more forward liaisons and some number of teams, as appropriate to the purpose of the operation.

Uncertain Environment

In an uncertain environment, host government forces, whether opposed or receptive to operations a unit intends to conduct, do not have totally effective control of the territory and population in the intended operational area. Forward-deployed naval forces are frequently called upon to conduct crisis response operations, such as noncombatant evacuation or embassy reinforcement, in an uncertain environment. They may also be called upon to combine with additional forces to conduct larger missions, such as the 1995 amphibious withdrawal of United Nations forces from Somalia. Furthermore, an increased number of ungoverned or undergoverned areas throughout the world are being exploited as safe havens by terrorists, weapons traffickers, pirates, and other criminal elements. Amphibious forces may conduct counterterrorism, counterproliferation, and counterpiracy missions, such as amphibious raids conducted for the purposes of destroying terrorists and their sanctuaries; capturing pirates or other criminals and seizing contraband; rescuing hostages; or securing, safeguarding, and removing materiel, to include weapons of mass destruction.

When conducting operations in an uncertain environment, landing forces will normally organize into a number of elements, which may include the following:

- A forward command element to provide on-scene command and control, to include direct liaison with Department of State personnel when required.
- A security element to isolate the objective area from external interference or attack.
- An assault element tasked to destroy, capture, rescue, or recover the intended target.
- A support element may serve a number of purposes. In a raid, it might provide direct fire for the assault force or, during a noncombatant evacuation operation, it might provide landing zone control or assist Department of State personnel in processing evacuees.

Hostile Environment

In a hostile environment, hostile forces have control, intent, and capability to effectively oppose or react to the operations a unit intends to conduct. The most common mission for amphibious forces in a hostile environment involves amphibious assaults, although withdrawals, demonstrations, and raids can also be expected. Large-scale amphibious assault provides the Nation's singular, sustainable capability for forcible entry, which is the seizing and holding of a military lodgment in the face of armed opposition. Regardless of the size or nature of the mission, the organization, capabilities, and techniques required to conduct large-scale amphibious assaults—with MEBs as the building blocks of the landing force—provide the basis for adaptation to conduct the other types of amphibious operations in a hostile environment.

Once a landing force has executed its initial mission ashore, it may remain ashore to support ongoing operations or re-embark in amphibious shipping to be available for a new mission. Marine Corps forces can provide great flexibility to a joint force commander when they are re-embarked aboard amphibious shipping and maneuver at sea to strike the enemy again.

Amphibious Operation Command Relationships

The joint force commander has the authority to organize forces to best accomplish the assigned mission based on the concept of operations. The organization should be sufficiently flexible to meet the planned phases of the contemplated operation and any development that may necessitate a change in the plan. The joint force commander establishes subordinate commands, assigns responsibilities, establishes or delegates appropriate command relationships, and establishes coordinating instructions for the component commanders. Sound organization should provide for unity of effort, centralized planning, and decentralized execution.

A landing force is a Marine Corps or Army task organization formed to conduct amphibious operations; an amphibious task force is a Navy task organization formed to conduct amphibious operations. An amphibious force consists of an amphibious task force and a landing force, together with other forces that organize, equip, and train for amphibious operations (see JP 3-02). Importantly, JP 3-02 explains that the terms commander, amphibious task force (CATF) and commander, landing force (CLF) do not confer titles or command relationships. In practice, commanders assigned amphibious responsibilities are referred to by either their command titles, such as Commanding General, 2d MEB, or assigned task force designators.

The command relationships established among the CATF, CLF, and other designated commanders of the amphibious force are important decisions. The type of relationship chosen by the common superior commander, or establishing authority, should be based on the mission, nature, and duration of the operation, force capabilities, command and control capabilities, operational environment, and recommendations from subordinate commanders. While the full range of command relationship options, as outlined in JP 1, are available in amphibious operations, Service component commanders normally retain operational control over their parent Services' forces and tactical control over other Services' forces attached or made available for tasking.

Typically, a support relationship is established between the commanders and is based on the complementary rather than similar nature and capabilities of the amphibious task force and landing force. However, it is not the intent to limit the common superior's authority to establish either an operational control or tactical control command relationship, as appropriate.

The command relationships are normally articulated in an initiating directive from the common superior commander. The initiating directive may come in the form of a warning order, an alert order, a planning order, or an operation order. Regardless of the command relationships, when the initiating directive is received, unique relationships are observed during the planning phase. The amphibious force commanders, designated in the initiating directive, are coequal in planning matters. Planning decisions must be reached on a basis of common understanding of the mission; objectives; and tactics, techniques, and procedures and on a free exchange of information. Some of these decisions are called primary decisions and are central to the planning of an amphibious operation. They may be either the responsibility of CATF or CLF or are mutual decisions of both the CATF and CLF, as shown in table 2-1 on page 2-28. Any differences between commanders that cannot be resolved are referred to the establishing authority. If a change in the mission occurs after commencement of operations or if an amphibious operation is initiated from an afloat posture, coequal planning relationships (either as described previously or as specified in the initiating directive) will apply to any subsequent planning. However, as the operational situation dictates, the commander delegated with operational control of the amphibious force may specify planning relationships to coordinate planning efforts, especially during crisis action planning under the provisions of the Chairman of the Joint Chiefs of Staff Manual 3122.01, *Joint Operation Planning and Execution System (JOPES), Volume I (Planning Policies and Procedures)*.

An establishing directive is essential to ensure unity of effort within the amphibious force. Normally, the commanders within the amphibious force will

Table 2-1. Primary Decisions for Amphibious Operations.

Primary Decision	May be in the Initiating Directive	Decision Authority
Determine amphibious force mission(s)	X	Mutual
Select amphibious force objective(s)	X	Mutual
Determine COA for development	X	Mutual
Select COA		Mutual
Select landing area		Mutual
Select landing beaches		Mutual
Determine sea echelon plan		CATF
Select landing force objectives		CLF
Select landing zones and drop zones		CLF
Select date and hour of landing	X	Mutual

develop a draft establishing directive during the planning phase to provide the specifics of the support relationship. The commanders within the amphibious force submit the draft establishing directive to the establishing authority for approval. The establishing directive normally specifies the purpose of the support relationship, the effect desired, and the scope of the action to be taken. It may also include the following:

- Forces and other resources allocated to the supporting effort.
- Time, place, level, and duration of the supporting effort.
- Relative priority of the supporting effort.
- Authority, if any, of the supporting commander to modify the supporting effort in the event of exceptional opportunity or an emergency.
- Degree of authority granted to the supported commander over the supporting effort.
- Establishment of air, sea, and ground maneuver control measures.
- Development of joint tactical airstrike requests and air support requests.
- Development of target nominations, establishment of fire support coordination measures, electronic order of battle, integration of air defense, and the role of the supporting arms coordination center.

- Development of the amphibious force intelligence collection plan.
- Nonorganic logistic support.
- Force protection responsibilities afloat and ashore.

Unless otherwise stated in the initiating directive for the amphibious operation or the establishing directive, the CATF and CLF will identify the events and conditions for any shifts of the support relationship throughout the operation during the planning phase and forward them to the establishing authority for approval. The establishing authority will resolve any differences among the commanders.

Phases of Amphibious Operations

Amphibious operations generally follow distinct phases, though the sequence may vary when amphibious forces are forward-deployed or subsequent tasks are assigned. Generally, forward-deployed amphibious forces use the following sequence: planning, embarkation, rehearsal (to include potential reconfiguration of embarked forces), movement to the operational area, and action. However, significant planning occurs prior to embarkation to anticipate the most likely missions and to load assigned shipping properly according to those missions.

Planning

The planning phase normally denotes the period starting from the issuance of an initiating directive for the operation and ending with the embarkation of landing forces. Planning, however, is continuous throughout the operation. Although planning does not cease with the termination of this phase, it is useful to distinguish between the planning phase and subsequent phases because of the change that may occur in the relationship between amphibious force commanders when the planning phase ends.

Embarkation

The embarkation phase begins when the landing forces, with their equipment and supplies, embark in assigned shipping. Organization for embarkation needs to be flexible enough to support changes to the original plan. The landing plan and scheme of maneuver ashore are based on conditions and enemy capabilities existing in the operational area before embarkation of the landing force. A change in conditions of friendly or enemy forces during the movement phase may cause changes in either plan with no opportunity to reconfigure the landing force. The extent to which changes in the landing plan can be accomplished may depend on the ability to reconfigure embarked forces.

Rehearsal

The rehearsal phase is the period during which forces rehearse the prospective operation to—

- Test the adequacy of plans, timing of detailed operations, and combat readiness of participating forces.
- Ensure all echelons are familiar with plans.
- Provide an opportunity to reconfigure embarked forces and equipment.
- Verify communications for commonality, redundancy, security, and reliability.

Rehearsal may consist of an actual landing or may be conducted as a command post exercise.

Movement

The movement phase is the period during which various elements of the amphibious force move from points of embarkation or from a forward-deployed position to the operational area. This move may commence from rehearsal, staging, or rendezvous areas. The movement phase completes when the various elements of the amphibious force arrive at their assigned positions in the operational area.

Action

The decisive action phase starts when the amphibious force arrives in the operational area. It ends with the accomplishment of the mission and termination of the amphibious operation.

MARITIME PREPOSITIONING FORCE OPERATIONS

The MPF is an integral part of the expeditionary capability of the Marine Corps. Rapid response to regional contingencies is its primary role. An MPF consists of the maritime prepositioning ships squadron (MPSRON), Navy support element, and MAGTF fly-in echelon. Together, they provide the joint force commander with a proven, flexible force that can quickly respond across the full range of military operations—from combat to humanitarian relief. Fundamental to the MPF is its interoperability with joint forces and its rapid introduction of combat forces into austere environments.

Three squadrons of specially-designed ships comprise the MPF. Each MPSRON carries equipment and supplies for 30 days of combat operations by a MEB.

When deployed together, the three MPSRONs provide equipment and supplies to support a MEF. At least two of these MPSRONs are forward-deployed in the Pacific and Indian Oceans to ensure rapid closure to likely crisis areas within a 5- to 14-day sailing period.

The MAGTF fly-in echelon and Navy support element personnel airlift to a previously seized lodgment, a benign or host nation port or airfield, or other intermediate location where they link up with equipment and supplies offloaded from the MPSRON. If a port is not available, the MPSRON may conduct an in-stream offload. A unique characteristic of the MPF is that the embarked equipment is maintained aboard ship and is combat-ready immediately upon offload.

Movement and arrival of an MPSRON, the Navy support element, and MAGTF fly-in echelon must be integral parts of the MAGTF commander's overall concept of operations in order to achieve the desired tempo of force buildup and sustainment ashore. Support packages can be tailored by MPFs to accommodate a variety of missions of varying scope and complexity across the range of military operations. Additionally, ongoing enhancements to maritime prepositioning are expanding the current in-stream offload capability for a more robust ability to conduct sea-based operations independent of local ports and airfields.

SUSTAINED OPERATIONS ASHORE

The Marine Corps also has the capability to operate independent of the sea to support sustained operations ashore with the Army or multinational partners. The Marine Corps provides the joint force commander with four options when conducting sustained operations ashore—enabling, decisive, exploitation, or sustaining forces.

Enabling Force

The enabling force sets the stage for follow-on operations by other joint force components. The amphibious landing and subsequent operations ashore on Guadalcanal (1942) set the stage for the arrival of other joint forces to complete the seizure of the island and the advance through the Solomon Islands toward Rabaul in 1943. Enabling actions are not limited to the opening phases of the campaign, such as establishing a lodgment, but may be conducted to divert attention from the main effort. An example of enabling actions is the role of I MEF in Operation Desert Storm (1991) in fixing the Iraqi forces in Kuwait and allowing United States Central Command's main effort, US Army VII Corps, to maneuver to envelop the enemy.

Decisive Force

The decisive force accomplishes the essential task required to achieve mission success. Decisive actions may include defeat of enemy military units, interdiction of critical lines of communications, or the evacuation of American and other country nationals from untenable urban areas. An example of such a decisive action is when the 1st MARDIV severed the North Korean lines of communications at Seoul, forcing their withdrawal from South Korea in 1950.

Exploitation Force

The exploitation force takes advantage of opportunities created by the activity of other joint force components. The joint force commander may exploit these opportunities through rapid and focused sea-based operations by the MAGTF that capitalize on the results of ongoing engagements to achieve decisive results. The 24th MEU served in this role during operations to seize Grenada and safeguard American citizens in 1983. While Army forces fixed the Cuban and Grenadian forces at one end of the island, the Marines landed and maneuvered freely across the island, accomplishing the joint force commander's objectives.

Sustaining Force

The sustaining force maintains a presence ashore over an extended period of time to support continued operations by the joint force commander within the joint area of operations. This force provides logistical sustainment to joint, allied, and/or coalition forces until theater-level sustainment is established. I MEF fulfilled this role in the early days of Operation Desert Shield (1990) in Saudi Arabia and Operation Restore Hope (1992–93) in Somalia by providing sustainment to joint and Army forces until arrangements for theater support were complete.

COMMAND AND CONTROL OF MARINE CORPS TACTICAL AIR DURING SUSTAINED OPERATIONS ASHORE

Joint doctrine states a joint force commander has full authority to assign missions, redirect efforts, and direct coordination among subordinate commanders. It also notes joint force commanders should allow Service tactical and operational assets and groupings to function generally as they were designed and organized, explaining that the intent is to meet the needs of the joint force commander while maintaining the tactical and operational integrity of the Service organizations. Given the unique nature of the MAGTF construct, JP 1 provides a specific policy for command and control of Marine Corps tactical air during sustained operations ashore. That policy states:

> The Marine air-ground task force (MAGTF) commander will retain operational control (OPCON) of organic air assets. The primary mission of the MAGTF aviation combat element is the support of the MAGTF ground combat element. During joint operations, the MAGTF air assets normally will be in support of the MAGTF mission. The MAGTF commander will make sorties available to the joint force commander (JFC), for tasking through the joint force air component commander (JFACC), for air defense, long-range interdiction, and long-range reconnaissance. Sorties in excess of MAGTF direct support requirements will be provided to the JFC for tasking through the JFACC for the support of other components of the joint force or the joint force as a whole.

The policy notes that sorties provided for air defense, long-range interdiction, and long-range reconnaissance are not excess sorties, inasmuch as they provide a distinct contribution to the overall joint force effort over which the joint force commander must exercise integrated control. Excess sorties are in addition to these sorties. Additionally, the policy provides the following caveat:

> Nothing herein shall infringe on the authority of the geographic combatant commander (GCC) or subordinate joint force commander (JFC) in the exercise of operational control (OPCON) to assign missions, redirect efforts (e.g., the reapportionment and/or reallocation of any Marine air-ground task force (MAGTF) tactical air (TACAIR) sorties when it has been determined by the JFC that they are required for higher priority missions), and direct coordination among the subordinate commanders to ensure unity of effort in accomplishment of the overall mission, or to maintain integrity of the force.

See JP 1 and MCWP 3-43.3, *Marine Air-Ground Task Force Fires.*

CHAPTER 3

Conducting Expeditionary Operations

"There wasn't any fuss about their mobilizing. There never is. Just an order issued and . . . one regiment after another are on their way to Cuba, or Mexico, or the world's end. Where they are going isn't the Marine's concern. Their business is to be always ready to go."

—An editorial from *Harper's Weekly*, 1912
Soldiers of the Sea

This chapter describes how Marine Corps commanders plan, execute, and assess expeditionary operations. It provides the tactical tenets that commanders consider when conducting those activities appropriate to each unique situation. This chapter links the maneuver warfare philosophy found in Marine Corps doctrinal publications with the techniques and procedures of planning, execution, and assessment.

PLANNING

For a planning process to be effective and enable the command's ability to adapt to and understand changing situations, the commander must ensure feedback loops that connect ongoing planning with execution results and other sources of information. Since perfect understanding is not possible and time is constrained, commanders must assume risk. They must act when they believe they have achieved sufficient understanding of the problem. Whether planning occurs at the strategic, operational, or tactical level, its key functions are to—

- Direct and coordinate actions.
- Develop a shared situational understanding.
- Generate expectations about how actions will evolve and how they will affect the desired outcome.
- Support the exercise of initiative.
- Shape the thinking of planners.

PLANNING TENETS

The planning tenets derive from the Marine Corps maneuver warfare philosophy. These tenets—top-down planning, single-battle concept, and integrated planning—guide the commander's use of his staff and subordinate units to plan and execute military operations.

- *Top-down planning.* Top-down planning is the active participation of commanders that drives the process at their respective levels to gain knowledge and promote understanding as a basis for decisionmaking.
- *Single-battle concept.* Single-battle is a unifying perspective of operations, which holds that actions anywhere in the operational environment can affect actions elsewhere. For example, early fires success in the deep fight facilitates rapid maneuver in the close battle, which exacerbates combat service support push over limited lines of communications.
- *Integrated planning.* Integrated planning is the application of a systemic and systematic approach to planning through the employment of a planning team that is composed of subject matter experts in appropriate disciplines to consider all relevant factors, reduce omissions, and share information.

THE MARINE CORPS PLANNING PROCESS

The Marine Corps Planning Process (MCPP) provides commanders and staffs at all levels a means to organize their planning activities, to transmit plans to subordinate units, and to share a common understanding of the mission and intent. The MCPP applies across the range of military operations. It applies equally to deliberate planning and continuous planning for ongoing operations.

There are six steps in the MCPP. While these steps appear in a particular sequence, planning seldom occurs in the same straightforward manner. Environmental factors, enemy action, updated intelligence, revised guidance, and feedback as a result of operations all contribute to making most planning endeavors highly complex and nonlinear in practice. The problem will evolve in the process of being solved. Above all else, planning is a dynamic learning process—one that improves the understanding of a situation even as the situation constantly evolves. For a detailed discussion of the MCPP, refer to MCWP 5-1, *Marine Corps Planning Process*. The six-step MCPP involves problem framing, COA development, COA war game, COA comparison and decision, orders development, and transition.

Problem Framing

Since no amount of subsequent planning can solve a problem insufficiently understood, framing the problem is critical. The purpose of problem framing is to gain an understanding of the environment as well as an understanding of the nature of the problem as a basis for possible solutions. This greater understanding allows a commander to visualize the operation and describe his conceptual approach, providing context for the examination of what the command must accomplish; when and where it must be done; and, most importantly, why—the purpose of the operation. To achieve this understanding, problem framing requires both the judgment of synthesis and the systematic study of analysis. Accordingly, problem framing consists of a commander-driven design supported by staff actions.

Design

As a form of conceptual planning, design *is the conception and articulation of a framework for solving a problem.* A design-inspired framework represents a broad operational approach conceived as a result of understanding gained largely through critical thinking and dialog—the basic mechanism of design—and articulated through the commander's intent and guidance. Design's ability to address complex problems lies in the power of organizational learning. Group dialog, when conducted within the proper command climate, can foster a collective level of understanding not attainable by any individual within the group regardless of experience or seniority. Short of direct interaction with object systems, such as the adversary or population, group interaction involving frank and candid interaction is the best way to replicate the nonlinear nature of conflicts and the actors involved.

To conceive of and articulate a framework for solving a problem, commanders must understand the environment and the nature of the problem. How a problem is understood points directly to possible solutions. For example, the challenge of insurgent murder and intimidation tactics is distinctly different—and suggests entirely different COAs—from the passive or active acceptance of the insurgents by the local villagers.

Understanding the environment is a critical aspect of design; it provides the context for understanding the problem. Critical thinking and open and frank dialog, while examining any number of factors, help expose a broad range of ideas to be considered in the identification of the problem. In the process, not only can design participants determine the relevant actors, but also the relationships between and among them. Such interactions include potentials, trends, tensions, strengths, and weaknesses. All of these dynamics help to identify the problem and suggest ways to interact not only with adversaries, but also with the population and other elements within the battlespace. In this manner, it is understandable how problem identification, or problem framing, and problem solving occur iteratively.

The problem is some aspect of the environment uniquely understood by the commander. Armed with an understanding of the environment and the problem, the commander gains an appreciation for the situation as it exists. Coupled with any assigned or anticipated tasks as well as guidance and intent from higher echelons, those conducting problem framing can determine a desired future state. The difference between the current and desired states is a catalyst in terms of envisioning a tentative configuration of actions suggested by the various ways in which the commander can interact within the battlespace.

Staff Actions

Staff actions provide the information the commander needs to help gain understanding and form his subsequent visualizations of the problem and how he sees the operation unfolding. Staff actions involve a number of activities, including intelligence preparation of the battlespace and task analysis. Commands normally receive tasks from which they use the more essential among them, along with the purpose and their understanding of the environment and problem, to form the mission statement, which is an action-based expression of the problem.

Course of Action Development

The development of a COA outlines one or more broad options for *how* the mission and commander's intent might be accomplished. Simply put, COA development and all subsequent steps are about providing options for the commander while continuing to refine the understanding of the problem. To be distinguishable, each COA must address the essential tasks determined during problem framing and incorporate the commander's guidance and intent.

Course of Action War Game

The COA war game critically examines and refines the broad options in light of enemy capabilities and potential actions or reactions as well as the characteristics peculiar to the operational environment. Planners wargame friendly COAs against selected adversary COAs through an iterative action-reaction-counteraction process. On larger staffs, a free-thinking red cell builds and "fights" the adversary COAs, while a green cell might be used to account for actions/reactions by other actors, such as host nation security forces, government agencies, host nation government, or the local population, to the friendly and enemy actions. This form of interaction introduces the nonlinear, unpredictable nature of war into the learning process, seeking to strengthen the friendly COAs. The results of COA war games include greater understanding of the problem, identification of potential branches and sequels, and recognition of required modifications to each COA.

Course of Action Comparison and Decision

With estimates of supportability from his staff and subordinate commanders, the commander reviews the pros and cons of the broad options and decides how he will accomplish the mission. The commander either approves a COA as formulated or assimilates what has been learned into a new COA, which planners should develop, wargame, and compare against previous COAs prior to moving to an approved concept of operations and orders development.

Orders Development

Orders development translates the commander's decision into oral, written, and/or graphic communication sufficient to guide implementation and initiative by subordinates. Orders development often involves additional detailed planning. When completed, the operation plan or operation order becomes the principal means by which the commander expresses his decision, intent, and guidance.

Transition

Transition may involve a wide range of briefs, drills, or rehearsals necessary to ensure a successful shift from planning to execution, subject to the variables of echelon of command, mission complexity, and, most importantly, time. At a minimum, the transition step includes a concept of operations brief along with the handover and explanation of any execution tools developed during the previous planning steps, such as a decision support matrix and execution checklist. If time and resources allow, the transition step may include rehearsal of concept drills and confirmation briefs by subordinate units. More than likely, higher headquarters will require subordinate commanders to brief their plans prior to execution.

PLANNING CONSIDERATIONS

Design does not end in problem framing. Every planning step furthers the design effort by deepening the understanding of the environment and the problem. Because the situation is constantly evolving, design must be dynamic; it requires continuous assessment of the situation in light of the mission and the changing conditions within the battlespace. The commander, based on his visualization, directs the conduct of operations by issuing orders, assigning tasks and priorities, assessing results, and adjusting as necessary.

When commanders receive orders consistent with existing conditions, planners should proceed directly to staff actions. Whenever the paradigm or the understanding of the paradigm changes, commanders will need to reframe the problem.

A commander must be constantly aware of and optimize the time each problem allows for planning. Whether planning is deliberate or rapid, the commander must display an acute awareness of the time available and ensure he accounts for the time needed for dissemination and understanding of his plan as well as the time needed by subordinate commanders to plan their operations.

Operational Environment

The operational environment is a composite of the conditions, circumstances, and influences that affect the employment of capabilities and bear on the decisions of the commander. The term operational environment was introduced by JP 3-0 to encourage a more thorough examination of the battlespace based on lessons learned from Operations Iraqi Freedom and Enduring Freedom. Understanding friendly and enemy forces is not enough; other factors, such as culture, language, tribal affiliations, and human environment, can be equally important. The term operational environment is consistent with the need to study and learn as much as possible about a situation. Essentially, commanders analyze the operational environment in order to determine the physical dimensions of their battlespace in the form of areas of interest, influence, and operations.

Battlespace

Battlespace includes areas of interest, influence, and operations. Operational areas for MAGTFs are usually areas of operations. Commanders must develop an appreciation of how conditions within the battlespace will impact and be impacted by friendly, enemy, and civilian actions. Commanders must consider how best to arrange friendly forces and execute actions within the battlespace to accomplish the mission.

Area of Interest

The area of interest contains friendly and enemy forces, capabilities, infrastructure, and terrain that concern the commander. This area includes the area of influence and those areas that contain current or planned objectives or enemy forces that are capable of endangering mission accomplishment. The size of the area of interest normally exceeds the commander's operational reach.

While the area of interest includes any assigned area of operations and area of influence, the area of interest may stretch far beyond the other parts of the commander's battlespace. The commander is unconstrained in determining his area of interest and may include noncontiguous areas. A forward-deployed MEF, for example, may have an area of interest that extends back to the continental United States during the execution of the time-phased force deployment. The commander may also have areas of interest around airbases in neighboring regions.

Area of Influence

The area of influence is that area which a commander can affect through maneuver, fires, and other actions of his force. Its geographical size is normally based on the physical limits of organic systems, such as fire support, aviation, mobility, or reconnaissance capabilities, and operational requirements identified within each of the warfighting functions (see app. B). However, actions within these areas may influence perceptions and events on a global scale. The area of influence normally reflects the extent of the force's operational reach. Because MAGTFs employing Marine fixed-wing aviation can extend their operational reach, their area of influence could be very large; however, determining the area of influence should not be based solely on the combat radius of the MAGTF's fixed-wing aircraft. The commander should consider his mission, forces, warfighting functions, and the area of operation to determine his area of influence. Understanding the area of influence allows the commander to assign subordinate areas of operations and focus intelligence collection and information operations.

Area of Operations

The joint force commander normally assigns areas of operations to land and maritime force commanders. Areas of operations are prescribed by physical boundaries and are normally large enough to allow commanders to accomplish their missions and to protect their force by employing their organic, assigned, and supporting systems to the limits of their capabilities. An area of operations is two-dimensional. Commanders of the MAGTF will need to request airspace above their assigned area of operations in order to properly employ the MAGTF.

The joint force commander or component commander normally assigns the MAGTF an area of operations. The MAGTF, in turn, will assign areas of operations to subordinate commanders whenever those commanders are assigned ground-based tactical tasks (see the list of tactical tasks in app. C). Such assignments are not limited to the GCE. Area of operations assignments can include the ACE, when tasked with screening or guarding the MAGTF flank, for example. They may also include the LCE when serving as the main effort for a noncombatant evacuation operation or foreign humanitarian assistance mission.

Commanders who are assigned an area of operations must develop their own plans for accomplishing assigned tasks, which may involve further subdivision of the area of operations and tasks to their subordinate commanders. These plans may include sizing the operation and determining their contiguous and noncontiguous boundaries.

The size of an area of operations will normally change over the course of an operation. Many factors can influence that change to include—

- Incorporating geopolitical constraints.
- Accomplishing objectives.
- Assuming a new task or mission.
- Shifting to a new phase of the operation.
- Anticipating exploitation and pursuit.
- Assuming the main effort.

Regardless of the MAGTF's size, its commander must be able to command and control his forces throughout the assigned area of operations. Commanders should neither seek nor assign areas of operations that are greater than the unit's area of influence.

A subordinate commander who is unable to directly influence his entire area of operations may have to request additional forces or assets that will extend his operational reach. Failing that, he may have to—

- Request a change in mission or tasks.
- Request a reduction in the size of his area of operations.
- Revise his concept of operations by phasing operations in such a way that he only needs to directly influence portions of his area of operations.
- Accept some degree of risk.

A contiguous area of operations is one in which all subordinate commands' areas of operations share one or more common boundaries. A noncontiguous area of operations involves one or more subordinate areas of operations do not share a common boundary. Commands with contiguous areas of operations are normally within supporting distance of one another. The commander establishes contiguous areas of operations when—

- The area of operations is of limited size to accommodate the force.
- Political boundaries or enemy dispositions require concentration of force.

- There is a risk of being defeated in detail by enemy forces or the enemy situation is not clear.
- Concentration of combat power along a single axis of advance or movement corridor is required.

A noncontiguous area of operations, shown in figure 3-1, is normally characterized by a 360-degree boundary. Because units with noncontiguous areas of operations must provide all-around security, such situations allow for less concentration of combat power along a single axis. There is additional risk for units operating in noncontiguous areas of operations because they are normally out of supporting range of each other. The commander establishes noncontiguous areas of operations when—

- Limited friendly forces must occupy or control widely separated key terrain.
- Subordinate units do not need to provide mutual support.
- Dispersed enemy or population centers throughout the area of operations require a corresponding dispersal of friendly units.

Operations in areas not included in assigned noncontiguous areas of operations are the responsibility of the common higher commander.

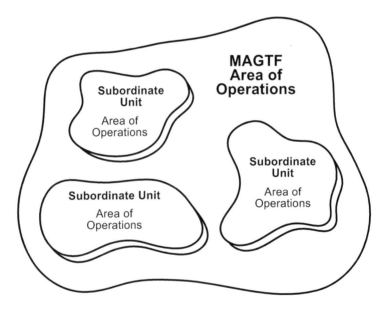

Figure 3-1. Noncontiguous Areas of Operations.

Battlespace Framework

The battlespace framework depicts how the commander may organize his battlespace so he can relate his forces to one another in time, space, event, and purpose. The battlespace framework consists of envisioned deep, close, and rear operations (shown in fig. 3-2) as well as the organization of the force into the main effort, reserve, and security. The nature of the mission may also mean organizing into contiguous or noncontiguous deep, close, and rear areas. The battlespace framework provides the commander and his staff with a means to ensure they consider all essential elements of military operations while in the planning and execution phases.

> JP 3-10, *Joint Security Operations in Theater*, changes joint rear area to joint security area. The Marine Corps continues to use the security area in the traditional sense (see chapters 8 and 9 of this publication), using the term rear area to mean the area to the rear of the main battle area where logistic and administrative functions are normally the dominant activity.

Deep Operations

Deep operations afford commanders an opportunity to shape or prevent future close battles. Deep operations can strip away enemy capabilities, force an early culmination, or otherwise attack the enemy system so friendly forces can handle what remains when the enemy forces become a part of the close battle. By conducting deep operations, the commander can seize the initiative, create windows of opportunity for decisive action, restrict the enemy's freedom of action, and disrupt the cohesion and tempo of enemy operations. Because of its operational reach, deep operations are primarily conducted by the ACE, although the GCE and LCE may play significant roles as well. The MAGTF intelligence assets, such as reconnaissance and signals intelligence, contribute to the conduct of deep operations. Also contributing to deep operations are ACE and GCE surveillance and reconnaissance assets, such as unmanned aircraft systems and ground surveillance radars.

Deep operations normally focus on the enemy's follow-on and supporting forces, command and control nodes, and key lines of communications or facilities. Deep operations may require coordination and integration with national-level assets and joint forces. They may include—

- Interdiction through fire and maneuver.
- Surveillance, reconnaissance, and target acquisition.

Marine Corps Operations

- Information operations integrating deception and military information support operations.
- Offensive antiair warfare.
- Electronic warfare.

Close Operations

Close operations project power against enemy forces in immediate contact. These operations require speed and mobility to rapidly concentrate overwhelming combat power at the critical time and place. Fire and maneuver conducted by combined arms forces from the GCE and the ACE supported by the LCE dominate close operations. Combined arms forces maneuver to enhance the effects of their fires and conduct fire support operations to enhance their ability to maneuver. Commanders weight the main effort and focus combat power to create effects that lead to a decision.

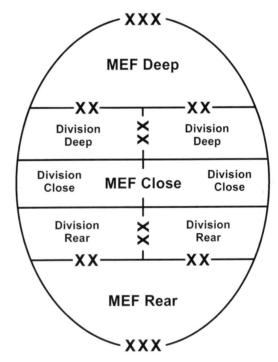

Figure 3-2. Battlespace Organization.

Rear Operations

All MAGTF elements conduct rear operations. Sustainment and security are normally the dominant rear area activities to ensure the freedom of action of the force and continuity of operations, logistics, and command and control. The MAGTF commander may need to provide commanders in the rear area additional capabilities, such as a tactical combat force, fire support assets, and associated command and control. To minimize the logistical footprint, rear operations may exploit seabasing, host nation support, and existing infrastructure.

As the operation progresses, the geographic location, command and control structure, and the organization of the rear area will likely change. The broad functions of rear area operations include—

- Communications.
- Intelligence.
- Sustainment.
- Security.
- Movement.
- Area management.
- Infrastructure development.
- Host nation support.

To provide command and control of rear area operations, the commander may assign a rear area coordinator or commander with specific, designated functions. That individual usually establishes a rear area operations center to assist in the conduct and coordination of assigned functions.

Battlespace Considerations

Battlespace framework allows a commander to relate his forces to one another in time, space, and purpose; however, past operations in such places as Somalia, Afghanistan, and Iraq challenge traditional notions of deep, close, and rear areas. Irregular warfare can involve areas of operations where deep, close, and rear all share the same space, which compresses the time between tactical actions and strategic effects. In counterinsurgency or other types of irregular warfare, deep operations may be more a function of time or activity than space. In this construct, various stability-related activities—such as economic development or support to governance—may not yield immediate results. Instead, the desired result may be a product of numerous small successes over an extended period of time.

Alternatively, commanders may choose to view and organize their battlespace through such activities as shaping, sustaining, and decisive actions. Ideally, in planning, the decisive action is envisioned first, allowing planners to determine the shaping actions, such as fires and intelligence, needed to set conditions for success. Similarly, Marines conduct sustaining actions, such as planning, logistics, rehearsals, or force protection, in support of friendly forces.

Maneuver Control and Fire Support Coordination Measures

Commanders use control measures to assign responsibilities, coordinate fire and maneuver, and control combat operations. These measures delineate areas of operations or other areas in which commands will conduct their operations or coordinate maneuver or fires between adjacent units. Each of these measures has specific purposes. Therefore, it is critical Marines use these measures as they were designed and clearly articulate to all affected higher, adjacent, and subordinate units any modifications to the doctrinally-based measures.

Boundaries are the basic maneuver control measures used by commanders to designate the geographical area for which a particular unit is tactically responsible. They affect fire support in two ways—

- They are *restrictive* in that no fire support means may deliver fires across a boundary unless those fires are coordinated with the force having responsibility for the area within that boundary.
- They are *permissive* in that the maneuver commander has complete freedom of fire and maneuver within his boundaries, unless otherwise restricted by higher headquarters. Many times, boundaries negate the need for fire support coordination measures.

As shown in figure 3-3, on page 3-14, fire support coordination measures facilitate the rapid engagement of targets while providing safeguards for friendly forces. They ensure fire support will not jeopardize the safety of personnel, will interface with other fire support means, and/or will not disrupt adjacent unit operations.

Centers of Gravity and Critical Vulnerabilities

An important aspect of the commander's visualization includes his analyses of centers of gravity and critical vulnerabilities. These analyses assist the commander in visualizing the relative strengths and weaknesses of the enemy and friendly forces.

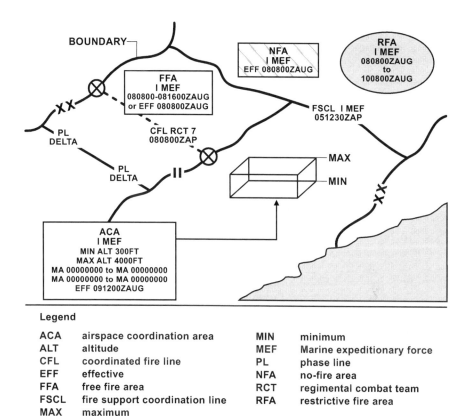

Figure 3-3. Unit Boundaries and Fire Support Coordination Measures.

A center of gravity is a source of power that provides moral or physical strength, freedom of action, or will to act. Depending on the situation, centers of gravity may be intangible characteristics, such as resolve or morale; they may be military units, such as armored forces or aviation; or they may be the cooperation between two arms, the relations in an alliance, or forces occupying key terrain that anchor an entire defensive system. In counterinsurgency operations, the center of gravity may be the support of the local population.

As they explore options for attacking an adversary's source of power, commanders ask themselves, "Where is the enemy vulnerable?" Of all the vulnerabilities a commander may seek to exploit, some are more critical than others. The commander should focus his efforts against a critical vulnerability that, if exploited, will do the most significant damage to the enemy.

Center of gravity and critical vulnerability are complementary concepts. The former looks at the problem of how to attack the enemy system from the perspective of seeking a source of strength, the latter from the perspective of seeking weakness. A critical vulnerability is a pathway to attacking the center of gravity.

The center of gravity and critical vulnerability analyses are ongoing processes. The commander's thinking on these items may be radically altered during the planning process, once the plan is executed, or as the situation changes and the conflict transitions to a new phase of the operation.

Commander's Intent

Commander's intent is the commander's personal expression of the purpose of the operation. It must be clear, concise, and easily understood two levels down. It may also include end state or conditions that, when satisfied, accomplish the purpose. Commander's intent helps subordinates understand the larger context of their actions and guides them in the absence of orders. It allows subordinates to exercise judgment and initiative—in a way that is consistent with their higher commander's aims—when the unforeseen occurs. This freedom of action, within the framework of commander's intent, creates tempo during planning and execution.

Commander's Guidance

Commander's guidance provides specific information that focuses the planning effort. As planning progresses, the nature of the commander's guidance will vary based on the stage of planning and his understanding of the situation. Early in planning, the commander's guidance is conceptual. He shares his understanding of the environment and problem and a broad operational framework for solving the problem. The latter stages of the planning process focus on the specifics of implementation. Accordingly, the commander's guidance will be more detailed.

Of all the guidance the commander provides, COA development guidance provides the method—how the commander envisions solving the problem. The commander should articulate his commander's concept, a clear and concise expression of what he intends to accomplish and how it will be done using available resources. As planning continues, this concept enables the planners to develop and refine COAs. This visualization reflects the commander's understanding of the situation and a hypothesis for achieving the overall purpose. Based on a variety of considerations, such as available time or understanding of the problem and its complexity, the commander's guidance may be narrow and directive or it may be broad and inquisitive. The former may include development of a single COA, while the latter may direct exploration of several COAs. Specific guidance can be in terms of warfighting functions, types or lines of operations, or forms of maneuver. Course of action development guidance should include the commander's vision of decisive and shaping actions, which assists the staff in determining the main effort, parts of the operation, location of critical events, and other aspects the commander deems pertinent to COA development.

Decisive Action

The purpose of all military operations is mission success. For any given mission, there is normally a decisive event or activity that is critical to success. In counterinsurgency, it may be isolating the insurgents from the populace. In a small unit engagement, it may be destroying a particular enemy weapon or position. In a major operation, it may be defeating a particular unit. In foreign humanitarian assistance, it may be reopening a host nation port or airfield. Ideally, Marines seek to achieve a decision with the least loss of time, equipment, and, most importantly, life.

A tactical engagement should lead to achieving operational and strategic goals. The goal is not just for the commander to achieve a decision, but to ensure it has greater meaning by contributing to the success of his senior commander's operation or campaign. For an action to be truly decisive, it must lead to a result larger than the action itself.

Decisive action may occur anywhere and at any time in the single battle. Any of the MAGTF's major subordinate commands/elements may conduct decisive actions. The commander considers the following in planning decisive action:

- What are the enemy's capabilities?
- Given his capabilities, what is the enemy's most dangerous COA?
- Given his capabilities, what is the enemy's most likely COA?
- What are the centers of gravity and critical vulnerabilities?
- What are the shaping requirements necessary to achieve a decision?
- Have I resourced the main effort for decisive action?
- Is the MAGTF prepared to shift priorities and resources to converge combat power?
- Can the MAGTF accomplish the mission without reaching a culminating point?
- Are we prepared to recognize and act on unforeseen opportunities caused by enemy or friendly actions?

Shaping Actions

The commander employs shaping actions to set the conditions for achieving a decision. Shaping actions are lethal and nonlethal activities conducted throughout the battlespace to attack an enemy capability or force or to influence the enemy commander's decisionmaking. Shaping actions can also protect friendly critical vulnerabilities or enhance friendly capabilities. In many cases, the MAGTF can achieve much of its own shaping. The objective of shaping actions can include—

- Limiting enemy freedom of action.
- Denying the enemy the capability to concentrate forces.
- Deceiving the enemy about friendly intentions.
- Destroying enemy capabilities.
- Altering the tempo of operations.
- Gaining and maintaining momentum.
- Influencing perceptions of the enemy, allies, and the local civilian population.

Shaping can have a favorable impact on friendly forces; the sense of being on the offensive and taking the fight to the enemy helps to maintain morale and foster an offensive spirit. For example, General Ulysses S. Grant, despite being cut off from resupply and facing an imposing defense during the 1863 siege of Vicksburg, kept his forces on the offensive throughout the winter, primarily to keep their spirits up and morale high.

Shaping incorporates a wide array of functions and capabilities to create desired effects and is more than just fires and targeting. It may include direct attack, military information support operations, electronic warfare, civil affairs, public affairs, and engineer operations. Information management; preventive medical services; and logistic operations, such as the marshalling of critical ammunition, fuel, and supplies to facilitate future operations, are also shaping actions. Because these shaping actions are directed at friendly forces, they are referred to as sustaining actions.

Shaping makes the enemy vulnerable to attack, impedes or diverts his attempts to maneuver, aids the MAGTF's maneuver, and otherwise dictates the time and place for decisive action. It forces the enemy to abandon his COA and adopt a COA favorable to the MAGTF. Shaping actions must be relevant to the envisioned decisive action. The commander attempts to shape events in a way that allows him several options, so that, by the time the moment for decisive action arrives, he is not restricted to only one means of achieving it. Ideally, when the decisive moment arrives, the issue has been resolved. Actions leading to this point have so shaped the conditions that the result is a matter of course.

Lines of Operations

A line of operations helps define the orientation of the force. In conventional operations, lines of operations connect actions related in time and space to an objective. During counterinsurgency or other irregular warfare operations, lines of operations focus on major stability-related objectives, such as security, restoration of essential services, and training host nation military and police forces. In either case, lines of operations reinforce the idea of the single battle, since success or failure in any line of operations will have an impact on the other lines of operations. There is more information on this topic in MCWP 3-33.5, *Counterinsurgency*.

Commander's Critical Information Requirements

The commander's critical information requirements (CCIRs) are those information requirements identified by the commander as being significant to timely decisionmaking. The CCIRs identify information on friendly activities, enemy activities, and the environment. Commanders use CCIRs to help confirm their vision of the battlespace, assess desired effects, and determine how they will achieve a decision to accomplish their mission or to identify significant deviations from that vision.

Not all information requirements directly support the commander's decisionmaking, so CCIRs must link to the critical decisions the commander anticipates making, thereby driving the command's collection efforts. The number of CCIRs must be limited to only those that support the commander's critical decisions. Too many CCIRs can diffuse the staff's focus and overwhelm the collection effort. In many cases, such as during Operation Iraqi Freedom, many of the CCIRs were significant notification events. Significant notification events identify a requirement for *more* information or the need to provide information of a strategic communication nature to higher headquarters; whereas, CCIRs identify the need for the commander to make a decision.

These requirements help the commander tailor his command and control organization and are central to effective information management. While the staff can recommend CCIRs, only the commander can approve them. The commander must continually review and update his CCIRs to reflect the changing situation.

Planning generates many information requirements. Those that are answered inform planning, while those that remain unanswered require assumptions to allow planning to continue. In some cases, planning-related information requirements can evolve into CCIRs, while some may also emerge from the COA war game and link to decision points the commander will have to address during execution.

There are two categories of CCIRs—priority intelligence requirements and friendly force information requirements. A priority intelligence requirement is an adversary- or environment-based intelligence requirement associated with a decision that will affect the success of the command's mission. A friendly force information requirement is information the commander needs about friendly forces to make effective decisions. Depending on the circumstances, information on unit location, composition, readiness, personnel status, and logistic status could become a friendly force information requirement.

Information Operations

Information operations are the integrated employment, during military operations, of information-related capabilities with other lines of operation to influence, disrupt, corrupt, or usurp the decisionmaking of adversaries and potential adversaries while protecting our own. Marines conduct information operations across the range of military operations and at every level of war. They are well-suited to support the MAGTF's expeditionary operations, since information operations can project the influence of the United States and be tailored to create measured effects in a specific mission or situation. They are scalable, allowing the commander to increase or decrease the level of intensity to reflect a changing situation. Information operations must be closely coordinated with joint force commander information operations and adjacent commanders to ensure unity of effort and to avoid undermining the effects desired by higher headquarters. Information operations require a thorough understanding of the culture of the target audience in order to produce the desired effect by communicating messages in the right cultural context and using the appropriate means.

The primary focus of MAGTF information operations is at the operational and tactical levels of war. Information operations in offensive operations may focus on command and control targets, disrupting or denying an enemy's use of information and information systems to achieve the commander's objectives. The MAGTF relies primarily on electronic warfare and physical destruction to attack command and control, intelligence, and other critical information-based targets the enemy needs to conduct operations. The MAGTF can also employ deception operations to deceive the enemy commander's intelligence collection, analysis, and dissemination systems. Information operations in defensive operations may protect information and information systems the MAGTF commander requires to plan and execute operations. Information operations include perception management or those actions taken to influence selected groups and decisionmakers. Perception management combines informational activities, truth projection, operations security, military deception, and military information support operations. It encompasses all actions taken to convey or deny selected information to an audience and can be a key contributor to shaping efforts.

In some environments, information operations capitalize on the growing sophistication, connectivity, and reliance on information technology. It focuses on the vulnerabilities and opportunities presented by the increasing dependence of the United States and its adversaries on information and information systems.

In other situations, information operations may mean employing low-tech means to facilitate civil-military operations, influence selected target audiences, or support military deception. Whatever the nature of the conflict, information operations target information or information systems to affect the adversary's decisionmaking process. Information operations may, in fact, have their greatest impact as a deterrent in peace and during the initial stages of crisis, discouraging adversaries from initiating actions detrimental to the United States.

Forward-deployed MAGTFs, coordinated and integrated with public affairs and defense support to public diplomacy, exploit the full range of their information operations capabilities in support of a communication strategy. When appropriate, MAGTFs will develop and nest with communication strategy programs, plans, objectives, themes, messaging, and images at the operational and tactical levels, leaving them to exploit success attained and exponentially shape the battlespace for future operations. The intent of these operations is to develop a relative advantage over the adversary and selected groups in the information environment and create an operational advantage (information superiority) at a specific time and location. An operational advantage may be in the form of adversarial decisionmaking or targeted audience behaviors. This advantage enables the MAGTF to maneuver and execute actions relatively unchallenged because the adversary does not have populace support or cannot communicate timely, accurate guidance or direction to its own forces. On the other hand, an operational advantage may be one that permits the MAGTF commander to make more timely and accurate decisions than the adversary, resulting in an advantage in initiative, tempo of operations, and momentum. Ultimately, the aim of information operations is to impact the content and flow of information to an adversary or neutral and friendly audiences (non-US citizens).

Cyberspace Operations

Cyberspace may be described as a global domain that leverages information and telecommunication technologies to create an environment of interdependent computer and telecommunication networks, including command and control systems, which can be used to produce outcomes in virtual and physical realms.

The ability to operate in cyberspace is critical to strategic, operational, and tactical successes. Without secure computerized technologies, many weapon and command and control systems will not function properly; intelligence, surveillance, and reconnaissance systems will be ineffective; and sensitive information will be at risk of compromise. The Marine Corps and other Services depend on cyberspace operations for speed, precision, and lethality. Adversaries recognize that much of the United States' economic and military dominance relies upon the technology, communications, and automated systems that cyberspace enables. Ease of access and rate of technological change combine to make dominance in this domain tenuous and invite asymmetric challenges. Challenges range from recreational hackers to self-styled cyber-vigilantes, groups with nationalistic or ideological agendas, terrorist organizations, transnational actors, international corporations with ties to other governments, and nation states.

Cyberspace operations involve the employment of cyber capabilities where the primary purpose is to create military objectives or effects in or through cyberspace. Cyberspace operations comprise five broad categories—Department of Defense network operations, defensive cyber operations, offensive cyber operations, computer network exploitation, and information assurance.

- Network operations are Department of Defense-wide operational, organizational, and technical capabilities employed to operate and defend the Department of Defense information network. This network is the globally interconnected, end-to-end set of information capabilities for collecting, processing, storing, managing, and disseminating information on demand to warfighters, policy makers, and support personnel. Marine Corps network operations include day-to-day operations required to maintain the Marine Corps Enterprise Network and protect it from both external and internal threats.
- Defensive cyber operations involves actions taken to protect, monitor, analyze, detect, and respond to unauthorized activity within Department of Defense information network. Defensive cyber operations employs information technology, information assurance, intelligence,

counterintelligence, law enforcement, and other military capabilities to defend Department of Defense information network.

- Offensive cyber operations includes the use of computer networks to disrupt, deny, degrade, or destroy information resident in computers and computer networks, within the computers and networks themselves, or to enable future offensive operations. Computer network attack is a subset of offensive cyberspace operations where the anticipated effect of the operation is equivalent to a military attack.
- Computer network exploitation is intelligence collection activities conducted through the use of computer networks to gather data from target or adversary automated information systems or networks.
- Information assurance includes measures that protect and defend information and information systems by ensuring their availability, integrity, authenticity, confidentiality, and nonrepudiation. These measures include providing for restoration of information systems by incorporating protection, detection, and reaction capabilities.

Given the scope and complexity of cyberspace operations, they must be carefully integrated into the overall joint and Marine Corps operational planning and effectively coordinated to achieve designated operational and tactical objectives.

EXECUTION

Execution of operations is the concerted action of the commander and his forces to conduct operations based on the operation plan or operation order, modified as the current tactical situation dictates, to achieve the commander's intent and accomplish the mission. Similarly, execution is the commitment of capabilities to interactions with selected elements within the battlespace. In viewing the enemy as part of a system, Marines invest energy into the system during execution in order to influence how that system evolves. The commander and his forces must gain and retain the initiative, create overwhelming tempo, establish and maintain momentum, create desired effects, exploit success, and successfully finish the operation.

The commander, assisted by his deputy commander and staff, oversees the activities of the MAGTF. These activities include the movement and maneuver of the force, coordination and control of fires, collection of intelligence, sustainment and protection of the force, and assessment of these activities to determine the progress of the command in achieving the desired end state.

Command and Control

No activities in war are more important than command and control. Through command and control, the commander recognizes what needs to be done and sees to it that appropriate actions are taken. Command and control provides purpose and direction to the varied activities of a military unit. If done well, command and control add to the strength of the force.

Decentralizing decisionmaking authority allows commanders on the scene and closest to the events the latitude to deal with the situation on their own authority—but in accordance with the higher commander's intent. In a decentralized approach, control of an operation rests, in large part, with subordinate units working together laterally and from the bottom up to accomplish tasks that fulfill the commander's intent while providing feedback. Acting in this manner places the friendly system under control.

Commanders must determine where to locate in order to observe and make timely and relevant decisions. For component and MAGTF commanders, who are hierarchically and geographically removed from the scene of the action, they mostly observe the operation vicariously, most notably through their subordinate units who are closer to the action. Component and MAGTF commanders have three basic methods for observation—the commander's battle rhythm, collection plan, and feedback, such as combat reporting.

The commander's battle rhythm is an important aspect of command and control. The battle rhythm will contain the venues that augment his battlefield circulation and provide him critical information. It will likely include meetings with higher and adjacent commanders, visits to subordinate commands where he can personally observe the operation, and interactions with his staff. The collection effort is a source of information, whether conducting "front-end" collection (such as answering CCIRs), locating and validating targets, or collecting post-event information (such as bomb damage assessments). Finally, feedback is a critical resource that identifies the difference between the situation as it exists and the desired end state.

Information Management

The rate and amount of change occurring during execution and the staffs' efforts to record and report on that change generates an overwhelming amount of information that must be managed. Accordingly, information management includes the processes and techniques the command uses to obtain, handle, direct, control, and safeguard information. Commanders develop information management processes to ensure access to timely and useful information, enabling them to make decisions. Sound information management practices facilitate the rapid, distributed, and unconstrained flow of information in all directions—to higher headquarters, adjacent units, and subordinate commanders. Information management policies and procedures enable the staff to determine the importance, quality, and timeliness of information to provide the commander with refined and focused data and prevent information overload. Fundamental to a sound and productive information management program is basic staff tactics, techniques, and procedure excellence. This excellence includes the mastery of the various information systems that helps staffs manage information. Based on the commander's observation of the operation, he must orient to the changing situation to assess its meaning to him and his command so he can continue to adapt in a relevant manner faster than the enemy, adversaries, or competitors.

ASSESSMENT

Assessment is the continuous monitoring and evaluation of the current situation and progress of an operation. It is the basis for adaptation, keyed to the overall purpose, oriented on the future, and focused on emerging opportunities. Successful assessment requires the commander's situational understanding and his recognition of the difference between planned goals and the situation as it exists. This difference between what was planned and what actually happened becomes the catalyst for decisionmaking, either to correct deficiencies or seize opportunities. An effective assessment process requires four elements:

- A basis for comparisons in the form of planning goals, which include tasks, purpose, conditions, and effects.
- Feedback that allows approximation of the situation as it exists.
- Analysis and synthesis to determine the causes and difference between plans and execution.
- Recommendations for change.

Planning for Assessment

The hierarchical layering of tasks and purposes in military plans and orders provides a natural framework for assessment. As planners determine specific planning goals, the plan or order may contain sufficient information for assessment, particularly during conventional operations where so much of the operation is observable and measurable. However, in some cases, a more detailed assessment process may be needed due to operational complexity, the commander's desire for more detailed information, staff experience, or the detailed reporting requirements of higher headquarters.

Assessment Cell

On larger, more senior staffs, the commander may form an assessment cell. This assessment cell normally shadows the planning effort, looking for areas of the plan that may require assistance in measuring progress toward planned goals and the purpose of the operation. Since some conditions are necessarily complex, commanders and their staffs, to include an assessment cell, may use measures of performance and effectiveness to determine the degree to which a condition has been satisfied.

Measures of Performance and Measures of Effectiveness

Measures of performance help assess friendly actions tied to measuring task accomplishment. They help answer the question, "Are we doing things right?" Measures of effectiveness help assess changes in system behavior, capability, or operational environment that are tied to measuring the attainment of an end state, achievement of an objective, or creation of an effect. They help answer the question, "Are we doing the right things?" The measures of performance and measuress of effectiveness provide the commander with tangible indicators of how close he is to achieving his planned goals. To be meaningful, measures of performance and measures of effectiveness need to be observable, measurable, and relevant.

Assessment Considerations

Assessment, like the planning process, should be driven top-down by the commander. His assessment guidance could begin as early as his commander's orientation. Similarly, he needs to provide his information requirements to guide the assessment effort.

While measures of performance and measures of effectiveness may inform the assessment effort, they also impose collection requirements. Like CCIRs, too many measures of performance and measures of effectiveness can overwhelm the collection effort and diffuse the staff's focus. Staffs must avoid the tendency to unnecessarily complicate the assessment process.

When developing orders and planning for assessment, measures of performance and measures of effectiveness must be carefully crafted. Tactical tasks have precise definitions that describe what is to be accomplished. Planners should select the most appropriate tactical task and stick with it to avoid confusion and possible mission creep.

Tactical tasks can have major resource implications. One of the most costly in terms of time, resources, and risk to friendly forces is the tactical task *destroy*. For example, before committing resources to "destroy 50 percent of all artillery in zone," planners should seek alternative solutions or a different tactical task that can still contribute to the commander's intent without obligating an inordinate amount of the command's resources and capabilities.

Joint Publications 3-0 and 3-60, *Joint Targeting*, portray tactical level assessment as being primarily in the spatial/physical realm focused mostly on lethal fires. While lethal fires can be a large and important part of tactical operations, the greatest effect of fires is generally not the amount of physical destruction they cause, but the effect of that destruction on the enemy's moral strength. Because it is difficult to quantify mental and moral forces, it is tempting to exclude them from the assessment effort. However, any assessment process that neglects these factors ignores the greater part of the nature of war—the human element.

Military operations do not subscribe to the additive properties of math. Accordingly, any assessment-related, color-coded charts that reflect a numerical sum or average of discrete values is fundamentally flawed. If the color coding represents better or worse, less or more, or other analogic indicators, then they may have merit with respect to the determination of progress or the lack thereof and the reasons why. The most insightful assessment reporting lies in the narrative. What are commanders, staffs, or assessment officers saying in their reports, whether written or verbal? Their comments should reflect the *why* behind the information in the charts. They are more likely to reflect knowledge or understanding, which is a requirement for relevant change. In the end, assessment is a *qualitative* event, requiring commanders to balance the science of quantifiable information with the art of intuition and judgment to arrive at an understanding of the situation that fosters timely and relevant decisions.

TACTICAL TENETS

Actions at the tactical level of war are the building blocks used to achieve operational success and fulfill the joint force commander's operational goals. Every action the MAGTF commander and the major subordinate commanders take is aimed at achieving the senior commander's goals and accomplishing the mission. The tactical level of war is the province of combat. It includes the maneuver of forces to gain a positional advantage, the use and coordination of fires, the sustainment of forces throughout the area of operations, the immediate exploitation of success, and the combination of different arms and weapons—all to cause the enemy's defeat. The MAGTF conducts these tactical operations through the major subordinate commands that execute them.

Successful execution of Marine Corps tactics requires the thoughtful application of a number of tactical tenets to succeed in the battlespace. Among those tenets, achieving a decision, gaining advantage, tempo, adapting, and exploiting success and finishing are key. They do not stand alone; rather, they merge to create an effect greater than each one applied separately. Part of the art of tactics is knowing where and when to apply these tenets and how to combine them to create the desired effect.

Achieving a Decision

The objective of tactics is to achieve military success through a decision in battle. In combat, the success the commander seeks is victory—not a partial or marginal outcome, but a victory that settles the issue in his favor and contributes to the success of the overall operation or campaign.

Achieving a decision is not easy. The enemy's skill and determination may prevent even a victorious commander from achieving the decision he seeks. Commanders must not engage in battle without envisioning a larger result for their actions.

Commanders must be prepared to act decisively. Key to this effort is identifying enemy critical vulnerabilities, shaping the operating area to gain an advantage, designating a main effort to focus the MAGTF's combat power, and acting in a bold and relentless manner.

Forcing a successful decision requires the commander to be bold and relentless. Boldness refers to daring and aggressiveness in behavior. It is one of the basic requirements for achieving clear-cut outcomes. The commander must have a desire to "win big," even if he realizes that in many situations the conditions for victory may not yet be present. Relentlessness refers to pursuing the established goal single-mindedly and with dogged perseverance. Once he has an advantage, he should exploit it fully, increasing the pressure as he goes. Victory in combat is rarely the product of the initial plan; rather, it is because of a relentless exploitation of any advantage, no matter how small, until the mission succeeds.

Gaining Advantage

Some of those exploitable advantages include the use of maneuver and surprise whenever possible. The commander employs complementary forces as combined arms; he exploits the terrain, weather, and times of darkness to his advantage; he traps the enemy by fire and maneuver; he fights asymmetrically to gain added advantage; and he strives to gain an advantage over the enemy by exploiting every aspect of a situation to achieve victory, not just by overpowering the enemy's strength with his own.

Combined Arms

Combined arms, a Marine Corps core competency, is an important means of gaining advantage. Combined arms presents the enemy not merely with a problem, but with a dilemma—a no-win situation. The commander combines supporting arms, organic fires, and maneuver in such a way that any action the enemy takes to counteract one makes him more vulnerable to another.

Modern combined arms tactics combine the effects of various arms—infantry, armor, artillery, aviation, and information operations—to create the greatest possible effect against the enemy. The strengths of the arms complement and reinforce each other. At the same time, weaknesses and vulnerabilities of each arm are protected or offset by the capabilities of the other.

The MAGTF is a perfect example of a combined arms team. For example, an entrenched enemy discovers that if he stays in fighting holes, Marine ground forces will maneuver into a position of advantage and, if necessary, will close with and destroy him. If he comes out to attack, the enemy becomes susceptible to the lethal fires of Marine artillery and aviation. If he tries to retreat, Marine motorized/mechanized and aviation forces will pursue him to his destruction. Combined arms tactics is standard practice and second nature for all Marines.

Exploiting the Environment

The use of the environment offers tremendous opportunities to gain advantage over the enemy. Marines must train for and understand the characteristics of any environment where they may have to operate, such as jungle, desert, mountain, arctic, riverine, urban, and information. More importantly, Marines must understand how the terrain, weather, and periods of darkness or reduced visibility impact their own and the enemy's ability to fight.

In addition to the physical aspects of the environment, Marines must consider the impact on the operation by the people and the culture, political and social organization, and any external agencies or organizations that exist within the area of operations. These aspects will have differing effects in the information environment due to beliefs, ability to pass information, collect information, and understand the information available. Since most expeditionary operations take place in the world's littoral regions, which are more urban and densely populated, Marines must plan for and be prepared to conduct more urbanized and civil-military operations.

Marine Corps Operations

Complementary Forces

Complementary forces—the idea of fix-and-flank—are an important way of gaining advantage. The commander seeks to crush the enemy—as between a hammer and an anvil—with two or more actions. With its two combat arms, the MAGTF has organic complementary and asymmetric forces. Ground combat forces may attack an enemy in one direction and dimension, while aviation combat forces attack from another. This capability places the enemy in a dilemma. The opponent is now vulnerable to one or the other of the two combat forces. He has no protection against both; no matter how he moves, he is exposed.

One of the complementary forces may take a direct, obvious action to fix the enemy. The other force takes the unexpected or extraordinary action. These two actions work together against the enemy. The two actions are inseparable and can be interchangeable in battle. The concept is basic, but it can be implemented in a variety of combinations limited only by imagination.

Surprise

Achieving surprise can greatly increase advantage. In fact, surprise can often prove decisive. The commander tries to achieve surprise through information operations that result in deception, stealth, and ambiguity.

The commander uses deception to mislead the enemy about his real intentions and capabilities. By employing deception, he tries to cause the enemy to act in ways that will eventually prove prejudicial for them. He may use deception to mislead the enemy about the time and location of a pending attack or to create the impression his forces are larger than they really are. Forces used to support deception operations must be appropriate and of sufficient size to make the deception credible. Ideally, by the time the enemy discovers the deception, it will be too late for him to react effectively.

Surprise can be generated through stealth, an advantage when maneuvering against an enemy. It provides less chance of detection by the enemy, leaving him vulnerable to surprise action for which he may be unprepared.

The commander can also achieve surprise through ambiguity. It is usually difficult to conceal all friendly movements from the enemy, but the commander can sometimes confuse him about the meaning of what he sees, especially his awareness of where the main effort is or where the commander has placed his bid for a decision. Clearly, the ambiguity created in the minds of the Iraqi high command by the amphibious force contributed to fixing the Iraqi forces, allowing coalition forces to succeed in Operation Desert Storm.

Asymmetry

Fighting asymmetrically means gaining advantage through imbalance, applying strength against an enemy weakness in an unexpected way. At the tactical level, fighting asymmetrically means using dissimilar techniques and capabilities to maximize the MAGTF's strengths while exploiting enemy weaknesses. By fighting asymmetrically, the MAGTF does not have to be numerically superior to defeat the enemy. It only has to be able to exploit the enemy's vulnerabilities. In MAGTF operations, using tanks to fight enemy artillery or attack helicopters against enemy tanks are examples of fighting asymmetrically. In these examples, the greater speed and mobility of the tanks and aircraft provide an advantage over the enemy. Fast-moving tanks operating in the enemy's rear against stationary or slow-moving artillery can disrupt the enemy's cohesion. Ambushing tanks with attack helicopters in terrain that hampers tank maneuver provides even greater effect and generates even more advantage. United States attack helicopters assisted in blunting a rapid and powerful North Vietnamese advance and destroyed the enemy's armor using just such tactics during the Easter Offensive (1972) in the Republic of Vietnam.

Commanders must anticipate asymmetric actions and take measures to reduce the adversary's advantage. An adversary may counter MAGTF strengths asymmetrically by conducting insurgency or terrorist operations, such as the terrorist bombing of the Marine barracks in Beirut, Lebanon (1983). The adversary may also try to use information operations to undermine alliances and influence public opinion.

Tempo

One of the most powerful weapons available to the commander is speed. The unit that can consistently move and act faster than its enemy has a powerful advantage. The ability to plan, decide, execute, and assess faster than the enemy creates advantages commanders can exploit.

In a military sense, there is more to speed than simply going fast and there is a vital difference between acting rapidly and acting recklessly. Speed and time are closely related. In tactics, time is always of the utmost importance. Time that cannot be spent in action must be spent preparing for action and shaping conditions for decisive actions. If speed is a weapon, so is time. Speed and time create tempo. Tempo is the rate of military action and has significance only in relation to that of the enemy. When friendly tempo exceeds that of the enemy to react, friendly forces seize and maintain the initiative and have a marked advantage. The advantage of tempo applies across the range of military operations. During counterinsurgency operations, for example, when the results of friendly actions can take a long time to occur, the tempo competition still applies. Advantage is gained through a tempo or rhythm of adaptation that is beyond the other side's ability to achieve or sustain.

Tempo is not merely a matter of acting fastest or at the earliest opportunity; it is also a matter of acting at the right time. The commander must be able to generate and maintain a fast pace when the situation calls for it and to recover when it will not hurt. Timing means knowing when to act and, equally important, when not to act. To be consistent, superiority in tempo must continue over time. It is not enough to move faster than the enemy only now and then. When the friendly force is not moving faster, the advantage and initiative pass to the enemy. Most forces can manage an intermittent burst of speed, but must then halt for a considerable period to recover; it is then when they are likely to lose their advantage. While a force cannot operate at full speed indefinitely, the challenge is to be consistently faster than the enemy.

To act consistently faster than the enemy, it is necessary to make rapid transitions from one action to another. While there are many types of transitions in combat, the important thing to remember is that transitions produce friction. Reduction of friction minimizes the loss of tempo that is generated at the point of transition. A unit that can make transitions faster and more smoothly than another can be said to have greater relative speed.

Adapting

War is characterized by friction, uncertainty, disorder, and rapid change. Each situation is a unique combination of shifting factors that cannot be controlled with precision or certainty. A tactically proficient leader must be able to adapt actions to each situation. For adaptation to be effective, commanders must readily exploit the opportunities that arise during execution. While making the best possible preparations, commanders must welcome and take advantage of unforeseen opportunities.

There are two basic ways to adapt—anticipation and improvisation. Sometimes the commander has enough situational awareness to understand a situation in advance and take preparatory action—anticipation. At other times, he has to adapt to the situation on the spur of the moment without time for preparation—improvisation. A successful commander must be able to do both.

To anticipate, the commander must forecast future actions. Forecasts are usually based on past experiences and learned through trial and error in training, exercises, and actual combat. Planning is a form of anticipatory adaptation—adapting actions in advance. Another form of adaptation is immediate-action drills or standing operating procedures. These tools allow Marines to react immediately in a coordinated way to a broad variety of tactical situations. They provide the basis for adaptation.

Improvisation requires creative, intelligent, and experienced leaders who have an intuitive appreciation for what will work and what will not. Improvisation is critical to increasing speed. It requires commanders with a strong situational awareness and a firm understanding of their senior commander's intent so they can adjust their own actions in accordance with the higher commander's desires.

Exploiting Success and Finishing

The successful commander repeatedly exploits any advantage aggressively and relentlessly until the opportunity arises for the finishing stroke. He uses any advantage to create new opportunities. The commander builds on successfully exploited advantages to create new ones, reflecting the changing situation that results from both friendly and enemy adaptation. Advantages don't have to be large; small, favorable circumstances exploited repeatedly and aggressively can quickly multiply into decisive advantages. In the same way, the commander exploits opportunities to create others. Victories are usually the result of aggressively exploiting some advantage or opportunity until the action becomes decisive.

Such victories are realized through development and maintenance of momentum and the successful attack of enemy critical vulnerabilities. Momentum is the increase of combat power, gained from seizing the initiative and attacking aggressively and rapidly. Once the commander decides to exploit an advantage, he makes every effort to build momentum until the offensive becomes overwhelming and the objective is achieved. He should not sacrifice momentum to preserve the alignment of advancing units and he should drive hard at gaps in the enemy defense. The commander should not waste time or combat power on enemy units that cannot jeopardize the overall mission, choosing instead to fix them with minimal forces and bypass them with his main force. The commander exploits enemy weaknesses, such as tactical errors, faulty dispositions, assailable flanks, poor or no preparation, lack of support, numerical and equipment inferiority, low morale, and predictable operational patterns.

Subordinates must be accustomed through practice and training to seize opportunities on their own initiative. For example, a major subordinate commander should have a complete understanding of the MAGTF commander's intent so he can recognize a decisive opportunity and have the confidence to rapidly exploit it without further orders from the MAGTF commander. The commander exploits opportunities by conducting consolidation, exploitation, or pursuit.

Exploiting advantages without applying the finishing stroke to defeat the enemy or achieve the objective will not be decisive. Once the commander has created the opportunity to deliver the decisive blow, he must strike the enemy vigorously and relentlessly until the enemy is defeated. At the same time, the commander must exercise judgment to ensure the force committed to the decisive action is not unduly or unintentionally made vulnerable to enemy counteraction. Rapid and accurate assessment by the MAGTF commander and his major subordinate commanders is critical in determining the appropriate time and place of the decisive action.

Tactical excellence is the hallmark of a Marine Corps leader. Marines fight and win in combat through the mastery of both the art and science of tactics. The art of tactics involves the creative and innovative use of maneuver warfare concepts, while the science of tactics requires skill in basic warfighting techniques and procedures. Marine leaders must work continuously to develop tactical proficiency within themselves and their Marines.

CHAPTER 4

Military Engagement, Security Cooperation, and Deterrence

". . . all of these people here know that without the security provided by United States Marines, none of this would be happening. The NGO and civilian doctors would have been afraid to show up, for fear of Abu Sayyaf."

—Lieutenant Colonel Dennis Downey,
US Army Imperial Grunts

"Lying offshore, ready to act, the presence of ships and Marines sometimes means much more than just having air power or ship's fire, when it comes to deterring a crisis. And the ships and Marines may not have to do anything but lie offshore. It is hard to lie offshore with a C-141 or C-130 full of airborne troops."

—General Colin Powell,
US Army Congressional Testimony, 1990

Forward-postured naval forces conduct a wide array of activities and operations designed to build the partnerships that promote a collective approach to mutual security concerns, as called for in the national strategy documents identified in chapter 1. The imperative to build and sustain partnerships that contribute to collective security, deterrence, and combat effectiveness comes at a time when sensitivity to US bases overseas is rising and the overall number of US forces stationed on foreign soil is much lower than during the Cold War. In this context, sea-based forward presence provides the opportunity to conduct cooperative activities with allies and an expanding set of international partners, while minimizing the political, economic, cultural, and social impacts sometimes associated with forward-stationed US forces.

Military engagement, security cooperation, and deterrence activities encompass a wide range of actions where the military instrument of national power prevents and deters conflict. These actions generally occur regularly in all geographic combatant commanders' areas of responsibility regardless of other ongoing contingencies, major operations, or campaigns. They include partnership activities designed to collectively address mutual security concerns as well as actions to alleviate or mitigate sources of conflict. They usually involve a combination of military forces and capabilities separate from and integrated with the efforts of other government agencies and intergovernmental organizations—generically referred to in joint doctrine as interorganizational partners—in a complementary fashion.

Because the Department of State plays a major role in many of these activities, joint force commanders maintain a working relationship with the chiefs of the US diplomatic missions in their areas. Similarly, Marine Corps component commanders, subordinate commanders, and staffs tasked with conducting these activities should establish contact and maintain a dialogue with pertinent interorganizational partners to share information and facilitate operations.

Military engagement is the routine contact and interaction between individuals or elements of the US Armed Forces and either the armed forces of another nation or foreign and domestic civilian authorities or agencies. This contact is designed to build trust and confidence, share information, coordinate mutual activities, and maintain influence. Military engagement occurs as part of security cooperation, but also extends to interaction with domestic civilian authorities.

Security cooperation involves all Department of Defense interactions with foreign defense establishments to build defense relationships that promote specific US security interests, develop allied and friendly military capabilities for self-defense and multinational operations, and provide US forces with peacetime and contingency access to a host nation. Security cooperation is a key element of global and theater shaping operations. The geographic combatant commanders shape their areas of operations through security cooperation activities by continually employing military forces to complement and reinforce other instruments of national power. The geographic combatant commander's theater campaign plans provide a framework within which Marine Corps components and subordinate echelons engage regional partners in cooperative military activities and development. Ideally, security cooperation activities lessen the causes of potential crises.

Deterrence is the prevention from action by fear of the consequences—a state of mind brought about by the existence of a credible threat of unacceptable counteraction. Naval forces have historically contributed to that form of deterrence by providing the nuclear strike and conventional power projection capabilities that discourage acts of aggression. Recognizing some rogue states or nonstate actors may not be deterred by nuclear or conventional retaliation and may actually seek to elicit reprisals to support their own strategic objectives, the United States has developed an expanded form of deterrence. It now includes promoting a collective approach to mutual defense concerns among international partners, denying rogue states or nonstate actors the likelihood of success. This expanded form of deterrence also includes addressing the local conditions that generate conflict, thereby eroding support for such actors within the populace. In this form of deterrence, military engagement and security cooperation activities provide an important, proactive complement to retaliatory deterrence capabilities.

The expeditionary character and forward posture of the Marine Corps—maintained through rotational and permanently forward-deployed forces—have proven to be critical enablers of rapid crisis response. Concurrently, these qualities also enable military engagement, security cooperation, and deterrence. Some of these activities involve larger formations—such as MEFs and MEBs—conducting large-scale multilateral or bilateral exercises. More often, they require a larger number of smaller, more dispersed formations composed of personnel with regional expertise and cultural savvy who establish effective relationships with their international partners. Recent force structure enhancements—such as intelligence; explosive ordnance disposal; civil affairs; foreign military training units; and irregular warfare training and education initiatives in culture, languages, and foreign advisory duties—allow for greater participation in the military engagement, security cooperation, and deterrence operations across the range of military operations.

Sea-based Marine Corps forces demonstrate commitment to partners without imposing a lasting footprint ashore—persistent presence without permanence. Often embarked aboard amphibious ships, Marines are ideally suited to conduct an expanding array of activities that prevent, deter, or resolve conflict. Examples include forward-deployed ARG/MEUs, SPMAGTFs afloat, Marine detachments aboard a wider variety of Navy ships, and Marine Corps training assistance groups.

Regardless of the size of the units involved or means of deployment and employment, the Marine Corps component commanders play a key role in identifying and satisfying geographic combatant commander requirements for security cooperation, which includes educating joint force and other component staffs regarding Marine Corps capabilities that may have utility in achieving a given set of geographic combatant commander objectives. It also includes gaining similar expertise with regard to the capabilities resident in other components, with a view toward task-organizing Service-unique capabilities in complementary, innovative ways to better satisfy operational requirements. The ability to plan, execute, support, sustain, and command and control Marine Corps capabilities task-organized with those of other components, including the ability to employ Marines from a wider variety of Navy ships, is essential to meeting increasing geographic combatant commander requirements.

Even when the United States is not conducting limited contingency operations, major operations, or campaigns, numerous routine military engagement, security cooperation, and deterrence activities are occurring under the general heading of *engagement*. In some cases, what begins as an engagement activity, such as limited support to a counterinsurgency through a security assistance program, can expand to a limited contingency operation or even a major operation when the President commits US forces. Engagement activities generally are governed by various directives and agreements and do not require a joint operation plan or operations order for execution.

The following paragraphs identify the types of military operations and activities Marine Corps commands may conduct to meet geographic combatant commander military engagement, security cooperation, and deterrence objectives. They are presented in the order of likelihood, as determined through a combination of historical experience and assessments of the unfolding 21st-century security conditions.

NATION ASSISTANCE

Nation assistance includes civil/military assistance rendered to a nation by foreign forces within that nation's territory during peacetime, crises or emergencies, or war based on agreements mutually concluded between nations. Nation assistance programs include humanitarian and civic assistance, support to foreign internal defense, security assistance, and other United States Code, Title 10 programs and activities performed on a reimbursable basis by Federal agencies or intergovernmental organizations.

Humanitarian and Civic Assistance

Humanitarian and civic assistance to the local populace is predominantly provided by US forces in conjunction with military operations and exercises. This assistance is specifically authorized by United States Code, Title 10, sec. 401, and funded under separate authorities. Marine Corps forces often provide this type of assistance in conjunction with MEF-level bilateral exercises, such as Cobra Gold; regularly scheduled ARG/MEU deployments; or smaller security cooperation missions, such as those conducted by SPMAGTF Unitas.

Support to Foreign Internal Defense

Foreign internal defense involves participation by civilian and military agencies of a government in any of the action programs taken by another government or other designated organization to free and protect its society from subversion, lawlessness, and insurgency. Forward-deployed MEUs, SPMAGTFs, and other task-organized Marine Corps forces routinely conduct a variety of foreign internal defense tasks.

Security Assistance

Security assistance includes a group of programs authorized by United States Code, Title 22, *Foreign Relations and Intercourse*, as amended, by which the United States provides defense articles, military training, and other defense-related services by grant, loan, credit, or cash sales to further national policies and objectives. Only those Marine Corps organizations and personnel specifically authorized to do so can conduct security assistance.

MARITIME SECURITY OPERATIONS

Maritime security operations protect sovereignty and resources, ensure free and open commerce, and counter maritime-related terrorism, transnational crime, piracy, environmental destruction, and illegal seaborne immigration. Marines may participate in maritime security operations by conducting visit, board, search, and seizure operations, as in 2010 when elements of 15th MEU recaptured the *MV Magellan Star* and rescued its crew from Somali pirates.

COMBATING TERRORISM

Combating terrorism actions are taken to oppose terrorism throughout the entire threat spectrum. They include antiterrorism and counterterrorism.

Antiterrorism

Antiterrorism consists of defensive measures used to reduce the vulnerability of individuals and property to terrorist acts. These defensive measures include limited response and containment by local military and civilian forces, such as fleet antiterrorism security teams.

Counterterrorism

Counterterrorism operations include the offensive measures taken to prevent, deter, pre-empt, and respond to terrorism. Marine Corps forces may conduct a variety of counterterrorism tasks or provide capabilities in support of other forces engaged in counterterrorism. Operations by Task Force 58 (2001) during the initial phases of Operation Enduring Freedom demonstrated the flexibility of forward-deployed amphibious forces in counterterrorism operations.

Show of Force Operations

Show of force operations demonstrate US resolve. These operations involve increased visibility of deployed forces in an attempt to defuse a specific situation that, if allowed to continue, may be detrimental to US interests or national objectives. These operations often involve the overt repositioning of forward-deployed forces, such as ARG/MEUs; the pairing of offloaded MPF assets with a fly-in echelon; multinational training exercises; rehearsals; forward deploying additional units; or the buildup of forces within a theater. In 1990, for example, Amphibious Group Two and 4th MEB conducted Operation Imminent Thunder in the Arabian Gulf. By design, the location of this amphibious exercise and its accessibility for coverage by the world media were a signal to Saddam Hussein that the international coalition was serious about forcing his withdrawal from Kuwait. Two years later, 11th MEU conducted another show of force operation in the same region to again signal US intentions to a re-assertive regime.

Arms Control

Arms control includes those activities by military forces to verify conventional, chemical, biological, radiological, or nuclear arms control agreements; seize or destroy weapons; dismantle or dispose of weapons and hazardous materials; and escort deliveries of weapons. It encompasses any plan, arrangement, or process controlling the numbers, types, and performance characteristics of any weapon system. These activities help reduce threats to regional security and assist in implementing arms agreements. Marine Corps forces may conduct arms control inspections or may provide command and control, logistic, or intelligence support to verification and inspection teams. They may also seize, secure, or recover weapons or support other organizations in those efforts.

Sanctions Enforcement/Maritime Interception Operatiions

Enforcement of sanctions includes coercive measures to interdict the movement of designated items in or out of a nation or specified area to compel a country or group to conform to the objectives of the nation or international body that establishes the sanctions. Maritime interception operations include efforts to monitor, query, and board merchant vessels in international waters to enforce sanctions and/or prevent the transport of restricted goods. As part of a larger naval force, Marines can help establish a barrier, detect blockade runners, and intercept and search such vessels to enforce the sanction. These operations allow authorized cargo and persons to pass through while preventing material and persons under sanctions from passing, as demonstrated during the maritime interception operations conducted in the 1990s in the Arabian Gulf against Iraq.

PROTECTION OF SHIPPING

Protection of shipping involves the use of proportionate force by US warships, military aircraft, and other forces, when necessary, to protect US flag vessels and aircraft and US citizens (whether embarked in US or foreign vessels) and their property against unlawful violence. This protection may extend (consistent with international law) to foreign flag vessels, aircraft, and persons. When necessary, Marine Corps forces can protect US flag vessels, citizens, and their property embarked on US or foreign vessels from unlawful violence in and over international waters. Protection can take the form of embarked Marines providing security on board the vessel or from other ships or convoy escorts. Protection can also be combat air patrols by Marine aviation and the recovery of hijacked vessels by Marine Corps security forces. A MAGTF can also protect US shipping by eliminating the threats of land-based antiship missiles, coastal guns, and hostile naval forces operating in the littorals. In 1988, for example, a SPMAGTF operating from the *USS Trenton* conducted Operation Praying Mantis to prevent the Iranians from using the Sassan oil platform to target shipping in the Arabian Gulf.

FREEDOM OF NAVIGATION AND OVERFLIGHT

Freedom of navigation and overflight operations demonstrate US or international rights to navigate sea or air routes in accordance with international law. Marine Corps electronic warfare aircraft participated in Operation Attain Document, a series of freedom of air and sea navigation operations against Libya in the Gulf of Sidra. Marines can conduct operations to seize and control critical chokepoints on sea lines of communications to help ensure unimpeded use of the seas. Marine aviation can assist the combatant commander by providing combat air patrol or strikes against antiair missiles and guns to ensure use of air routes in accordance with international law.

DEFENSE SUPPORT TO PUBLIC DIPLOMACY

Defense support to public diplomacy includes those activities and measures taken by Department of Defense components to support and facilitate the public diplomacy efforts of the US Government. For example, in 1990 the Marine Corps provided a SPMAGTF afloat to support a Presidential visit to Colombia. More recently, in 2010 the *USS Peleliu* ARG/15th MEU provided support to the US Secret Service during the Presidential visit to India.

EXCLUSION ZONES ENFORCEMENT

Exclusion zone enforcement operations employ coercive measures to prohibit selected activities in a specific geographic area. A sanctioning body establishes an exclusion zone to persuade a nation or a group to modify its behavior to meet the desires of the sanctioning body or face either continuing sanctions or the use or threat of force. As demonstrated in Operation Southern Watch (Iraq) and Operation Deny Flight (Bosnia), Marine Corps forces, including Marine aviation, enforced exclusion zones.

DEPARTMENT OF DEFENSE SUPPORT TO COUNTERDRUG OPERATIONS

The Department of Defense supports federal, state, local, and foreign law enforcement agencies in their efforts to disrupt the transfer of illegal drugs into the United States. Military forces assist in detecting and monitoring drug trafficking, support interdiction efforts, provide intelligence and logistic support, and integrate communications and intelligence assets dedicated to interdicting the movement of illegal drugs into the United States. Marines frequently support Department of Defense counterdrug activities, such as the Joint Task Force-North operations along the US-Mexico border, by providing observation, radar support, and cargo inspection.

SUPPORT TO INSURGENCY

An insurgency is an organized use of subversion and violence by a group or movement that seeks to overthrow or force change of a governing authority. Insurgency can also refer to the group itself. (JP 1-02) It uses a mixture of political, economic, informational, and combat actions to achieve its political aims. It is a protracted politico-military struggle designed to weaken the control and legitimacy of an established government, an interim governing body, or a peace process while increasing insurgent control and legitimacy—the central issues in an insurgency. The United States may support an insurgency against an oppressive regime. Because support for an insurgency is often covert, many of the operations connected with it are conducted by special operations forces. Marine Corps forces may be called upon to conduct or support these operations, providing logistic and training support as they did for the Mujahidin resistance in Afghanistan during the Soviet occupation in the 1980s. In certain circumstances, the United States can provide direct combat support, as a small number of Marines did with the French Resistance in World War II.

CHAPTER 5

Crisis Response and Limited Contingency Operations

> "An amphibious force of modern type, operating from the sea and equipped with helicopters, is free from dependence on airfields, beaches, ports, land-bases—with all their logistical and political complications. The use of an airborne force, or of any land-based force, is a more irrevocable step, since its commitment is more definite and its withdrawal more difficult. A self-contained and sea-based amphibious force, of which the U.S. Marine Corps is the prototype, is the best kind of fire extinguisher—because of its flexibility, reliability, logistic simplicity, and relative economy . . . . Amphibious flexibility is the greatest strategic asset that a sea-based power possesses."
>
> —Sir B. H. Liddell Hart, 1960
> *Deterrence or Defense*

> "Before their coming, sanitation, save in the crudest and most unsatisfactory forms, was unknown; fevers and epidemics were as plentiful as revolutions, a press gang was in vogue and the country was the victim of continuous uprisings engineered by political scoundrels, each of whom ravaged the customs money drawer as each in turn came into short-lived power. The entry of the United States Marines ended this sorry story."
>
> —Right Reverent Charles B. Colmore, Episcopal Bishop of Haiti, 1916
> *Soldiers of the Sea*

The vast majority of the Marine Corps' expeditionary service has involved crisis response and limited contingency operations, usually conducted in periods when the Nation has ostensibly been at peace. Some of these were relatively short-term rescue or punitive expeditions. Others evolved from rapid crisis response operations into contingencies that were limited in force size, but not duration, complexity, and level of integration with the other elements of national power. Such expeditions provided the source of our institutional "small wars" expertise, so much so that a previous generation of Marines was often referred to as "State Department troops."

Recognizing the need for/benefit of expeditionary responsiveness and operational versatility, the 1952 Congress (through the Douglas-Mansfield Act) codified that the Marine Corps should provide the Nation an expeditionary force in readiness, "the most ready when the nation is least ready," to "prevent the growth of potentially large conflagrations by prompt and vigorous action during their incipient stages" and to "suppress or contain international disturbances short of large scale war."

Crisis response and limited contingency operations encompass a variety of military actions, often in support of other government agencies, to contain or mitigate the effects of natural disasters or calamitous human events. They erupt episodically and may occur in any area of operations, requiring a military response regardless of ongoing operations elsewhere. They may occur alongside a variety of nongovernmental organizations or the forces of other nations operating—at least initially—without benefit of a commonly stated purpose or formally established divisions of responsibility and authority. Additionally, they may occur in uncertain or hostile environments subject to the threat of armed opposition by state or nonstate actors whose objectives are contrary to those of the United States or the international community.

A *crisis* is an incident or situation involving a threat to a nation, its territories, citizens, military forces, possessions, or vital interests that develops rapidly and creates a condition of such diplomatic, economic, political, or military importance that commitment of military forces and resources is contemplated to achieve national objectives. A *contingency* is a situation requiring military operations in response to natural disasters, terrorists, subversives, or as otherwise directed by appropriate authority to protect US interests.

United States military forces need to be able to respond rapidly to crises, either unilaterally or as a part of an interagency or multinational effort, when directed by the President or Secretary of Defense. The United States, by responding rapidly with appropriate options to potential or actual crises, contributes to regional stability. Crisis response and limited contingency operations are typically limited in scope and scale and conducted to achieve a very specific strategic or operational objective. They vary greatly, however, regarding the level of complexity, duration, resources, and degree of cooperation with or participation by other organizations and countries. These operations may stand alone in response to a crisis, such as noncombatant evacuation operations, or be an element of a larger, more complex joint or combined campaign or operation.

The expeditionary character and forward posture of the Marine Corps are proven critical enablers of rapid crisis response. Forward-postured forces—especially ARG/MEUs—play a key role in responding to crises. Their inherent mobility, operational flexibility, and lethality provide the geographic combatant commanders a quick and effective means of intervening to deny an adversary the time to accomplish his objectives. The ARG/MEUs can mitigate the effects of a natural or manmade disaster and facilitate the introduction of additional relief capabilities provided by interorganizational partners and other forces, including Marine Corps forces surged from other global locations.

Marine Corps forces maintain a very high state of expeditionary readiness—additional forces and capabilities can deploy swiftly to crisis areas worldwide. This expeditionary readiness includes the ability to deploy by both sea and air and is further enhanced by the ability of troops to marry up with equipment forward-based in cooperative security locations overseas or forward-postured aboard MPF squadrons.

When the geographic combatant commanders conduct crisis action planning, the Marine Corps component commanders play a key role providing advice regarding the additional forces and capabilities that can rapidly be brought into action, such as alert contingency MAGTFs deployed by organic or intertheater airlift and the equipment sets and supplies embarked aboard prepositioning ships. The geographic combatant commanders have often tasked MAGTF command elements, given their expeditionary responsiveness and command and control capabilities, to provide the nucleus of a joint or combined headquarters. In 2004, III MEF Command Element performed such a role in Operation Unified Assistance after a tsunami ravaged portions of Southeast Asia. The establishment of 3d MEB Command Element under Commander, MARFORPAC; 2d MEB Command Element under Commander, MARFORCOM; and 5th MEB Command Element under Commander, Marine Corps Forces, Central Command as standing headquarters, as well as the embedding of 4th MEB Command Element within the Commander, United States Marine Corps Forces, Africa staff, provides the respective geographic combatant commanders immediate access to additional tactical headquarters for similar purposes.

The following paragraphs identify the types of military operations and activities that Marine Corps forces may conduct within the context of crisis response and limited contingencies. With the exception of consequence management—which is not readily predictable, but certainly a national priority—they are presented in the order of likelihood, as determined through a combination of historical experience and assessments of the unfolding 21st-century security conditions.

CONSEQUENCE MANAGEMENT

Consequence management consists of actions taken to maintain or restore essential services and manage and mitigate problems resulting from disasters and catastrophes, including natural, manmade, or terrorist incidents. When conducted within the continental United States or on US installations overseas, consequence management is closely aligned with military support to civil authorities. The laws of the United States assign primary authority to the states to respond to the consequences of terrorism; the federal government provides assistance, as required. When conducted outside the continental United States in support of a host nation, consequence management closely aligns with foreign humanitarian assistance. The Department of State generally serves as the lead federal agency and will coordinate the actions of Department of Defense elements in support of foreign consequence management activities.

Though each MAGTF maintains an organic capability to perform chemical, biological, radiological, and nuclear consequence management, the Marine Corps may provide additional chemical, biological, radiological, and nuclear response support through the employment of CBIRF or its elements. The Marine Corps trains, organizes, and equips CBIRF to provide rapid response to chemical, biological, or radiological incidents. The CBIRF is well-suited for operations in a wide range of contingencies when designated by the President, the Secretary of Defense, or the geographic combatant commander to which assigned or allocated.

FOREIGN HUMANITARIAN ASSISTANCE

Foreign humanitarian assistance operations relieve or reduce the results of natural or manmade disasters that might present a serious threat to life or result in extensive damage to or loss of property. Humanitarian assistance provided by US forces is generally limited in scope and duration. The assistance is designed to supplement or complement the host nation civil authority's efforts when the need is gravely urgent and when the humanitarian emergency overwhelms normal relief agencies.

Foreign humanitarian assistance operations may be directed by the President or the Secretary of Defense when a serious international situation threatens the political or military stability of a region considered of interest to the United States. Assistance may also occur when the humanitarian situation itself may be sufficient and appropriate to use US forces. The Department of State or the US ambassador in the affected country is responsible for declaring a foreign disaster or situation that requires humanitarian assistance. The Department of State then requests Department of Defense assistance from the Secretary of Defense.

United States military forces participate in three basic types of foreign humanitarian assistance operations—United Nations-led, United States action in concert with other multinational forces, and United States unilateral action. Through the provisioning of security, logistic, engineering, medical support, command and control, and communications capabilities, the Marine Corps can respond rapidly to emergencies or disasters and assist the restoration of order in austere locations. A foreign humanitarian assistance mission could also include securing an environment to allow humanitarian relief efforts. In Operation Provide Comfort (1991), the 24th MEU Special Operations Capable provided security, shelter, food, and water to the dissident Kurdish minority in northern Iraq. The 5th MEB, during Operation Sea Angel (1991), assisted Bangladesh in the aftermath of a devastating tropical cyclone by distributing food and medical supplies and repairing the country's transportation infrastructure. In late 2004 and early 2005, III MEF provided the core of Joint Task Force/Combined Support Force 536 to oversee Operation Unified Assistance, which provided assistance to Indonesia and neighboring areas following an earthquake and subsequent tsunami.

NONCOMBATANT EVACUATION OPERATIONS

Noncombatant evacuation operations involve the use of Department of Defense forces under the direction of Department of State or other authorities for the evacuation of individuals, normally US citizens, who are located in a foreign country and faced with the threat of hostile or potentially hostile actions. Such operations may also include the evacuation of US military personnel, citizens of the host country, and third country nationals friendly to the United States, as determined by the Department of State.

The Department of State is responsible for protecting and evacuating American citizens abroad and for guarding their property. The Department of Defense advises and assists the Department of State in preparing and implementing plans for evacuating US citizens. The US ambassador or chief of the diplomatic mission is responsible for preparing emergency action plans that address the military evacuation of US citizens and designated foreign nationals from a country. Military operations to assist implementation of emergency action plans are the responsibility of the geographic combatant commander.

Characterized by uncertainty, the requirement to conduct a noncombatant evacuation operation may arise without warning because of sudden changes in a country's government, a reoriented political or military relationship with the United States, a sudden hostile threat to US citizens from elements within or external to a foreign country, or a natural disaster. Diplomatic considerations can significantly influence the tactics, methods, and timing of noncombatant evacuation operations. Under ideal circumstances, there may be little or no opposition; however, commanders should anticipate opposition and plan accordingly.

Similar to raids, noncombatant evacuation operations involve swift insertion of a force (normally preceded by an advance party), temporary occupation of objectives, and a planned withdrawal. They differ from raids by the size and purpose of the force. Forces penetrating foreign territory to conduct a noncombatant evacuation operation should be kept to the minimum consistent with mission accomplishment. Forward-deployed MAGTFs, sea-based and task-organized, provide the geographic combatant commanders with multiple response options. Examples of Marine Corps noncombatant evacuation operations are Operations Assured Response (Liberia, 1996), Noble Obelisk (Sierra Leone, 1997), and Silver Wake (Albania, 1997). A MAGTF might conduct the entire operation itself or provide support forces.

STRIKES AND RAIDS

A strike is an attack to damage or destroy an objective or a capability for political purposes. An example of a strike is Operation Praying Mantis (1988), during which a SPMAGTF destroyed two oil platforms that Iran was using to coordinate attacks on merchant shipping. In recent years, MEU aircraft flying from ARG shipping attacked targets ashore in support of Operations Deliberate Force (Bosnia, 1995), Noble Anvil (Yugoslavia, 1999), Enduring Freedom, and Iraqi Freedom.

A raid is an operation to temporarily seize an area in order to secure information, confuse an adversary, capture personnel or equipment, or destroy a capability. It ends with a planned withdrawal upon completion of the assigned mission. Operations of this type include amphibious raids, such as those conducted by 13th MEU in 1991 to destroy enemy equipment on Umm Al Maradim Island and to capture prisoners on Faylakah Island during Operation Desert Storm.

EMBASSY DEFENSE

Detachments from the Marine Corps Embassy Security Group provide *internal* security services to selected Department of State embassies, consulates, and legations. They prevent the compromise of classified material and equipment and protect United States citizens and Government property. Each of these diplomatic posts normally relies on host nation law enforcement or military forces to provide external security. When periods of civil unrest, revolution, and lawlessness exceed the host nation's abilities to contain, Marine Corps forces have often been called upon to defend US diplomatic posts and personnel against *external* danger, such as during Operations Sharp Edge (Liberia, 1990), Quick Response (Central African Republic, 1996), and Resolve Resolute (Albania, 1998). Embassy defense operations are frequently conducted in conjunction with noncombatant evacuation operations.

RECOVERY OPERATIONS

Recovery operations search for, locate, identify, rescue, and return personnel or human remains, sensitive equipment, or items critical to national security. Hostile forces may oppose recovery operations. One aspect of recovery operations is personnel recovery, which is an implicit requirement in all combat operations. All elements of the MAGTF possess the ability to support personnel recovery, or participate in the recovery of isolated personnel. The primary Marine Corps method for personnel recovery is the tactical recovery of aircraft and personnel.

Tactical recovery of aircraft and personnel includes rescue or extraction, by surface or air, of downed aircraft/personnel and equipment; aircraft sanitization; and advanced trauma life support in a benign or hostile environment. Tactical recovery of aircraft and personnel examples include the *USS Kearsarge* ARG/24th MEU's rescue of a downed US Air Force pilot in Bosnia in 1995 and the rescue of another US Air Force pilot in Libya in 2011 by the *USS Kearsarge* ARG/26th MEU.

DEFENSE SUPPORT OF CIVIL AUTHORITIES

Defense support of civil authorities involves temporary military support when permitted by law and normally occurs when an emergency overwhelms the capabilities of the civil authorities. Support of civil authorities may be as diverse as temporary augmentation of government workers during strikes, restoration of law and order in the aftermath of riots, protecting life and property, or providing humanitarian relief after a natural disaster. Limitations on military forces providing support to civil authorities include the United States Code, Title 18, *Crimes and Criminal Procedure*, sec. 1385, which prohibits the use of federal military forces to enforce or otherwise execute laws unless expressly authorized by the Constitution or by an act of Congress.

During disaster relief operations, Marine Corps forces have provided military support to civil authorities. For example, following Hurricane Andrew in Florida in 1992, a SPMAGTF established and maintained a temporary city for 2,500 displaced civilians, distributed supplies, and helped restore power to Dade County. Marines also supported relief efforts after Hurricane Katrina in Louisiana in 2003. Marine forces are called upon almost yearly to fight wildfires in California.

Peace Operations

Peace operations broadly refer to those military, multiagency, and multinational actions to contain conflict, redress the peace, and shape the environment to support reconciliation and rebuilding, and facilitate the transition to legitimate governance. Peace operations include peacekeeping, peace enforcement, peacemaking, peace building, and conflict prevention efforts. Peace operations occur under the provisions of the United Nations Charter. The specific United Nations resolution may dictate rules of engagement, use of combat power, and type of units deployed. See General Zinni's 22 principles for peace operations at the end of this chapter.

Peacekeeping

Peacekeeping operations are military operations undertaken with the consent of all major parties to a dispute. These operations monitor and facilitate implementation of an agreement, such as a cease fire or truce, and support diplomatic efforts to reach a long-term political settlement. Peacekeeping operations involve high levels of mutual consent and strict impartiality by the intervening force and are authorized under Chapter VI of the United Nations Charter. Forces conducting peacekeeping operations must be prepared to transition rapidly to peace enforcement operations as conditions change or one or more of the belligerents withdraw its consent. Preparation should include planning, task organization, equipment, and appropriate force protection measures. An example of peacekeeping is the deployment of Marine Corps forces to Lebanon in 1982–83. This mission began as a peacekeeping operation, but evolved into a peace enforcement operation.

Peace Enforcement

Peace enforcement is the application of military force, or the threat of its use, normally pursuant to international authorization to compel compliance with resolutions or sanctions designed to maintain or restore peace and order. Unlike peacekeeping, peace enforcement neither requires the consent of the states involved nor of other parties to the conflict. Furthermore, the intervening force is not necessarily considered impartial. Such operations qualify under the mandate of Chapter VII of the United Nations Charter. The purpose of peace enforcement is to maintain or restore peace and support diplomatic efforts to reach a long-term settlement. Peace enforcement operations include intervention operations, as well as operations to restore order, enforce sanctions, forcibly separate belligerents, and establish and supervise exclusion zones to create an environment for a truce or cease fire. A MAGTF must deploy sufficient combat power to present a credible threat, protect the force, and conduct the full range of military operations necessary to restore order and separate the warring factions, if necessary. Examples of peace enforcement are Operation Power Pack (Dominican Republic, 1965) and the initial phase of US involvement in Haiti during Operation Uphold Democracy (1995).

Peacemaking

Peacemaking is the process of diplomacy, mediation, negotiation, or other forms of peaceful settlements that arranges an end to a dispute and resolves issues that led to it. Military activities supporting peacemaking include security assistance and military-to-military relations.

Peace Building

Peace building refers to stability actions, predominately diplomatic and economic, that strengthen and rebuild governmental infrastructure and institutions in order to avoid a relapse into conflict. These activities include restoring civil authority, rebuilding physical infrastructure, and re-establishing civil institutions, such as schools and medical facilities.

Conflict Prevention

Conflict prevention is a peace operation employing complementary diplomatic, civil, and, when necessary, military means, to monitor and identify the causes of conflict and act in a timely manner to prevent the occurrence, escalation, or resumption of hostilities. Activities aimed at conflict prevention are often conducted under Chapter VI of the United Nations Charter. Conflict prevention can include fact-finding missions, consultations, warnings, inspections, and monitoring.

General Anthony Zinni's 22 Principles for Peace Operations

One of the US military's most experienced leaders in the field of irregular warfare, General Anthony Zinni, USMC (Retired), developed the following considerations for humanitarian assistance, peacekeeping, and peace enforcement operations:

Each operation is unique. We must be careful what lessons we learn from a single experience.

Each operation has two key aspects: (1) the degree of complexity of the operation and (2) the degree of consent of the involved parties and the international community for the operation.

The earlier the involvement, the better the chance for success.

Start planning as early as possible, including everyone in the planning process.

Make as thorough an assessment as possible before deployment.

Conduct a thorough analysis, determining the centers of gravity, end state, commander's intent, measures of effectiveness, exit strategy, and the estimated duration of the operation.

Stay focused on the mission. Line up military tasks with political objectives. Avoid mission creep and allow for mission shifts. A mission shift is a conscious decision, made by the political leadership in consultation with the military commander, responding to a changing situation.

Centralize planning and decentralize execution of the operation. This allows subordinate commanders to make appropriate adjustments to meet their individual situations or rapidly changing conditions.

Coordinate everything with everbody. Establish coordination mechanisms that include political, military, nongovernmental organizations, international organizations, and other interested parties.

Know the culture and the issues. We must know who the decisionmakers are. We must know how the involved parties think. We cannot impose our cultural values on people with their own culture.

Start or restore key institutiions as early as possible.

Don't lose the initiative and momentum.

Don't make unneccessary enemies. If you do, don't treat them gently. Avoid mindsets or using words that might come back to haunt you.

Seek unity of effort and unity of command. Create the fewest possible seams between organizations and involved parties.

Open a dialogue with everyone. Establish a forum for each of the involved parties.

Encourage innovation and nontraditional responses.

Personalities often are more important than processes. You need the right people in the right places.

Be careful whom you empower. Think carefully about those you invite to participate, use as a go-between, or enter into contracts with since you are giving them influence in the process.

Decide on the image you want to portray and keep focused on it. Whatever the image, humanitarian or as firm, but well-intentioned, agents of change, ensure your troops are aware of it so they can conduct themselves accordingly.

Centralize information management. Ensure that your public affairs and psychological operations are coordinated, accurate, and consistent.

Seek compatibility in all operations; cultural and political compatibility and military interoperability are crucial to success. The interest, cultures, capabilities, and motivations of all the parties may not be uniform, but they cannot be allowed to work against each other.

Senior commanders and their staffs need the most education and training in nontraditional roles. The troops need awareness and understanding of their roles. The commander and the staff need to develop and apply new skills, such as negotiating, supporting humanitarian organizations effectively and appropriately, and building coordinating agencies with humanitarian goals.

CHAPTER 6

Major Operations and Campaigns

"Military campaigns are not conducted in a vacuum. Military power is employed in conjunction with other instruments of national power—diplomatic, economic, and informational—to achieve strategic objectives. Depending upon the nature of the operation, the military campaign may be the main effort, or it may be used to support diplomatic or economic efforts. The military campaign must be coordinated with the nonmilitary efforts to ensure that all actions work in harmony to achieve the ends of policy."

—MCDP 1-2

When required to achieve national strategic objectives or protect national interests, the United States may conduct a major operation or campaign. These are large-scale, long-duration operations that typically include multiple phases. They usually involve warfare—armed conflict between or among various combatants, whether nation-states or nonstate groups.

A *major operation* is a series of tactical actions, such as battles, engagements, or strikes, conducted by combat forces of one or several Services. It is coordinated in time and place to achieve strategic or operational objectives in an operational area. These actions can occur simultaneously or sequentially in accordance with a common plan.

A *campaign* is a series of related major operations aimed at achieving strategic and operational objectives within a given time and space. Campaigns are joint in nature—functional and Service components conduct supporting operations in support of campaigns. They are often the most extensive joint efforts in terms of time, the size of the forces involved, and the commitment of other resources.

The principal tool by which commanders translate national strategic goals into tactical action is the campaign plan. Like planning at any level, framing the problem is critical to successful campaign planning. An essential aspect of problem framing at this level is recognition of the military strategy and forms of warfare the combatants employ.

A military strategy of annihilation is used to achieve an unlimited political objective, such as the overthrow of the enemy leadership or its unconditional surrender. A strategy of erosion may be used to achieve a limited political objective by wearing down an adversary's will to continue the struggle. Alternatively, a strategy of annihilation can also be used to achieve a limited political objective if it is believed that the enemy will continue to resist as long as he has any means to do so.

Joint doctrine delineates two basic forms of warfare—*traditional* and *irregular*—but acknowledges this naming convention is not ideal. It describes traditional warfare as a violent struggle for domination between nation-states or coalitions and alliances of nation-states. Irregular warfare is described as a violent struggle among state and nonstate actors for legitimacy and influence over the relevant population(s). It must be recognized, however, that "traditional" and "irregular" conflict in pure form are rare. World War II is generally considered a traditional conflict because it largely involved conventional combat among the forces of nation-states, yet it also had irregular aspects that included partisans in the Philippines, France, and Yugoslavia as well as nonstate entities, such as the Chinese Communists, fielding major forces to oppose both their nationalist countrymen and the Japanese. Conversely, the war in Vietnam is generally viewed as irregular, yet Marines were often heavily engaged in conventional combat against large formations of North Vietnamese Army regulars. As these examples illustrate, naming conventions may help inform understanding of a conflict, but they cannot fully define it. As noted in MCDP 1, "War is both timeless and ever changing. While the basic nature of war is constant, the means and methods we use evolve continuously."

A combatant's military strategy and forms of warfare are closely intertwined and must be understood to successfully frame the problem. During the American Revolution, for example, a succession of British commanders employed a traditional form of warfare in pursuit of a strategy of annihilation. Failing to recognize that their opponent was employing both traditional *and* irregular forms of warfare in a strategy of erosion, they won a succession of tactical victories, but failed at achieving their national strategic goal of retaining the American colonies.

Campaign plans rooted in national strategic goals establish the necessary context for tactical actions. Failure to understand the basic strategic approach (annihilation or erosion) and the form(s) of warfare (traditional, irregular, or a hybrid of the two) will prevent the development of a coherent campaign plan and may cause military and diplomatic leaders to work at cross-purposes. While these factors drive campaign planning, which drives tactical actions, the reverse is also true. Tactical results generate modifications to the campaign plan, which may have strategic implications.

The art of campaigning requires understanding when military force is the main effort and when it is acting in support of some other instrument of national power. Lower-echelon commanders must understand the strategic context of their tactical missions if they are to provide useful feedback to higher levels on the effectiveness of their operations. Consequently, commanders must clearly communicate strategic goals to every level.

Given their size, scope, and duration, major operations and campaigns involve a complex, interwoven, and evolving blend of many different types of operations. Counterinsurgency operations, for example, will normally involve a mixture of stability operations and defensive measures to protect friendly forces, material assets, and infrastructure. Offensive actions may occur only sporadically as a result of actionable intelligence.

In a more traditional conflict, while one command might be conducting an attack, there may be other units conducting security operations to protect the command's flanks and lines of communications. Meanwhile, adjacent units may be on the defense, while others are retiring following a relief in place. Still other units could be conducting stability operations within captured or liberated areas.

Activities and operations associated with major operations and campaigns have applicability throughout the range of military operations. For example, Marine Corps forces often conduct multilateral and bilateral exercises focused on developing interoperability and combined warfighting skills. These large-scale cooperative security events have significant deterrence value as well. Similarly, crisis response and limited contingency operations conducted in uncertain or hostile environments may be heavily reliant on the combat capabilities, tactics, techniques, and procedures developed primarily for major operations and campaigns.

Commanders must be capable of orchestrating—and Marine Corps forces must be capable executing—innumerable combinations of activities and operations, discussed in more detail in subsequent chapters.

COUNTERINSURGENCY

Counterinsurgency refers to those military, paramilitary, political, economic, psychological, and civic actions taken by a government to defeat an insurgency. Counterinsurgency and insurgency reside within a broad category of conflict known as irregular warfare.

DEFENSEIVE OPERATIONS

Although offensive action is generally viewed as the decisive form of combat, it may be necessary, or appropriate, to conduct defensive operations. There are three types of defensive operations—the area defense, the mobile defense, and retrogrades.

OFFENSIVE OPERATIONS

Offensive operations seek to gain, maintain, and exploit the initiative, causing the enemy to react. Offensive operations focus on the enemy. There are four types of offensive operations—movement to contact, attack, exploitation, and pursuit. These types may occur sequentially, simultaneously, or independently throughout the depth of the battlespace.

OTHER TACTICAL OPERATIONS

Other tactical operations include passages of lines, linkups, reliefs in place, obstacle crossings, and breakouts from encirclement. Each of these operations is complex. They require detailed planning and close coordination.

RECONNAISSANCE AND SECURITY OPERATIONS

Reconnaissance operations use visual observation or other detection methods to obtain information about the activities and resources of an enemy or adversary. Commanders use that information to help them understand the larger environment and the nature of the problem. Reconnaissance can help reduce uncertainties about an area and an enemy who is actively concealing information about his forces and intentions. Counterreconnaissance consists of all active and passive measures taken to prevent hostile observation of a force or area.

Security operations are an essential component of all operations. They involve measures taken by a military unit, activity, or installation to protect itself against all acts designed to, or which may, impair its effectiveness. As the definition implies, security operations can be defensive in nature, such as elements of the GCE preventing the enemy from collecting friendly information, protecting the force from surprise, or deceiving the enemy about friendly capabilities and intentions. Security operations can also involve significant offensive actions, such as the ACE conducting shaping actions in the MAGTF's deep area to intercept, engage, delay, or disorganize the enemy. There are three types of security missions—screen, guard, and cover.

STABILITY OPERATIONS

Stability operations encompass various military missions, tasks, and activities conducted outside the United States in coordination with other instruments of national power to maintain or re-establish a safe and secure environment and/or provide essential governmental services, emergency infrastructure reconstruction, and humanitarian relief. They occur throughout all phases of conflict and across the range of military operations. The magnitude of stability operations missions may range from small-scale, short-duration to large-scale, long duration. Marine Corps forces may support stability operations led by other US Government departments or agencies, foreign governments and security forces, international governmental organizations, or when otherwise directed. In some circumstances, Marine Corps forces may lead stability operations until they transition lead responsibility to one of the aforementioned organizations.

SUSTAINMENT OPERATIONS

Sustainment is the ability to ensure combat forces are provided the support required until the mission is completed. Marine Corps forces normally organize as self-contained and self-sustaining organizations with sufficient logistic capabilities to accomplish assigned missions.

CHAPTER 7

Counterinsurgency Operations

> *"The first, the supreme, the most far-reaching act of judgment that the statesman and commander have to make is to establish... the kind of war on which they are embarking; neither mistaking it for, nor trying to turn it into, something that is alien to its nature. This is the first of all strategic questions and the most comprehensive."*
> —Carl von Clausewitz, *On War*

> *"Essential though it is, the military action is secondary to the political one, its primary purpose being to afford the political power enough freedom to work safely with the population."*
> —David Gallula, *Counterinsurgency Warfare*, 1964

Insurgency is the organized use of subversion and violence by a group or movement that seeks to overthrow or force change of a governing authority. Insurgency can also refer to the group itself. Each insurgency is unique in terms of purpose and scope, and a given insurgency might pursue political, ideological, or criminal objectives on a local, national, regional, or transnational level. Counterinsurgency involves comprehensive civilian and military efforts taken to defeat an insurgency and to address any core grievances. Political power is the central issue in insurgencies and counterinsurgencies; each side aims to get the people to accept its governance or authority as legitimate. Insurgents use politics, diplomacy, information—including appeals to religious, ethnic, or ideological beliefs—military actions and economics to overthrow the existing authority. Counterinsurgents use all instruments of national power to sustain the established or emerging government.

Counterinsurgency is an extremely complex form of warfare that often requires actions counterintuitive to traditional warfare (see the end of the chapter for paradoxes of counterinsurgency). At its core, counterinsurgency is a struggle for the population's support. The protection, welfare, and support of the people are vital to success. Gaining and maintaining that support is a formidable challenge. Achieving these aims requires integrating the efforts of many nonmilitary and host nation agencies in a comprehensive approach.

Designing operations that achieve the desired end state require counterinsurgents to understand the culture and the problems they face. Both insurgents and counterinsurgents are fighting for the support of the populace; however, insurgents are constrained by neither the law of war nor the bounds of human decency as Western nations understand them. In fact, some insurgents are willing to commit suicide and kill civilians in carrying out their operations—and deem this a legitimate option. They also will do anything to preserve their greatest advantage, the ability to hide among the people. These amoral and often barbaric enemies survive by their wits, constantly adapting to the situation. Successfully countering them requires developing the ability to learn and adapt rapidly and continuously.

Popular support allows counterinsurgents to develop the intelligence necessary to identify and defeat insurgents. Designing and executing a comprehensive campaign to secure the populace and then gain their support requires carefully coordinating actions over time to produce success. One of these actions is developing host nation security forces that can assume primary responsibility for combating the insurgency.

Long-term success in counterinsurgency depends on the local population taking charge of its own affairs and accepting the government's rule. Achieving this condition requires the government to eliminate as many causes of the insurgency as feasible, including eliminating those violent extremists whose beliefs prevent them from ever reconciling with the government. Over time, counterinsurgents aim to enable a country or regime to provide the security and rule of law that allow establishment of social services and growth of economic activity. Therefore, counterinsurgency involves the application of national power in the political, military, economic, social, information, and infrastructure fields. Political and military leaders and planners should never underestimate the scale and complexity of counterinsurgency; moreover, they should recognize that military forces cannot succeed in counterinsurgency without the active involvement of other government agencies. Purely military solutions to counterinsurgency operations are unlikely to succeed. Peacekeeping and stability operations that support counterinsurgency often depend on other government agencies, such as Department of State, and host nation government stability and legitimacy. Counterinsurgency campaigns are generally long, complex undertakings.

CONTEMPORARY IMPERATIVES OF COUNTERINSURGENCY

Recent counterinsurgency experiences have identified an important set of additional imperatives to consider for success in counterinsurgency operations.

Manage Information and Expectations

Information and expectations are related; skillful counterinsurgents must manage both. To limit discontent and build support, the host nation government and any counterinsurgents create and maintain a realistic set of expectations among the populace, friendly military forces, and the international community. Information operations, including military information support operations, and the related activities of public affairs and civil-military operations are key tools to achieve steady progress toward a set of reasonable expectations. These expectations can increase the populace's tolerance for the inevitable inconveniences entailed by ongoing counterinsurgency operations. Where a large US force is present to help establish a regime, such progress can extend the period before the populace views a force of liberation as a force of occupation.

United States forces start with a built-in challenge because of their reputation for accomplishment, what some call the "man on the moon syndrome." This idea refers to the expressed belief that a nation able to put a man on the moon can quickly restore basic services. Therefore, US agencies trying to fan enthusiasm for their efforts should avoid making unrealistic promises. In some cultures, failure to deliver promised results is automatically interpreted as deliberate deception, rather than good intentions gone awry. In other cultures, exorbitant promises are normal and people do not expect them to be kept. Effective counterinsurgents understand local norms; they use locally tailored approaches to control expectations. Managing expectations also involves demonstrating economic and political progress to show the populace how life is improving. Increasing the number of people who feel they have a stake in the success of the village, province, or nation and its government is a key to successful counterinsurgency operations. In the end, victory comes, in large measure, by convincing the populace that their lives will be better under the host nation government than under an insurgent regime.

To better manage expectations, both counterinsurgents and the host nation government must ensure their deeds match their words. They also must understand action has an information reaction. Counterinsurgents and the host nation government must carefully consider that impact on the many audiences involved in the conflict and on the sidelines. They work actively to shape responses via a communication strategy to further their goals. In particular, messages to different audiences must be consistent. In the global information environment, people in the area of operations can access the Internet and satellite television to determine the messages counterinsurgents are sending to the international community and the US public. Any perceived inconsistency reduces credibility and undermines counterinsurgency efforts.

Use the Appropriate Level of Force

Any use of force generates a series of reactions. There may be times when an overwhelming effort is necessary to destroy or intimidate an insurgent entity and reassure the populace. Extremist insurgent combatants often have to be killed; however, counterinsurgents should calculate the type and amount of force applied and who wields it for any operation. An operation that kills five insurgents is counterproductive if collateral damage leads to the generation of fifty new insurgents.

In a counterinsurgency environment, it is vital for military commanders to adopt appropriate and measured levels of force and apply that force precisely and proportionally to accomplish the mission without causing unnecessary destruction of infrastructure, suffering, or loss of life. Normally, counterinsurgents use force continuum procedures to minimize potential loss of life. These procedures are especially appropriate during convoy operations and at checkpoints and roadblocks. Force continuum refers to using lesser means of force when such use is likely to create the desired effects without endangering their own forces, others, or mission accomplishment. Escalation of force continuum procedures do not limit the right of self-defense, including the use of deadly force, when such force is necessary to defend against a hostile act or demonstrated hostile intent. Commanders must ensure their Marines are properly trained in such procedures and, more importantly, in methods of shaping situations so that small unit leaders have to make fewer split-second, life-or-death decisions.

Who wields force is also important. If the host nation police have a reasonable reputation for competence and impartiality, it is better for them to execute urban raids. Local circumstances affect this decision; if the police are seen as part of an ethnic or sectarian group oppressing the general population, their use may be counterproductive. Effective counterinsurgents must understand the character of the local police and popular perceptions of both police and military units. This understanding helps ensure the application of force is appropriate and reinforces the rule of law.

Learn and Adapt

An effective counterinsurgent force is a learning organization. Insurgents constantly shift between military and political phases and tactics. In addition, networked insurgents constantly exchange information about the enemy's vulnerabilities, even with insurgents in distant theaters. However, skillful counterinsurgents can adapt at least as fast as insurgents. Every unit needs to observe, draw, and apply lessons, and then assess results. Commanders must develop an effective system to circulate best practices throughout their command. Combatant commanders might also need to seek new laws or policies that authorize or resource necessary changes. Insurgents shift their areas of operations looking for weak links, so competence and adaptability are critical throughout the counterinsurgent force.

Attack the Network

Insurgencies are normally directed, supported, and sustained through a network of key individuals. These include leaders, recruiters, financiers, logistical facilitators, weapons providers, human smugglers, and, in some cases, individuals who produce/smuggle illicit drugs. Understanding the insurgent network requires infiltration, intelligence sharing, and mapping of network nodes. These activities resemble police work and are long, complex endeavors that can take months or years. Once critical actors and physical targets are identified, they are attacked through arrests or lethal operations, preferably accomplished in simultaneous raids in order to dismantle the network at one time.

Empower at the Lowest Levels Through Mission Command

Mission command is the conduct of military operations through decentralized execution based upon mission type orders. Successful mission command results from subordinate leaders at all echelons exercising disciplined initiative within the commander's intent. It requires an environment of trust and mutual understanding and is the preferred method of the Marine Corps for commanding and controlling forces during all types of operations. Under mission command, commanders provide subordinates with a mission, their commander's intent, a concept of operations, and resources adequate to accomplish the mission. Higher commanders empower subordinates to make decisions within the framework of their intent. They leave details of execution to their subordinates and expect them to use initiative and judgment to accomplish the mission.

Mission command is ideally suited to the mosaic nature of counterinsurgency operations. Local commanders have the best grasp or understanding of their situation. Under mission command, they have access to or control of the resources needed to produce timely intelligence, conduct tactical operations, and manage information and civil-military operations. Effective counterinsurgency operations are decentralized, and higher commanders owe it to their subordinates to push as many capabilities and authorities as possible to their level. Mission command encourages subordinate initiative and facilitates learning at every level. It is a major characteristic of a counterinsurgency force to be able to adapt and react at least as quickly as the insurgents.

Support the Host Nation

United States forces committed to a counterinsurgency effort assist a host nation government. The long-term goal is to prepare a government to stand by itself. In the end, the host nation has to win on its own. Achieving this victory requires viable local leaders and institutions. United States forces and agencies can help, but host nation elements must accept responsibilities to achieve real victory. While it may be easier for US military units to conduct operations themselves, it is better to strengthen local forces and institutions and subsequently assist them. The temptation will be to train host nation forces "in our own image," but Marines must resist this urge and train forces in a manner appropriate to their situation and purpose. Host nation governments ultimately have to solve their problems. Eventually all foreign forces are seen as interlopers or occupiers; the sooner the main effort can transition to host nation institutions without unacceptable degradation, the better.

Establish Genuine Partnerships

Partnering is an arrangement between US and host nation forces in which they operate together to achieve missions success while building capability and capacity. Partnering should be a real union of the organizations involved. It cannot be done on occasion, when convenient, or as time permits. Nor should it be limited to periodic or occasional combat operations. Real partnering is messy and hard—a continuous, collective, and collaborative effort on both large and small tasks toward a common goal. It requires mutual respect despite differences in size, skill, training, capability, or culture. In every partnership, each participant has relative strengths. Effective partnering will exploit all these relative strengths and overcome respective weaknesses. It also requires flexible and innovative leaders capable of forging strong personal relationships—which are a key to successful counterinsurgency efforts. Ultimately, however, successful counterinsurgency partnerships are designed to end as host nation forces gain the capability and capacity to stand alone.

SUCCESSFUL AND UNSUCCESSFUL COUNTERINSURGENCY PRACTICES

Successful practices of counterinsurgency include—

- Emphasizing intelligence.
- Focusing on the population, its needs, and its security.
- Establishing and expanding secure areas.
- Isolating insurgents from the populace.
- Conducting effective, persuasive, and continuous military information support operations.
- Providing amnesty and rehabilitation for those willing to support the government.

- Pacing host nation police in the lead with military support as soon as the security situation permits.
- Expanding and diversifying the host nation police force.
- Training military forces to conduct counterinsurgency.
- Embedding quality advisors with the host nation forces.
- Denying sanctuary to insurgents.
- Encouraging strong political and military cooperation and information sharing.
- Securing host nation borders.
- Protecting key infrastructure.

Unsuccessful practices of counterinsurgency include—

- Overemphasizing killing and capturing the enemy rather than securing and engaging the population.
- Conducting large-scale operations as the norm.
- Concentrating military forces in large bases for protection.
- Focusing special operations forces primarily on raiding.
- Placing low priority on assigning quality advisors to host nation forces.
- Building and training host nation security forces in the US military's image.
- Ignoring peacetime government processes, including legal procedures.
- Allowing open borders, airspace, and coastlines.

Paradoxes of Counterinsurgency Operations

In many ways, the conduct of counterinsurgency is counterintuitive to the traditional US view of war—although counterinsurgency operations have actually formed a substantial part of the US military experience. The following paradoxes of counterinsurgency operations are examples of the different mindset required. These paradoxes are offered to stimulate thinking, not to limit it. The applicability of the thoughts behind the paradoxes depends on a sense of the local situation and, in particular, the state of the insurgency. For example, the admonition, "Sometimes, the more force used, the less effective it is." does not apply when the enemy is coming over the barricades; however, that thought is applicable when increased security is achieved in an area. In short, these paradoxes should not be reduced to a checklist; rather, they should be used with considerable thought.

The Host Nation Doing Something Tolerably Is Normally Better Than Us Doing It Well

It is just as important to consider who performs an operation as it is to assess how well it is done. When the United States is supporting a host nation, long-term success requires establishing viable host nation leaders and institutions that can carry on without significant US support. The longer that process takes, the more US public support will wane and the more the local populace will question the legitimacy of their own forces and government. General Creighton Abrams, the US commander in Vietnam in 1971, recognized this fact when he said, "There's very clear evidence, . . . in some things, that we helped too much. And we *retarded* the Vietnamese by doing it. . . . *We* can't run this thing. . . . *They've* got to run it. The nearer we get to that, the better off *they* are and the better off *we* are."

T.E. Lawrence made a similar observation while leading the Arab Revolt against the Ottoman Empire in 1917: "Do not try to do too much with your own hands. Better the Arabs do it tolerably than that you do it perfectly. It is their war, and you are to help them, not to win it for them." A key word in Lawrence's advice is "tolerably." If the host nation cannot perform tolerably, counterinsurgents supporting the host nation may have to act. Experience, knowledge of the area of operations, and cultural sensitivity are essential to deciding when such action is necessary.

The More Successful The Counterinsurgency Is,
The Less Force Can Be Used And The More Risk Must Be Accepted

As the level of insurgent violence drops, the requirements of international law and the expectations of the populace lead to a reduction in direct military actions by counterinsurgents. More reliance is placed on police work, rules of engagement may be tightened, and troops may have to exercise increased restraint. Marines may also have to accept more risk to maintain involvement with the people.

Sometimes Doing Nothing Is The Best Reaction

Often insurgents carry out a terrorist act or guerrilla raid with the primary purpose of enticing counterinsurgents to overreact or at least to react in a way that insurgents can exploit—for example, opening fire on a crowd or executing a clearing operation that creates more enemies than it takes off the streets. If an assessment of the effects of a COA determines that more negative than positive effects may result, an alternative, such as *not* acting, should be considered.

Tactical Success Guarantees Nothing

As important as they are in achieving security, military actions by themselves cannot achieve success in counterinsurgency. Insurgents that never defeat counterinsurgents in combat still may achieve their strategic objectives. Tactical actions must be linked not only to strategic and operational military objectives, but also to the host nation's essential political goals. Without those connections, lives and resources may be wasted for no real gain.

> ## PARADOXES OF COUNTERINSURGENCY OPERATIONS—Continued
>
> **If A Tactic Works This Week, It Might Not Work Next Week;**
> **If It Works In This Province, It Might Not Work In The Next**
> Competent insurgents are adaptive. They are often part of a widespread network that communicates constantly and instantly. Insurgents quickly adjust to successful counterinsurgency practices and rapidly disseminate information throughout the insurgency. Indeed, the more effective a counterinsurgency tactic is, the faster it may become out of date because insurgents have a greater need to counter it. Effective leaders at all levels avoid complacency and are at least as adaptive as their enemies. There is no "silver bullet" set of counterinsurgency procedures. Constantly developing new practices is essential.
>
> **Sometimes, The More Force Used, The Less Effective It Is**
> Any use of force produces many effects, not all of which can be foreseen. The more force applied, the greater the chance of collateral damage and mistakes. Using substantial force also increases the opportunity for insurgent propaganda to portray lethal military activities as brutal. In contrast, using force precisely and discriminately strengthens the rule of law that needs to be established. As noted previously, the key for counterinsurgents is knowing when more force is needed—and when it might be counterproductive. This judgment involves constant assessment of the security situation and a sense of timing regarding insurgents' actions.
>
> **Sometimes, The More You Protect Your Force, The Less Secure You May Be**
> Ultimate success in counterinsurgency is gained by protecting the populace, not the counterinsurgency force. If military forces remain in their compounds, they lose touch with the people, appear to be running scared, and cede the initiative to the insurgents. Aggressive saturation, patrolling, ambushes, and listening post operations must be conducted; risk shared with the populace; and contact maintained. The effectiveness of establishing patrol bases and operational support bases should be weighed against the effectiveness of using larger unit bases. These practices ensure access to the intelligence needed to drive operations. Following them reinforces the connections with the populace that help establish real legitimacy.
>
> **Often, The Most Effective Weapons For Counterinsurgents Do Not Shoot**
> Counterinsurgents often achieve the most meaningful success in garnering public support and legitimacy for the host nation government with activities that do not involve killing insurgents, though killing clearly will often be necessary. Arguably, the decisive battle is for the people's minds; hence, synchronizing military information support operations with other efforts is critical. Every action, including uses of force, must be "wrapped in a bodyguard of information." While security is essential to setting the stage for overall progress, lasting victory comes from a vibrant economy, political participation, and restored hope. Particularly after security has been achieved, dollars and ballots will have more important effects than bombs and bullets. This is a time when "money is ammunition." Depending on the state of the insurgency, therefore, Marines should prepare to execute many nonmilitary missions to support counterinsurgency efforts.
>
> **Many Important Decisions Are Not Made By Generals**
> Successful counterinsurgency operations require competence and judgment by Marines at all levels. Indeed, young leaders—the "strategic corporals"—often make decisions at the tactical level that have strategic consequences. Senior leaders set the proper direction and climate with thorough training and clear guidance; then, they trust their subordinates to do the right thing. Leaders must be trained and educated to adapt to their local situations, understand the legal and ethical implications of their actions, and exercise initiative and sound judgment in accordance with their senior commanders' intent.

CHAPTER 8

Defensive Operations

"A sudden powerful transition to the offensive—the flashing sword of vengeance—is the greatest moment for the defence [sic]."

—Carl von Clausewitz
Warriors' Words

"Counterattack is the soul of defense . . . We wait for the moment when the enemy shall expose himself to a counter-stroke, the success of which will so far cripple him as to render us relatively strong enough to pass to the offensive ourselves."

— Sir Julian S. Corbett
Warriors' Words

The Marine Corps forces conduct defensive operations, often in combination with offensive operations, to defeat an enemy attack, gain time, or economize forces. During the early days of the Korean War (1950–53) the 1st Marine Brigade (Provisional) participated in defensive operations along the Pusan Perimeter. These operations gave the 1st MARDIV extra time to embark and deploy to Korea where it conducted an amphibious assault at Inchon to kick off the United Nation's long awaited offensive.

While opposing forms, the offense and defense are not mutually exclusive. In fact, they cannot exist separately. (MCDP 1) For example, during the first 38 days of Operation Desert Storm, I MEF/United State Marine Corps Forces, Central Command's aviation forces conducted offensive operations while the other elements of the MAGTF completed preparations for the ground assault from defensive positions.

Defensive operations require agility and flexibility since the defender is constantly seeking to regain the initiative. An effective defense will normally involve the following:

- Use of intelligence assets to locate enemy forces.
- Combined use of fire and maneuver to blunt the enemy's momentum.
- Speed that facilitates transition of friendly forces to the offense.

While the defense can deny victory to the enemy, it rarely results in victory for the defender. The defense, however, tends to be the more efficient form of warfare, expending less energy than the offense. For example, favorable and familiar terrain, friendly civilian populations, known enemy operational patterns subject to exploitation, and interior lines may prompt a commander to assume the defense to reduce enemy capabilities that are essential to his success. The attacking enemy usually chooses the time and place he will strike the defender. The defender uses his advantages of prepared defensive positions, concentrated firepower, obstacles, and barriers to slow the enemy's advance and disrupt the flow of his assault. Marines exploited these advantages in the defense of the Khe Sanh Combat Base, Republic of South Vietnam, during the Tet Offensive of 1968. Using aggressive defensive tactics and well-placed obstacles supported by responsive and continuous fires, the 26th Marines (Reinforced) destroyed two North Vietnamese army divisions.

While in the defense, the commander conducts shaping actions, such as attacking enemy forces echeloned in depth and/or his sustainment capabilities. These shaping actions help to set the conditions for decisive action, such as the defeat of the enemy's main effort by a counterattack that could allow the friendly force to transition to offensive operations.

ORGANIZATION OF THE DEFENSE

As in the offense, the MAGTF commander must also consider the organization of the battlespace and the force for the defense. As with other types of operations, the MAGTF commander organizes his battlespace for the defense into three areas—deep, close, and rear—in which the defending force performs specific functions.

Deep Area

The MAGTF conducts security operations in its deep area consistent with the security missions of screen, guard, and cover. Accordingly the MAGTF commander seeks to gather, gain, and maintain contact (visual or physical); protect the force by fighting to gain time; and/or to intercept, engage, delay, and disorganize the enemy to facilitate GCE success during close operations should they be required. Security operations in the MAGTF deep area (spatial reference) are a form of shaping operations (purpose base).

The MAGTF deep area includes all the battlespace not assigned to subordinate units. Unless designated to subordinate units, the MAGTF command element is responsible for the conduct of all operations in the deep area. For the MAGTF commander, the operational reach of the ACE allows him to create depth to the defense by extending the deep area as far forward as is tactically feasible. During the stability and support phase of Operation Iraqi Freedom (subsequent Operation Iraqi Freedom rotations) following the fall of Baghdad and the Hussein government, the Marine Corps-led Multinational Force-West established a security area as part of its deep operations. It included vast areas of largely unpopulated terrain within Al Anbar Province. The MEF (Fwd) command element, as Multinational Force-West, tasked the ACE to conduct reconnaissance to track activity in that area, and it occasionally conducted limited duration and limited objective operations in the security area to disrupt enemy safe havens and lines of communications.

Close Area

The close area is normally the province of the GCE(s). The MAGTF's role in the close area is to monitor, facilitate, and support the GCE operations primarily through resource allocation. The GCE will typically organize for the defense with security, main battle, and rear areas (see fig. 8-1). The GCE commander typically positions forces in the main battle area to defeat, destroy, or contain enemy assaults. Reserves/counterattack force may employ in the main battle area to destroy enemy forces, reduce penetrations or regain lost terrain, execute a

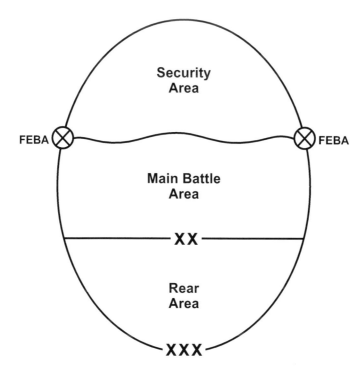

Figure 8-1. Organization of the Battlespace.

counterattack, or exploit weakness in the attack that hastens defeat of the enemy's attack. The MAGTF may establish a separate reserve or dual-designate the GCE reserve. If the latter, the MAGTF commander must articulate who can commit the reserve. See MCWP 3-1, *Ground Combat Operations*, for more information regarding the GCE in defense.

Rear Area

The MAGTF rear area extends forward from the command's rear boundary to the rear of the area assigned to the command's subordinate units. Rear area operations include those functions of security and sustainment required to maintain continuity of operations by the entire force. Rear area operations protect the sustainment effort as well as deny use of the rear area to the enemy. The rear area may not always be contiguous with the main battle area.

TYPES OF DEFENSIVE OPERATIONS

There are three fundamental types of defense—the *mobile defense,* the *area defense*, and *retrogrades*. In practice, Marine Corps commanders may use them in combination. Mobile defense orients on the destruction of the attacking force by permitting the enemy to advance into a position that exposes him to counterattack by a mobile reserve. An area defense orients on retention of terrain by absorbing the enemy in an interlocking series of positions and destroying him largely by fires. Retrogrades seek to reposition friendly forces to improve an operational or tactical situation and often involve trading space for time in order to prepare a decisive counterstroke. Combining these three types of defense can be very effective as the commander capitalizes on the advantages of each and the strengths and capabilities of his subordinate units.

Although these descriptions convey the general pattern of each type of defense, all may involve static and dynamic elements. Mobile defenses may employ static defensive positions to help control the depth and breadth of enemy penetration and ensure retention of ground from which to launch counterattacks. In area defenses, commanders may employ patrols, intelligence units, and reserve forces to cover the gaps among defensive positions, reinforcing as necessary and counterattacking from defensive positions as directed.

In retrogrades, commanders may employ dynamic elements to draw an adversary into a positional disadvantage as well as relatively static elements to wear an adversary down. Defending commanders may combine all three patterns, using static elements to delay, canalize, and halt the attacker, while using dynamic elements, such as spoiling attacks and counterattacks, to strike and destroy enemy forces. The balance of these patterns depends on the enemy, mission, force composition, mobility, relative combat power, and the nature of the conflict.

The specific design and sequencing of defensive operations is an art largely conditioned by experience; force capability; and mission, enemy, terrain, troops and support available-time available (METT-T). The MAGTF commander may elect to defend well forward with strong covering forces by striking the enemy as he approaches or he may opt to fight the decisive battle by facilitating GCE operations within the main battle area. If the MAGTF commander does not have to hold a specified location, he may draw the enemy deep into its defenses and then strike his flanks and rear. The MAGTF commander may even choose to preempt the enemy with spoiling attacks in the deep or security area if conditions favor such tactics.

A key characteristic of defensive operations is the ability of the commander to take offensive action and wrest the initiative from the enemy. With this in mind, the decision to conduct a hasty or deliberate defense is based on the time available or the requirement to quickly resume the offense.

A hasty defense normally occurs while in contact with the enemy or when contact is imminent and time available for organization is limited. It usually requires defensive strength, such as emplacements and obstacles. The hasty defense normally allows for only a brief leaders' reconnaissance and may entail the immediate engagement by security forces to buy time to establish the defense.

A commander may establish a deliberate defense when not in contact with the enemy or when contact is not imminent and time for organization and preparation is available. A deliberate defense normally includes fortifications, strong points, extensive use of barriers, and fully integrated fires. The commander normally is free to make a detailed reconnaissance, select the terrain on which to defend, identify key terrain, establish mutually supporting defensive positions, and determine the best distribution of forces.

Mobile Defense

A mobile defense uses maneuver and fires with terrain to seize the initiative from the enemy. The mobile defense destroys the attacking enemy through maneuver and offensive action. The commander allocates the bulk of his combat power to mobile forces to strike the enemy where he is most vulnerable and when he least expects attack. Minimum forces positioned forward canalize, delay, disrupt, and deceive the enemy about the actual location of the defensive positions. Retaining his mobile forces until the critical time and place are identified, the commander can focus combat power in a single or series of violent and rapid counterattacks throughout the depth of the battlespace, as illustrated in figure 8-2 on page 8-6.

A mobile defense requires mobility greater than that of the attacker. Marines generate the mobility advantage necessary in the mobile defense with organic mechanized and armor forces and Marine aviation. The commander must have sufficient depth within the area of operations to trade space and draw the enemy into the defensive area, causing the enemy commander to overextend his force and expose his flanks and lines of communications to attack. The success of the mobile defense often presents the opportunity to resume the offense.

In mobile defense, the MAGTF commander—

- Commits minimum forces to fixed locations.
- Positions maximum combat power to catch the enemy as he attempts to overcome that part of the force in fixed locations.

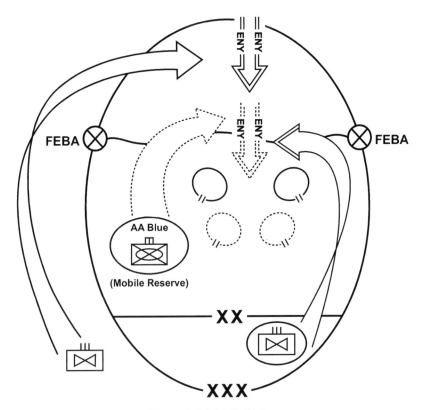

Figure 8-2. Mobile Defense.

- Takes advantage of terrain in depth, obstacles, and mines, while employing firepower and maneuver to wrest the initiative from the attacker.
- Employs a strong counterattack force to strike the enemy at his most vulnerable time and place.
- Uses reconnaissance and surveillance assets to track the enemy, identifying critical enemy nodes, such as command and control, radars, logistic trains, and indirect fire support elements.

Area Defense

The area defense denies the enemy critical terrain or facilities for a specified time. An area defense is suitable for the following conditions.

- The force must defend specific terrain that is militarily and politically essential.
- The defender possesses less mobility than the enemy.
- Maneuver space and depth of the battlespace is limited or the terrain enables mutual support to the defending forces.

An area defense focuses on the retention of terrain by absorbing the enemy into a series of interlocked positions from which, through friendly maneuver and fires, he can be destroyed. As shown in figure 8-3, on page 8-8, the area defense relies on the ability of the defenders to maintain their positions and to control the terrain among them. An area defense uses battle positions and strong points in combination with obstacles and barriers to slow, canalize, and defeat the enemy attack. The array of forces within these defensive positions allows for depth and mutual support of the force.

While a mobile defense requires considerable depth, an area defense will vary in depth according to the situation. For example, a significant obstacle to the front such as a river, built-up area, swamp, or escarpment favors an area defense. Such an obstacle adds to the relative combat power of the defender. Obstacles support static elements of the defense and slow or canalize the enemy through vital areas.

The commander positions the bulk of his ground combat power in static defensive positions and employs a small mobile reserve. He depends on his static forces to defend their positions and uses his reserves to blunt and contain penetrations, to counterattack, and to exploit opportunities presented by the enemy.

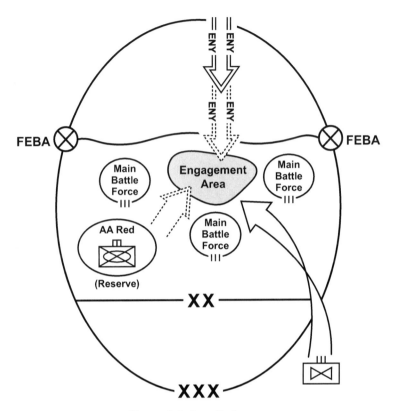

Figure 8-3. Area Defense.

Retrograde

A retrograde involves organized movement away from the enemy. These movements may involve delaying an adversary's advance, withdrawal of forces in contact, or the retirement of forces not in direct contact and various combinations thereof. All retrograde operations seek to improve an operational or tactical situation. These operations—

- Reduce the enemy's offensive capabilities.
- Draw the enemy into an unfavorable situation.
- Enable combat under conditions favorable to friendly forces.
- Gain time.
- Disengage from contact with the enemy.
- Reposition forces for commitment elsewhere.
- Shorten lines of communications.

Retrograde operations will usually involve all MAGTF elements. While the GCE is normally the main effort, the ACE and the LCE play major roles in setting the conditions for a successful retrograde. The ACE, operating from the sea or from bases beyond the reach of the enemy's artillery, interdicts enemy forces to disrupt and delay his advance. The ACE also provides close air support to ground forces in contact with the enemy and assault support to move troops, equipment, and supplies away from the enemy. The LCE continues to provide combat service support to the MAGTF and transportation to move troops, equipment, and supplies away from the enemy. It establishes new combat service support facilities in the rear to support future operations.

Delay

A delay involves a force under pressure trading space for time by slowing down the enemy's momentum. Its goal is to inflict maximum damage on the enemy without becoming decisively engaged. Forces execute delays when they have insufficient combat power to attack, to establish an adequate position or mobile defense, or when the plan calls for drawing the enemy into an area for counterattack, as illustrated in figure 8-4.

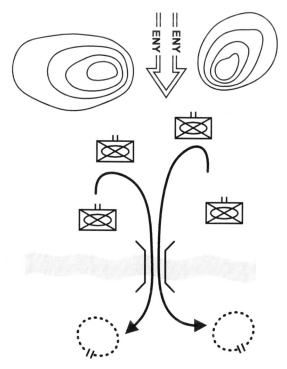

Figure 8-4. Delay.

The MAGTF commander may specify the amount of time to be gained or events to be accomplished by the delaying force to successfully accomplish the mission. Delays may be used in the deep area, main battle area, or close area or the rear area. Delaying operations require sufficient depth of area.

Commanders should plan for maximum use of terrain, barriers, and obstacles. Delaying forces must remain in constant contact with the enemy to ensure the enemy experiences continuous pressure and cannot bypass delaying units. The delaying force should make every effort to avoid becoming decisively engaged. Delays are conducted—

- When the force's strength is insufficient to defend or attack.
- To reduce the enemy's offensive capability by inflicting casualties.
- To gain time by forcing the enemy to deploy.
- To determine the strength and location of the enemy's main effort.
- When the enemy's intent is not clear and the commander desires intelligence.
- To protect and provide early warning for the main battle area forces.
- To allow time to re-establish the defense.

Withdrawal

Withdrawals are planned events in which a force in contact with the enemy disengages and moves in a direction away from the enemy. Ideally, a withdrawal occurs without the enemy's knowledge or before he can prevent or disrupt it. Conditions favorable to a withdrawal include—

- Danger of being defeated.
- Battle under unfavorable conditions.
- Opportunity to draw the enemy into terrain or a position that facilitates friendly offensive action.
- Reposition or redeployment of the force for employment elsewhere.

Some offensive operations, such as raids, also involve planned withdrawals. There are two types of withdrawal operations. They are distinguished by the enemy's reaction to the withdrawal—

- Withdrawal under enemy pressure, in which the enemy tries to prevent the disengagement by attacking.
- Withdrawal not under enemy pressure, in which the enemy does not or cannot try to prevent the withdrawal.

Regardless of the type of withdrawal, planning considerations are the same. A prudent commander always plans to execute a withdrawal under enemy pressure. He should anticipate enemy interference by fires, direct pressure, and envelopment. If the enemy interferes, security forces fight a delaying action as they move to the rear. If the enemy does not interfere, security forces disengage and withdraw on order.

The more closely a unit is engaged with the enemy, the more difficult it is to withdraw. Withdrawal is easiest after success in combat. If a unit cannot disengage from the enemy on its own, the commander may employ other units elsewhere to reduce enemy pressure on the withdrawing unit or he may employ additional combat power at the point of withdrawal for disengagement.

In any withdrawal, the commander should attempt to deceive the enemy about his intention to withdraw. Withdrawing during periods of reduced visibility facilitates disengagement from the enemy and conceals movement to a degree, but may make control more difficult. Due to the inherent difficulties of conducting a withdrawal, the commander must have the flexibility to switch to any other type of operation, such as delay, defend, or attack, as the situation demands.

Retirement

Retirements involve forces out of contact moving away from the enemy. A retirement may immediately follow a withdrawal and is normally protected by another unit between it and the enemy; however, the commander must still establish adequate security during the movement. Speed, control, and security are the most important considerations. Commanders retire units to—

- Position forces for other missions.
- Adjust the defensive scheme.
- Assist the delays and withdrawals of other units.
- Deceive the enemy.

DEFENSIVE METHODS

The six defensive methods—battle position, strong point, perimeter, linear, reverse slope, and sector—are the basic dispositions a commander may employ to array forces relative to the terrain and enemy. The defensive methods are normally employed in combination based on the mission; terrain; relative size and capabilities of the forces involved, especially in terms of mobility; and the type of defense selected by the MAGTF commander.

Battle Position

A battle position is a defensive position oriented on the most likely enemy avenue of approach from which a unit may defend or attack. The purpose of a battle position is to deny or delay the enemy the use of certain terrain or an avenue of approach. The size of a battle position can vary with the size of the unit assigned. For ground combat units, battle positions are usually hastily occupied, but should be continuously improved.

Strong Point

Usually heavily fortified and armed with automatic weapons, a strong point is a key point in a defensive position around which other positions are grouped to protect it. It is designed to deny the enemy certain terrain and the use of an avenue of approach. It differs from a battle position in that it is designed to be occupied for an extended period of time. It is established on critical terrain and must be held for the defense to succeed. A strong point requires all-around defense and should have sufficient supplies and ammunition to continue to fight even if surrounded or cut off from resupply. Strong points often require considerable time and engineer resources to develop.

Perimeter

A perimeter defense orients in all directions and applies to situations when a unit must hold critical terrain, such as a combat outpost, bridge, mountain pass, or airfield. Patrolling and security operations are usually prerequisites for a successful perimeter defense. A commander may also employ a hasty defensive perimeter when the unit has been bypassed and isolated by the enemy or when pausing to rearm or refuel during offensive operations.

Linear

A linear defense orients in a single direction to take advantage of a linear terrain feature, such as a river line or ridge, or when a wide area must be defended. It is characterized by the commitment of the preponderance of ground combat forces forward, strong mutual support between forward units, limited depth within the main battle area, and a relatively small reserve.

Reverse Slope

A reverse slope defense orients in a single direction and is organized on the portion of a terrain feature or slope with a topographical crest that masks the main defensive positions from enemy observation and direct fire. All or part of the defending ground forces may employ this method, which is normally applicable primarily at lower tactical levels due to terrain considerations. A reverse slope defense offers the opportunity to gain surprise and wrest the initiative from the attacker. Its success rests on denying the attacker control of the topographical crest.

Sector

A commander may assign subordinate commanders defensive sectors to provide them maximum latitude to accomplish assigned tasks. The extent of the assigned sector assigned is METT-T dependent, but as a general rule should be no larger than can be influenced by the unit.

CHAPTER 9

Offensive Operations

"Since I first joined the Marines, I have advocated aggressiveness in the field and constant offensive action. Hit quickly, hit hard and keep right on hitting. Give the enemy no rest, no opportunity to consolidate his forces and hit back at you. This is the shortest road to victory."

—General Holland M. Smith
Coral and Brass

The offense is the decisive form of warfare. While defensive operations can do great damage to an enemy, offensive operations are the means to a decisive victory. Offensive operations seize the initiative, gain freedom of action, and create effects to achieve objectives. Offensive operations allow the commander to impose his will on the enemy by shattering the enemy's moral, mental, and physical cohesion. The enemy loses his ability to fight as an effective, coordinated force as Marine Corps forces generate an overwhelming tempo by conducting a variety of rapid, focused, and unexpected offensive actions.

The offense gains, maintains, and exploits the initiative, causing the enemy to react. The focus of offensive operations is the enemy, not seizure of terrain. Even in the defense, a commander must take every opportunity to seize the initiative by offensive action. Offensive operations—

- Destroy enemy forces and equipment.
- Deceive and divert the enemy.
- Deprive the enemy of resources.
- Gain information.
- Fix the enemy in place.
- Seize key terrain.
- Force an enemy decision.
- Disrupt enemy actions or preparations.

Successful offensive operations—

- Avoid the enemy's strength and attack his weakness by focusing combat power against the enemy's critical vulnerabilities.
- Isolate the enemy from his sources of support, to include the population in counterinsurgency operations.

- Strike the enemy from unexpected directions, disrupting his plan.
- Exploit every advantage.
- Overwhelm the enemy commander's ability to observe, orient, decide, and act.

The Marine Corps warfighting philosophy is offensive in nature. It focuses on the enemy and uses speed to seize the initiative and degrade the enemy's ability to resist. To be decisive in offensive operations, the attacker weights the main effort. The fundamentals of offensive action are general rules evolved from the time-proven application of the principles of war. Many of the following fundamentals are related and reinforce one another:

- Orient on the enemy.
- Gain and maintain contact.
- Develop the situation.
- Achieve surprise.
- Exploit known enemy weaknesses.
- Seize or control key terrain.
- Gain and maintain the initiative.
- Neutralize the enemy's ability to react.
- Advance by fire and maneuver.
- Maintain momentum.
- Act quickly.
- Exploit success.
- Be flexible.
- Be aggressive.
- Provide for the security of the force.

ORGANIZATION OF THE OFFENSE

Leveraging the unifying perspective of the single-battle approach to operations, the commander organizes the battlespace and his forces in order to relate his forces to one another in time, events, space, or purpose. This chapter uses a spatial reference—deep, close, and rear construct—to discuss offensive operations. In other types of operations, a purpose-based construct—decisive, shaping, sustaining—may prove more useful.

Deep Operations

Conceptually, deep operations begin the process of attacking the enemy's mental, moral, and physical forces not so much to destroy them, but to isolate these components so they cannot be employed coherently. Deep operations create opportunities by addressing the enemy's potential. Specifically, deep operations help locate the enemy, restrict his freedom of action, disrupt the coherence and tempo of his operations, interdict his supplies, and isolate or destroy his forces.

Successful deep operations may defeat the enemy outright or, at a minimum, set the conditions for successful close operations. In doing so, deep operations can enable friendly forces to choose the time, place, and method for close operations.

Whether in the offense or defense, operations in the MAGTF deep area are very similar. For example, as part of security operations in the MAGTF deep area, the ACE will conduct deep air support just as it will for offensive operations. This is consistent with MCDP 1; there is no clear division between the offense and defense. They exist simultaneously as necessary components of each other. Another common trait to both the offense and defense in the MAGTF deep area is the responsibility of the MAGTF command element for the conduct of deep operations.

Close Operations

Due to the proximity of opposing forces, the intensity of operations dominated by fire and maneuver, and the potential for extreme rates of physical destruction, close operations will always be viewed as the decisive element in combat. It is during close operations that mission tactics and commander's intent serve their most vital role by empowering subordinates to exercise judgment and initiative to quickly adapt their actions to the changing situation.

Ideally, the commander, through his single-battle approach to operations, will have set the conditions for successful close operations. Shaping actions should strip away the enemy's capabilities and attack the enemy's mental, moral, and physical abilities to force him into predictable actions. Sustaining actions—logistics, force protection, planning—promote freedom of action and unity of effort and extend the MAGTF's operational reach.

Responsibility for offensive operations in the close area reside with the GCE. The MAGTF command element influences close operations primarily through resource allocation—battlespace; priority of fires; lift; or intelligence, surveillance, and reconnaissance—and whatever success it is achieving through shaping and sustaining actions in the deep and rear areas.

Rear Operations

Rear operations enhance a force's freedom of action and extend the force's operational reach both in time and space. While deep operations imply shaping actions, rear area operations are synonymous with sustaining actions that seek uninterrupted support to the force. The primary focus of rear area operations during the offensive is to maintain momentum and prevent culminating points.

TYPES OF OFFENSIVE OPERATIONS

There are four types of offensive operations—movement to contact, attack, exploitation, and pursuit. These operations may occur in sequence, simultaneously, or independently across the depth of the battlespace. For example, a movement to contact may be so successful that it immediately leads to exploitation or an attack may lead directly to pursuit as shown in figure 9-1.

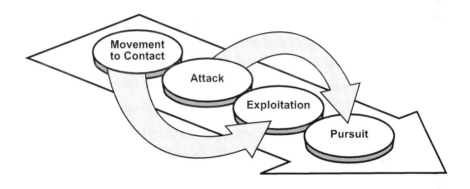

Figure 9-1. Types of Offensive Operations.

All four types of offensive operations rarely occur in one campaign or in the sequence presented in this chapter; moreover, the dividing lines between the types of offensive operations are not always distinct. The successful commander uses the appropriate type of offensive operation for his mission and situation, not hesitating to change as the situation dictates. The goal of offensive operations is to move to exploitation and pursuit as rapidly as possible. The commander seeks to take advantage of enemy weaknesses and maneuvers to a position of advantage, creating the conditions that lead to exploitation. For example, during Desert Storm, 1st and 2d MARDIV went directly into the attack from defensive positions in Saudi Arabia. After clearing the obstacle belts, the two divisions were mostly in pursuit of Iraqi ground forces while 3d MAW was conducting exploitation along what became known as the "Highway of Death."

Movement to Contact

Movement to contact is largely a GCE event supported by the other elements of the MAGTF. While the LCE provides sustainment, the ACE assists with assault support, reconnaissance, command and control, and offensive and antiair support. Because the ACE, in many cases, is already in contact with the enemy as a result of security/shaping operations, it can help develop the situation through interdiction and armed reconnaissance, as well as reporting on observations. See figure 9-2.

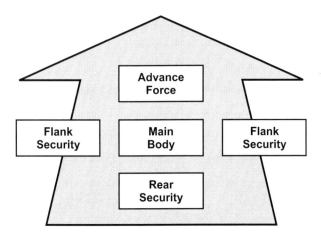

Figure 9-2. Movement to Contact.

Attack

An attack is an offensive operation of coordinated movement and maneuver supported by fire to defeat, destroy, or capture the enemy or seize/secure key terrain. Focusing combat power against the enemy with a tempo and intensity that the enemy cannot match, the commander attacks to shatter his opponent's will, disrupt his cohesion, and gain the initiative. If an attack is successful, the enemy is no longer capable of—or willing to offer—meaningful resistance.

The commander has a variety of attack options available to him. Types of attacks include hasty, deliberate, spoiling, counterattack, feint, demonstration, reconnaissance in force, and raids.

Hasty and Deliberate Attacks

Attacks can be hasty or deliberate based on the degree of preparation, planning, and coordination involved prior to execution. A hasty attack is when the commander trades preparation time for speed to exploit an opportunity. It takes advantage of audacity, surprise, and speed to achieve the commander's objectives before the enemy can effectively respond. The commander launches a hasty attack with the forces at hand and with little preparation before the enemy can concentrate forces or prepare to counter the attack effectively.

By necessity, hasty attacks do not employ complicated schemes of maneuver and require a minimum of coordination. Habitual support relationships, standing operating procedures, and battle drills contribute to increased tempo and the likelihood of success of the hasty attack. Unnecessary changes to the task organization of the force risks the loss of momentum.

A deliberate attack involves preplanned employment of firepower and maneuver and usually includes the coordinated use of all available resources. Deliberate attacks apply when there is no apparent advantage that can be rapidly exploited.

Spoiling Attack

A spoiling attack pre-empts the enemy who is in the process of forming or assembling for an attack.

Counterattack

A counterattack is a limited-objective attack conducted by part or all of a defending force to prevent the enemy from attaining the objectives of his attack. It may be the precursor to resuming offensive operations.

Feint

A feint is a limited-objective, supporting attack away from the main effort to distract the enemy's attention. A feint involves contact with the enemy and must be of sufficient strength to confuse the enemy about the location of the main attack. Ideally, a feint causes the enemy to commit forces to the diversion. A unit conducting a feint usually attacks on a wider front than normal with a consequent reduction in mass and depth to include a minimal reserve to deal with unexpected developments.

Demonstration

A demonstration is an attack or a show of force on a front where a decision is not sought. Its aim is to deceive the enemy. A demonstration, like a feint, is a supporting attack, but, unlike a feint, does not make contact with the enemy. The commander executes a demonstration by an actual or simulated massing of combat power, troop movements, or other activities designed to indicate the preparations for or beginning of an attack at a point other than the main effort.

Demonstrations can be a key aspect of an amphibious operation to draw enemy forces away from the actual landing beaches or to fix them in place. Demonstrations and feints increase the enemy's confusion while conserving combat power for the main and supporting efforts.

Reconnaissance in Force

A reconnaissance in force is a deliberate attack to obtain information and to locate and test enemy dispositions, strengths, and reactions. While the primary purpose of a reconnaissance in force is to gain information, the commander must be prepared to exploit opportunity. Reconnaissance in force usually develops information more rapidly and in more detail than other reconnaissance methods.

The commander may conduct reconnaissance in force as a means of keeping pressure on the defender by seizing key terrain and uncovering enemy weaknesses. The reconnoitering force must be of a size and strength to cause the enemy to react strongly enough to disclose his locations, dispositions, strength, planned fires, and planned use of the reserve.

Raid

A raid is an attack, usually small scale, involving a penetration of hostile territory for a specific purpose other than seizing and holding terrain. It ends with a planned withdrawal. Raids are characterized by surprise and swift, precise, and bold action. Raids typically—

- Destroy enemy installations and facilities.
- Disrupt enemy command and control or support activities.
- Divert enemy attention.
- Secure information.

Exploitation

Exploitation disorganizes the enemy in depth usually following a successful attack. The exploitation extends the initial success of the attack by preventing the enemy from disengaging, withdrawing, and re-establishing an effective defense.

The commander must prepare to exploit the success of every attack without delay. In the hasty attack, the force in contact normally continues the attack, transitioning to exploitation. In the deliberate attack, the commander's principal tool for the exploitation is normally the reserve. At the MAGTF level, aviation forces may support the reserve or assume the exploitation role. The commander retains only those reserves necessary to ensure flexibility and continued momentum. The reserve generally positions where it can exploit the success of the main effort or supporting attacks. Exploitation forces execute bold, aggressive, and rapid operations and thus require commensurate mobility.

The decision to commence the exploitation requires judgment, intuition, and situational understanding by the commander or the boldness and daring of a subordinate commander who recognizes an opportunity and acts on it. Conditions favorable for exploitation often include—

- Increased number of enemy prisoners of war.
- Absence of organized defenses.
- Absence of accurate enemy-massed direct and indirect fires.
- Loss of enemy cohesion upon contact.
- Capture, desertion, or absence of enemy commanders and senior staff officers.

Typical objectives for the exploitation force include command posts, reserves, seizure of key terrain, and the destruction of combat support and combat service support units located deep in the enemy's rear area. The destruction or defeat of these objectives further disrupts and disorganizes the enemy, preventing reconstitution. The commander must be prepared to assess the effects of his exploitation and determine when the time is at hand to pursue the enemy.

Pursuit

A pursuit is an offensive operation designed to catch or cut off a hostile force attempting to escape. Pursuit aims to destroy the enemy. Pursuits often develop from successful attack or exploitation operations when the enemy defenses begin to disintegrate. A pursuit may also occur when the enemy has lost the ability to fight effectively and attempts to withdraw.

Since the conditions that allow for pursuit are seldom predictable, a pursuit force is not normally established ahead of time. The commander must designate appropriate forces to conduct and support pursuit operations or the exploitation force may continue as the pursuit force. A pursuit is normally made up of a direct pressure force and an encircling force as illustrated in figure 9-3.

Pursuits challenge the utmost limits of endurance of troops/aircrew, equipment, and supplies to include ordnance and fuel. If the pursuit force pauses for any reason, the enemy has an opportunity to reorganize. Pursuit, like exploitation, must be relentless. Highly mobile and versatile combat service support forces are critical to sustaining a pursuit and preventing the MAGTF from reaching its culminating point before the enemy is completely defeated.

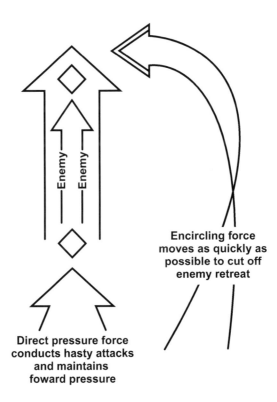

Figure 9-3. Pursuit.

FORMS OF MANEUVER

The six forms of offensive maneuver—frontal attack, flanking attack, envelopment, turning movement, infiltration, and penetration—are the basic techniques a force conducting offensive operations uses to gain advantage over the enemy. Each form of maneuver has a specific purpose relative to the enemy. The MAGTF commander chooses the form of maneuver that best accomplishes his mission.

The MAGTF commander organizes and employs the ACE, GCE, or LCE to best support the chosen form of maneuver. The GCE and ACE execute tactical actions to support or accomplish the MAGTF commander's mission. The MAGTF commander may task-organize aviation and ground combat units, along with combat service support units, under a single commander to execute the form of offensive maneuver selected.

Frontal Attack

A frontal attack is directed against the front of the enemy forces. It is used to rapidly overrun or destroy a weak enemy force or fix a significant portion of a larger enemy force to support a flanking attack or envelopment. Illustrated in figure 9-4, frontal attack is generally the least preferred form of maneuver because it strikes the enemy where he is the strongest. It can expose the attacker to the concentrated fires of the defender while limiting the effectiveness of the attacker's own fires. Commanders may opt for a frontal attack when they possess overwhelming combat power and the enemy is at a clear disadvantage. A frontal attack may also work because it is the last thing the enemy expects; the resulting shock and surprise could shatter the enemy's cohesion. Supporting efforts use frontal attacks to fix the enemy, enabling the main effort to maneuver to a position of advantage during an envelopment or a flanking attack.

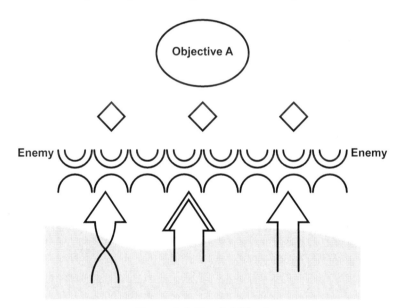

Figure 9-4. Frontal Attack.

Flanking Attack

A flanking attack pits our strength against the enemy's weakness in order to gain a position of advantage while avoiding the enemy's combat power. It is a form of offensive maneuver directed at the flank of an enemy force as illustrated in figure 9-5. A flank is a vulnerable aspect of an enemy formation. A flanking attack is similar to an envelopment, but generally not as deep. The purpose

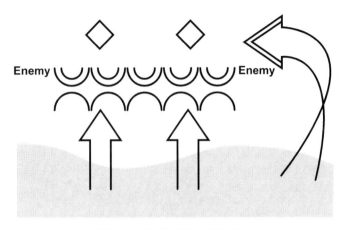

Figure 9-5. Flanking Attack.

of a flanking attack is to avoid the enemy's combat power in the process of defeating him.

Envelopment

Envelopment is an offensive maneuver in which the main attacking force passes around or over the enemy's principal defensive positions to secure objectives to the enemy's rear. During the execution of a single envelopment, as shown in figure 9-6 on page 9-12, the enemy's defensive positions may be bypassed using ground, waterborne, or vertical envelopment, compelling the defender to fight on the ground of the attacker's choosing. It requires surprise and superior mobility relative to the enemy. The operational reach and speed of aviation forces, coupled with their ability to rapidly mass fires on the enemy, make them an ideal force to conduct or support an envelopment. Envelopment is designed to—

- Strike the enemy where he is weakest, at critical vulnerabilities.
- Strike the enemy at an unexpected place.
- Attack at the enemy's rear area.
- Avoid the enemy's strengths.
- Disrupt the enemy's command and control.
- Disrupt the enemy's logistic effort.
- Destroy or disrupt the enemy's fire support assets.
- Sever the enemy's lines of communications.
- Minimize friendly casualties.

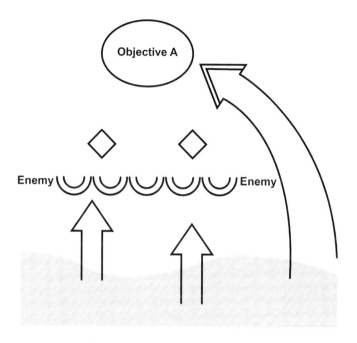

Figure 9-6. Single Envelopment.

Envelopments normally require a supporting effort to fix the enemy, prevent his escape or withdrawal, and reduce his ability to react against the main effort. They succeed by forcing the enemy to fight in multiple directions simultaneously or by deceiving him regarding the location, timing, or existence of the main effort. Success of the envelopment often depends on the effects created by the supporting effort.

Envelopments require sufficient depth so the enemy cannot reorient his defenses before the commander concentrates his force for the attack on the objective. Because of their ability to rapidly mass, aviation forces are particularly well-suited to function as the enveloping force or to enable the success of the enveloping force.

The commander may choose to conduct a double envelopment as illustrated in figure 9-7. A double envelopment is an offensive maneuver designed to force the enemy to fight in two or more directions simultaneously. It may lead to the encirclement of the enemy force so the commander must be prepared to contain and defeat any breakout attempts. The commander may select multiple objectives to the rear of the enemy's defense and the enveloping forces use different routes to attack, seize, or secure those objectives.

Marine Corps Operations

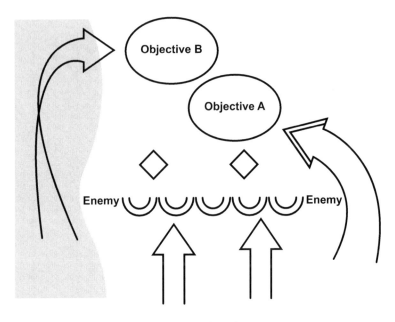

Figure 9-7. Double Envelopment.

Turning Movement

A turning movement is a variation of the envelopment in which the attacking force passes around or over the enemy's principal defensive positions to secure objectives deep in the rear area of the enemy. Normally, as shown in figure 9-8 on page 9-14, the main effort executes the turning movement as the supporting effort fixes the enemy in position. A turning movement differs from envelopment in that the turning force usually operates at such distances from the fixing force that mutual support is unlikely. The turning force must be able to operate independently. The turning movement, such as the Inchon landing, is an example of a loosely coupled plan where two independent forces linked through events, not specific time tables.

The goal of a turning movement is to force the enemy to abandon his position or reposition major forces to meet the adversary. Once "turned," the enemy loses his advantage of fighting from prepared positions on ground of his choosing.

Using the sea as maneuver space, the MAGTF is particularly well-suited to conduct a turning movement for the joint force commander. Through decentralized operations, the mobility of the ACE, and the use of the sea as

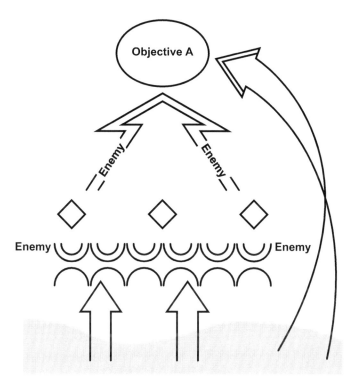

Figure 9-8. Turning Movement.

maneuver space, the MAGTF is capable of employing independent and distant forces from a variety of directions and means to positions well to the rear of the enemy's forces.

Infiltration

Infiltration is a form of maneuver in which friendly forces move through or into an area or territory occupied by either friendly or enemy troops or organizations. The movement occurs, either by small groups or by individuals, at extended or irregular intervals. When used in connection with the enemy, it implies contact is to be avoided. Forces move over, through, or around enemy positions without detection to assume a position of advantage over the enemy, as illustrated in figure 9-9. Infiltration is normally conducted in concert with other forms of maneuver.

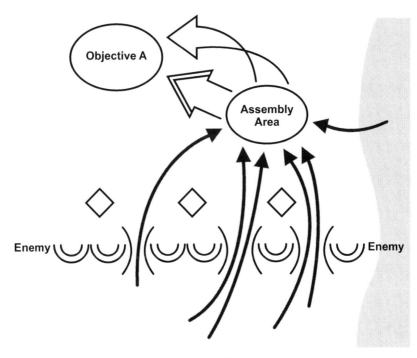

Figure 9-9. Infiltration.

The commander orders an infiltration to move all or part of his force through gaps in the enemy's defense to—

- Achieve surprise.
- Attack enemy positions from the flank or rear.
- Occupy a position from which to support the main attack by fire.
- Secure key terrain.
- Conduct ambushes and raids in the enemy's rear area to harass and disrupt his command and control and support activities.
- Cut off enemy forward units.

Infiltrations normally take advantage of limited visibility, rough terrain, or unoccupied or unobserved areas. These conditions often allow undetected movement of small elements when the movement of the entire force would present greater risks. The commander may elect to conduct a demonstration, feint, or some other form of deception to divert the enemy's attention from the area to be infiltrated.

To increase control, speed, and the ability to mass combat power, a force infiltrates with the largest possible units compatible with the need for stealth, enemy detection capabilities, and speed. Infiltrating forces may depend heavily on aviation forces for lift, aerial resupply, and close air support.

After infiltration, the infiltrating force may require a linkup or series of linkups to assemble for its subsequent mission. Infiltration requires extremely detailed and accurate information about terrain and enemy dispositions. The plan for infiltration must be simple, clear, carefully coordinated, and well understood by the executing force. Due to the need for linkup, close air support, and detailed planning, infiltrations are an example of a tightly-coupled plan. Infiltration operations are the most easily damaged and most difficult to repair. Accordingly, risk is a key consideration for this form of maneuver.

Penetration

A penetration is a form of maneuver in which an attacking force seeks to rupture enemy defenses on a narrow front to disrupt the defensive system. Penetrations apply when enemy flanks are not assailable or time, terrain, or the enemy's disposition does not permit the employment of another form of maneuver. Successful penetrations create assailable flanks and provide access to the enemy's rear. A penetration generally occurs in three stages—

- Rupturing the position.
- Widening the gap.
- Seizing the objective.

A penetration concentrates overwhelmingly superior combat power on a narrow front and in depth. As the attacking force ruptures the enemy's defenses, units secure the shoulders of the breach to widen the gap for follow-on units. Rupturing the enemy position and widening the gap are not inherently decisive; the attacker must exploit the rupture by attacking either into the enemy's rear area or attacking laterally to roll up the enemy's positions as shown in figure 9-10. The shock action and mobility of motorized, mechanized, and aviation forces are useful in rupturing the enemy's position and exploiting that rupture.

A commander may conduct multiple penetrations. Exploitation forces may converge on a single, deep objective or seize independent objectives. When unable to sustain more than one penetration, the commander generally exploits the success. Due to their inherent flexibility and ability to rapidly mass fires, aviation forces are well-suited for the role of a penetration. Because the force conducting the penetration is vulnerable to flanking attack, it must move rapidly. Follow-on forces must be close behind to secure and widen the shoulders of the breach.

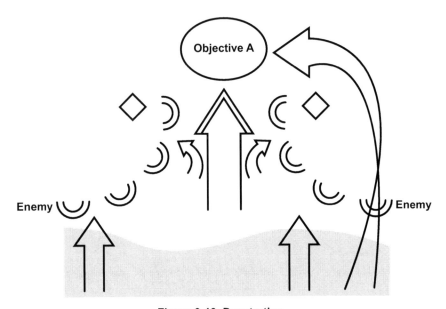

Figure 9-10. Penetration.

CHAPTER 10

Other Tactical Operations

> *"The operational tasks during the execution phase were extremely complex. We would conduct two night amphibious landings at the Mogadishu port and airfield; two reliefs in place of UN forces; a withdrawal and passage of lines by the Pakistani Brigade through our coalition lines (U.S. and Italian Marines); a day and night defense of the air- and seaports; a Non-combatant Evacuation of UN, media, and civilian agencies personnel; and two night amphibious withdrawals. These difficult tactical evolutions were tough enough, but the mix of coalition forces, the nighttime executions, and the prospect of doing these under fire compounded the difficulty exponentially."*
>
> —General Anthony Zinni, USMC, 2004
> *Battle Ready*

Other tactical operations—passages of lines, linkups, reliefs in place, obstacle crossings, and breakouts from encirclement—enable the MAGTF to execute a variety of missions. While other tactical operations primarily involve actions on the ground, they are not the exclusive province of the GCE. Depending upon their size, scope, and duration, all elements of the MAGTF may be involved in planning, coordinating, integrating, supporting, and conducting these operations.

In preparation for a relief in place, linkup, or passage of lines, the commander ordering the operation will specify responsibilities and procedures and resolve differences in methods of execution among subordinate commanders. The higher commander must establish measures to ensure continuous and effective fires and other support during the operation.

PASSAGE OF LINES

During a passage of lines operation, a force moves forward or rearward through another force's combat positions with the intention of moving into or out of contact with the enemy. The operation may be a forward or rearward passage of lines. It usually occurs within the context of another mission, such as an attack, exploitation, or security force mission.

A passage of lines, forward or rearward, is a complex and often dangerous operation, requiring thorough coordination. Inherent in the conduct of security operations, especially in the defense, is the requirement to execute a passage of lines. Faced with a superior enemy force or in the conduct of security operations in the defense, security forces must fall back and execute a rearward passage of lines, conducting battle handover with forces in the main battle area.

In the offense, security forces may fix enemy forces in place and allow the main force to pass through in the attack. In either instance, the commander may leverage additional capabilities, such as MAGTF fires, to support thestrong point operation.

The conduct of a passage of lines involves a stationary force and a moving force. In the offense, the moving force is normally the attacking force and organizes to assume its assigned mission after the passage. The stationary force facilitates the passage and provides maximum support to the moving force. Normally, the plans and requirements of the moving force have priority.

Normally, the responsibility for the zone of action transfers from the stationary force to the moving force. The timing or circumstances of that transfer require agreement by the two commanders or specified by higher authority. The attacking commander assumes responsibility at or before the time of attack. Responsibility may transfer before the time of attack to allow the attacking commander to control any preparatory fires. In this case, stationary force elements that are in contact at the time of the transfer operate under the control of the attacking commander. Liaison between the forces involved should occur as early as possible.

In the defense, a rearward passage of lines normally occurs during the withdrawal of a security force. The withdrawing force is the moving force and may pass through the stationary force en route to performing another mission or it may join the stationary unit. The common commander must specify any special command relationships and retain control of the passage. The executing commanders, preferably collocated, mutually decide on the actual transfer of responsibility for the sector. The withdrawing commander is responsible for identifying the last element of his command as it passes through the stationary unit. A detailed plan for mutual recognition, disseminated throughout both forces, is critical to the passage of lines. The stationary commander reports to his senior commander when he assumes responsibility for the sector. The withdrawing commander reports to the senior commander when his unit has completed the passage.

Due to the risks associated with a passage of lines (mainly enemy action to disrupt the passage or capitalize on the vulnerable forces), commanders normally execute passages of lines at night or during periods of reduced visibility. Risks include fratricide, exposure to enemy counteractions, loss of control during the transfer of sector responsibility, and the potential for uncoordinated movement of forces. Whether conducting a forward or rearward passage of lines, stationary and moving force commanders normally collocate their command posts to facilitate command and control of this demanding tactical operation.

Linkup

A linkup is an operation wherein two friendly forces join together in a hostile area. The purpose of the linkup is to establish contact between two forces. A linkup may occur between a helicopterborne force and a force on the ground, between two converging forces, or in the relief of an encircled force. The commander directing the linkup establishes the command relationships and responsibilities of the two units involved during and after the linkup to include responsibility for fire support coordination. If the linkup occurs between a Marine unit and a unit from another component of the joint or multinational force, the commander can employ MAGTF enablers, such as an air-naval gunfire liaison company, to provide a liaison capability and assist in the coordination of fires. Like a passage of lines, a linkup normally involves a stationary force and a moving force. If both units are moving, one is designated the stationary force and should occupy the linkup point at least temporarily to affect linkup. The commanders involved must coordinate their schemes of maneuver. They agree on primary and alternate linkup points where physical contact between the advance elements of the two units will occur. Linkup points must be easily recognizable to both units and where the routes of the moving force intersect elements of the stationary force. Commanders must coordinate fire support for the safety of both units.

Relief in Place

When directed by higher authority, a relief in place operation involves the replacement of all or part of a unit in a specific area by an incoming force. Mission responsibilities for the replaced elements and the assigned zone of action transfer to the incoming force. This transfer of authority is usually part of the relief in place operation and is termed a relief in place-transfer of authority (RIP-TOA). The incoming unit continues the operation as ordered. The relief must occur in an expeditious and orderly manner. Ideally, the RIP-TOA will take place without weakening the tactical integrity and security of the assigned area.

During a relief in place operation, the outgoing commander is responsible for the defense of his sector until transfer of authority. Both commanders should collocate throughout the operation to facilitate the transfer. The outgoing commander assumes command of any subordinate forces that have completed the relief in place. Following the transfer, the incoming commander assumes control of all elements of the outgoing force that have not yet been relieved. The incoming commander reports to higher headquarters upon completion of the RIP-TOA.

The relief can be simultaneous throughout the area of operation or staggered over time. Simultaneous reliefs take less time, but can cause greater congestion, threaten the readiness of the defense, and increase the likelihood of enemy detection due to the greater level of movement. By contrast, a staggered relief takes longer, but a larger portion of the force is prepared to conduct operations.

OBSTACLE CROSSING

An obstacle is any obstruction that disrupts, fixes, turns, or blocks the movement of an opposing force. The objective is to impose the loss of personnel, time, and equipment. Obstacles can be natural, manmade, or both. They are impediments to movement that usually require specific techniques and equipment to overcome. A series of such obstacles is called a barrier. Crossing obstacles is a common requirement in the offense. Though any obstacle can be crossed given sufficient time and resources, extensive preparation can help minimize losses from enemy action. Employment of obstacles covered by fires should be a normal element of the defense.

A critical requirement in any obstacle crossing is the reduction or elimination of the effects of enemy fire covering the obstacle. The goal is to cross the obstacle with minimum delay to maintain momentum and limit casualties.

Upon encountering an obstacle, the commander can bypass or breach. Intelligence can reveal the enemy's capability to oppose the crossing, the characteristics of the obstacle and crossing points, and the terrain on the far side. When possible, the attacker bypasses enemy obstacles, saving time, labor, and risk to personnel and equipment. However, the commander must exercise caution when bypassing, since obstacles can lead to predictability by canalizing forces. For example, a bypass route that at first appears desirable may lead to a kill zone.

A deliberate obstacle crossing should include a branch plan for a hasty attempt in the event the situation allows. The commander's options may be limited due to maneuver restrictions, the ability to deliver supporting fires, and the time required to move forces across or around the obstacle. The commander may conduct demonstrations and feints at locations away from the main crossing or breaching point to draw the enemy's attention and defenses or fires elsewhere.

The attacker advances to the obstacle quickly and on a broad front to increase the possibility of affecting a hasty crossing. The inherent capabilities of the ACE provide the MAGTF commander multiple options for moving on a broad front and rapidly crossing obstacles to establish security on the enemy side. The ACE can provide combat assault transport for MAGTF units attacking directly across the obstacle or carry MAGTF units far beyond the obstacle to bypass the enemy or conduct a turning movement.

Once forces and equipment commit to crossing, withdrawal or deviation from the initial plan is extremely difficult. During a crossing, a force is most vulnerable while astride the obstacle. After establishing units on the far side of the obstacle, the commander pushes his combat power across or through as quickly as possible.

Breach

A breach is the employment of any available means to break through or secure a passage through an enemy defense, obstacle, minefield, or fortification. The attacker attempts to breach an obstacle when it cannot be bypassed. A breach is the most common means of crossing an obstacle. The plan for breaching is based on the concept of operation on the far side. There are two types of breaching that generally correspond to hasty and deliberate attacks, with many of the same considerations, advantages, and disadvantages.

Hasty Breach

A hasty breach is the rapid creation of a route through a minefield, barrier, or fortification by any expedient method. It is a continuation of the operation underway with a minimum loss of momentum. A hasty breach involves speed and surprise, force dispersion, and decentralized control.

Deliberate Breach

A deliberate breach is the creation of a lane through a minefield or a clear route through a barrier or fortification. It requires a concentrated force to overcome the obstacle and enemy defenses on the far side. A deliberate breach requires extensive planning, detailed preparation, sustained supporting arms, and engineer support. When forced to conduct a deliberate breach, the attacker may lose momentum and the initiative.

River Crossing

Unfordable water obstacles have considerable influence on military operations due to their restrictions on movement and maneuver. They are obstacles in the attack and form natural lines of resistance for defense. The strength of a body of water as an obstacle increases with the width, depth, and velocity of the current.

A river crossing is a type of gap-crossing operation necessary for the projection of ground combat power on the other side. It is a centrally planned offensive operation that requires the allocation of external crossing means and a force dedicated to the security of the beachhead. The primary concern is the rapid buildup of combat power on the far side to continue offensive operations.

BREAKOUT FROM ENCIRCLEMENT

An encircled force normally attempts a breakout when it—

- Does not have sufficient relative combat power to defend itself against the enemy.
- Does not have adequate terrain to conduct its defense.
- Cannot sustain itself and needs relief by friendly forces.

The sooner the breakout occurs, the less time the enemy has to strengthen his position and the more organic resources and support the encircled force has available. The encircled force may receive fire support and diversions from other elements of the MAGTF, such as the ACE. Most importantly, the encircled force must maintain the momentum of the attack. If the breakout fails, the force will be more vulnerable to defeat or destruction than it was before the breakout attempt.

The encircled force normally conducts a breakout by task-organizing with a force to conduct the rupture, a main body, and a rear guard. If the commander has enough forces, he may organize separate reserve, diversionary, and supporting elements. Any of these forces may consist of appropriate combat service support and aviation or ground combat units with one or both as individual elements or as task-organized, combined arms teams.

CHAPTER 11

Reconnaissance and Security Operations

"The most certain method to uncover an enemy is to send scouts to visit suspected positions."

—Small Wars Manual, 1940

"Skepticism is the mother of security. Even though fools trust their enemies, prudent persons do not. The general is the principal sentinel of his army. He should always be careful of its preservation and see that it is never exposed to misfortune."

—Frederick the Great, 1747
Dictionary of Military and Naval Quotations

The fog and friction of war will never allow the commander to have a perfect picture of the battlespace. However, reconnaissance operations can reduce uncertainties about an unfamiliar area and an enemy who is actively trying to conceal information about his forces and intentions.

Reconnaissance of some type should always precede a commitment of forces. Failure to conduct a thorough reconnaissance may lead to the loss of initiative or an inability to exploit fleeting opportunities. Lack of reconnaissance can result in the enemy achieving surprise, inflicting unacceptable losses on friendly forces, and causing the failure of the mission. As part of the overall MAGTF intelligence effort, reconnaissance operations support the commander's decisionmaking process by collecting information to develop situational awareness and satisfy critical information requirements.

Security operations may occur in concert with a variety of MAGTF operations. They can reduce risk by providing the MAGTF commander with early warning and increased reaction time. They protect the force from surprise and attempt to eliminate the unknowns in any tactical situation. Security operations prevent the enemy from collecting information on friendly forces, deceive him about friendly capabilities and intentions, and prevent enemy forces from interfering with friendly operations.

Reconnaissance operations support security operations by providing information on enemy forces, capabilities, and intentions and by denying the enemy information about friendly activities through counterreconnaissance. To succeed, a MAGTF's security operations should be an integral element of its reconnaissance operations. Security operations are required during offensive, defensive, and other tactical operations.

RECONNAISSANCE ASSETS OF THE MAGTF

Reconnaissance attempts to answer the commander's questions about the enemy and the battlespace in which the MAGTF will operate. Reconnaissance is a mission—aerial, ground, or amphibious—undertaken to obtain, by visual or other detection methods, information about the activities and resources of the enemy or to secure data on the meteorological, hydrographic, electromagnetic, or geographic characteristics of a particular area. More simply, reconnaissance obtains information about the characteristics of a particular area and any known or potential enemy within it.

The commander uses reconnaissance to collect information and to gain and maintain contact with the enemy. Reconnaissance activities may range from passive surveillance to aggressive measures designed to stimulate an enemy response, such as reconnaissance by fire. Passive surveillance includes systematically watching an enemy force or named area of interest; listening to an area and the activities in it to help develop intelligence needed to confirm or deny adversary COAs; or identifying adversary critical vulnerabilities and limitations. All MAGTF elements have reconnaissance capabilities, but each has a unique capacity. Organic MAGTF chemical, biological, radiological, and nuclear reconnaissance and surveillance capabilities provide chemical, biological, radiological, and nuclear hazard information to the MAGTF commander's overall intelligence collection. These capabilities support chemical, biological, radiological, and nuclear passive defense and critical command decisions.

Command Element

The command element centralizes planning and direction of the entire reconnaissance effort for the MAGTF. The command element can task any MAGTF element to conduct reconnaissance to satisfy the commander's information requirements. It also directly controls MAGTF-level reconnaissance assets, such as radio battalion, force reconnaissance company, and the intelligence battalion.

Radio Battalion

The radio battalion provides ground-based signals intelligence, electronic warfare, communications security monitoring, and special intelligence communications capability to support MAGTF operations. It plans and coordinates the employment of its subordinate elements, to include radio reconnaissance and mobile electronic warfare support systems in light armored vehicles. The radio battalion is the focal point for MAGTF ground-based signals intelligence operations.

Force Reconnaissance Company

The force reconnaissance company is organized within the division reconnaissance battalion and is the MAGTF commander's ground reconnaissance asset. The company trains in unique insertion/extraction modes for deep reconnaissance. It receives operational guidance and tasking from the MAGTF commander.

Intelligence Battalion

The intelligence battalion provides remote sensor, imagery interpretation, and topographic intelligence support to MAGTF operations. In addition to the sensor control and management platoon, the force imagery interpretation unit, and the topographic platoon, the intelligence battalion establishes and staffs the MAGTF's surveillance and reconnaissance center. It plans, executes, and monitors MAGTF reconnaissance operations.

The intelligence battalion also provides human intelligence, counterintelligence, and interrogator-translator support to MAGTF operations. This support can include screening, interrogating, and debriefing prisoners of war and persons of intelligence interest; conducting counterintelligence force protection source operations; conducting counterintelligence surveys and investigations; preparing counterintelligence estimates and plans; translating documents; and exploiting captured material to a limited extent.

In addition to the specialized counterintelligence and interrogator-translator platoons, the battalion employs task-organized human intelligence exploitation teams in direct support of MAGTF subordinate elements. These exploitation teams combine counterintelligence specialists and interrogator-translators in one element, providing a unique and comprehensive range of counterintelligence/human intelligence services.

Ground Combat Element

The GCE has substantial organic reconnaissance assets. Those units in contact with the enemy, especially patrols, are among the most reliable sources of information. Combat engineers are also good sources of information. Engineer units often conduct engineer reconnaissance of an area and can provide detailed reporting on obstacles to lines of communications, such as roads, rivers, railroad lines, and bridges.

Ground reconnaissance provides immediate tactical ground reconnaissance and surveillance to the GCE. Like force reconnaissance, ground reconnaissance employs to observe and report enemy activity and other information of military significance. Their capabilities are similar to those of force reconnaissance.

The division reconnaissance battalion conducts close reconnaissance and surveillance in support of GCE operations. It uses insertion, patrolling, reporting, and extraction techniques to carry out amphibious reconnaissance, ground reconnaissance, and surveillance tasks in support of the GCE. The division also has other reconnaissance assets—light armored reconnaissance, counterbattery radar, and scout snipers.

Light Armored Reconnaissance

Light armored reconnaissance units usually operate in forward areas or along flanks and report early warning of contact with an enemy force. The Marines in each light armored vehicle train in information collection and reporting. These units are capable of a wide variety of missions due to their inherent mobility and organic firepower. The division light armored reconnaissance battalion provides the GCE with its light armored reconnaissance capability.

Counterbattery Radar

The counterbattery radar platoon, located within the artillery regiment's headquarters battery, uses mobile radars to detect and accurately locate enemy mortars, artillery, and rockets, permitting rapid engagement with counterfire. The GCE reports information on enemy order of battle and locations to the MAGTF command element based on information derived from counterbattery radar detections.

Scout Snipers

The scout sniper platoon is an organic collection asset of each infantry battalion. Although the platoon can employ in support of numerous tactical missions in defensive and offensive operations, they primarily employ to provide surveillance and tactical information and coordinate supporting arms and close air support. The scout sniper platoon provides the infantry battalion with extended area observation.

Aviation Combat Element

The capability of the ACE to observe the battlefield and report in near real time gives the MAGTF commander a multidimensional capability. Aviation combat units can span the entire area of operations, providing early indications, warning, and reconnaissance information essential to the success of the MAGTF. Each ACE aircraft, whether rotary-wing, fixed-wing, or tilt-rotor, can conduct visual observation of terrain and enemy forces. The ACE aircraft can engage enemy targets immediately or direct other supporting arms. The ACE manages the unmanned aircraft system, advanced tactical airborne reconnaissance system, and electronic reconnaissance and warfare assets.

Unmanned Aircraft Systems

Unmanned aircraft systems provide day-night, real-time imagery for reconnaissance, surveillance, and target acquisition. Their unique capabilities can also support real time target engagement and assist in the control of fires/supporting arms and maneuver. These systems provide high quality video imagery for artillery or naval gunfire adjustment, battle damage assessment, and reconnaissance over land or sea. They are capable of day and night operations using television or forward-looking infrared cameras. Unmanned aerial vehicle squadrons (VMU-1, VMU-2, and VMU-3) task-organize under the control of the ACE and provide sorties in general support of MAGTF collection requirements. Because of the limited number of unmanned aircraft system assets and the critical reconnaissance capabilities they provide to the entire force, the MAGTF command element collection management section coordinates unmanned aircraft system mission tasking.

Advanced Tactical Airborne Reconnaissance System

The F/A-18D can employ the advanced tactical airborne reconnaissance system, a real-time digital package providing day/night, all-weather imagery capability. The imagery provides sufficient detail and accuracy to permit delivery of appropriate air and ground weapons; assist with battle damage assessment; and provide tactical commanders with detailed information about the enemy's weapons, units, and disposition. Imagery resulting from collection can be digitally disseminated to the force imagery interpretation unit's tactical exploitation group for exploitation, printing, and dissemination.

Electronic Reconnaissance and Warfare

The EA-6B aircraft conducts aerial electronic reconnaissance and electronic warfare. Intelligence personnel can also process and disseminate information from digital tape recordings obtained during electronic warfare missions to update and maintain enemy electronic order of battle information. The sensors are passive systems that require active adversary emitters.

Through its ground-based, long-range radar, the ACE's tactical air operations center generates an air picture depicting friendly and enemy air activity. Through data links with other radars, the tactical air operations center can expand the field of view to include other areas of operation, as well as share the air picture with the ACE's tactical air command center for its use in the conduct of aviation operations.

Logistics Combat Element

The LCE has limited reconnaissance capabilities and no organic reconnaissance assets; however, it can conduct road and route reconnaissance with its engineer units, convoys, and military police.

NATIONAL AND THEATER ASSETS

The MAGTF can request reconnaissance support from national, theater, joint, other Service, and allied reconnaissance assets. When made available, these capabilities, such as Joint Surveillance Target Attack Radar System or Army signals intelligence aircraft, integrate fully into MAGTF reconnaissance operations. During forcible entry operations, the MAGTF integrates its amphibious reconnaissance capabilities with national, theater, and special operations forces. Some MAGTF reconnaissance assets, such as the radio battalion and the counterintelligence/human intelligence company, usually have direct connectivity with appropriate external agencies to coordinate tasking or support.

RECONNAISSANCE PLANNING

Reconnaissance supports the MAGTF commander by contributing to the commander's situational understanding and development. Reconnaissance assets support the specific CCIRs indicated by the commander's intent and subsequent unit intelligence and operations planning. Simultaneously, reconnaissance forces must remain alert to any developments that may cause the commander to reassess his intent.

Ideally, the MAGTF reconnaissance assets employ early to support the CCIRs and friendly COA development and selection. When reconnaissance occurs early in the planning cycle, planning and execution are driven by the flow of timely information and intelligence. If reconnaissance is delayed, situation development will generally be more uncertain. Reconnaissance assets are best employed in general support. The MAGTF reconnaissance units will most likely employ in rapidly developing and fluid situations. The main effort may shift quickly from one subordinate element to another. Such situations often require modifications or complete changes in the reconnaissance elements' missions.

The MAGTF commander and his staff are usually the individuals who are most capable of determining the best use of MAGTF reconnaissance assets at any given time to provide the necessary support and to integrate the results of reconnaissance information with other intelligence sources. Although placing reconnaissance assets in direct support of some subordinate element or even attaching them to specific units is occasionally appropriate, such support relationships generally make for inefficient use of specialized reconnaissance forces.

Reconnaissance requires time for detailed planning and preparation. Most reconnaissance focuses on the enemy's activities and intentions to satisfy the commander's need to exploit the enemy's vulnerabilities or to attack his center of gravity. This requirement frequently necessitates operating in and around the enemy's most critical and best-defended areas, over long distances, and well in advance of the commencement of the operations it will support. These conditions usually dictate specialized methods of transportation, communications system support, combat service support, equipment, and coordination.

Types of Reconnaissance Missions

There are four basic types of reconnaissance—route, area, zone, and force oriented. Each type provides specific details for mission planning and maintaining situational understanding.

Route Reconnaissance

Route reconnaissance is a directed effort to obtain detailed information about a specified route and all terrain from which the enemy could influence movement along that route. Route reconnaissance focuses along a specific line of communications, such as a road, railway, or waterway, to provide new or updated information on route conditions and activities. It normally precedes the movement of friendly forces and provides detailed information about a specific route and the surrounding terrain that could be used to influence movement along that route.

Area Reconnaissance

Area reconnaissance is a directed effort to obtain detailed information on the terrain or enemy activity within a prescribed area, such as a town, ridge line, woods, or other feature critical to operations. The focus in an area reconnaissance can be a single point, such as a bridge or installation, and could include hostile headquarters, key terrain, objective areas, or critical installations. Hostile situations encountered en route are developed only enough to allow the reconnoitering units to report and bypass; the unit's aim is to reach the area without being detected.

Zone Reconnaissance

Zone reconnaissance is a directed effort to obtain detailed information on all routes, obstacles (to include chemical or radiological contamination), terrain, and enemy forces within a zone defined by boundaries. A zone reconnaissance normally applies when the enemy situation is vague or when information on cross-country trafficability is desired.

Zone reconnaissance supports the total integrated intelligence picture of an area defined by length and width. The size of the area depends on the potential for information on hostile forces, terrain, and weather in the zone; the requirements levied by the commander; and the reconnaissance forces available to exploit the intelligence value in the zone.

Force-Oriented Reconnaissance

Force-oriented reconnaissance is a directed effort to find a specific enemy force quickly and stay with it wherever it moves on the battlefield. Force-oriented reconnaissance focuses on a specific enemy organization, wherever it is or may go. Force-oriented reconnaissance gathers intelligence information required about a specific enemy or unit. Reconnaissance assets orient on that specific force, moving when necessary to observe it and reporting all required information—information that has been requested as well as other pertinent observed and collected information.

RECONNAISSANCE PULL AND RECONNAISSANCE PUSH

A MAGTF can conduct reconnaissance using one of two basic methods—reconnaissance pull and reconnaissance push.

In operations based on *reconnaissance pull*, information derived from reconnaissance forces guides friendly force activities. Reconnaissance elements identify the surfaces and gaps in overall enemy dispositions and permit the commander to shape the battlespace. Making rapid decisions based on the flow of information, friendly combat forces are drawn to and through the weak spots in the enemy defense and seek to quickly exploit the advantages gained.

Reconnaissance pull requires early commitment of reconnaissance elements, allowance for the time to fully develop the reconnaissance picture, and a smooth flow of information from reconnaissance elements directly to higher and supported commanders and staffs in immediate need of reconnaissance data.

The landing at Tinian during World War II is an example of reconnaissance pull. Aerial and amphibious reconnaissance determined the Japanese defenders had largely ignored the northern beaches, while focusing most of their defensive effort on the most likely landing beaches in the southwest. The landing moved to the northern beaches. Coupled with a deception operation off the southern beach, the result was a complete surprise. Current concepts for MAGTF operations, such as operational maneuver from the sea, depend on the ability of the MAGTF to use reconnaissance pull to determine enemy dispositions and find or create exploitable gaps through which the MAGTF can pass while avoiding obstacles and strong points.

Reconnaissance pull requires a high tempo of intelligence operations to collect and report timely information. To sustain such operations, a reserve must be maintained to ensure fresh reconnaissance elements are always available to support developing situations. Maintenance of a reconnaissance reserve requires adequate consideration of the time required for reconnaissance unit preparation, insertion, mission execution, extraction, and recovery. Reconnaissance pull is easiest to execute early in an operation, but it is difficult to support over a lengthy period of high-tempo operations.

Operations based on *reconnaissance push* use reconnaissance elements more conservatively. They are often used as a tactical resource and generally with a shorter timeline. Reconnaissance push uses reconnaissance forces as the lead element of preplanned tactical operations, detecting enemy dispositions during the movement of the entire friendly force. The operations of I MEF in Operation Desert Storm (1991) were characterized by reconnaissance push. Reconnaissance forces, assisted by aggressive patrolling by combat forces, located Iraqi forces forward of advancing friendly forces in enough time to prevent them from interfering with I MEF operations.

Reconnaissance pull is preferred when the MAGTF can maneuver freely and exploit the enemy's weaknesses located by reconnaissance forces. It is the preferred method during offensive operations as it takes advantage of the MAGTF's inherent flexibility and reconnaissance capabilities. Reconnaissance push is more often used when the MAGTF is following a predetermined COA, targeting and destruction of enemy forces is a priority, freedom of maneuver is limited, and usually when on the defense.

Reconnaissance, although naturally oriented toward the battlespace beyond the forward edge of the battle area, should not ignore exposure of the rear area or command and control nodes, lines of communications, and logistic facilities. Devoting sufficient MAGTF reconnaissance capabilities to the rear area prevents the enemy from interfering with friendly combat operations.

Coordinating reconnaissance efforts between different echelons of command within the MAGTF as well as within the joint force avoids duplication of effort by scarce reconnaissance assets and facilitates turnover of reconnaissance responsibilities as units maneuver throughout the battlespace. Reconnaissance assets may be given the additional mission of engaging enemy forces with combined arms to disrupt and delay their advance. With advances in technology, there is now an emerging capability to directly communicate between a specific MAGTF reconnaissance asset through an automated data link and a fire support unit, such as sensor to shooter. Automatically transmitting target data from the sensor directly to the aircraft or firing unit brings combat power to bear against the enemy before the situation can change.

In counterinsurgency, stability, and other irregular warfare operations, reconnaissance forces provide a broad range of capabilities from direct-action combat missions to support for disaster relief and humanitarian operations. Irregular warfare calls for intelligence-collection accuracy and timely reporting to support the MAGTF's delivery of services, fires, or other support, and also usually calls for great restraint in the use of force.

Reconnaissance operations may emphasize objectives, such as the location and identification of lines of communications, services, and infrastructure, to support threatened civilian populations. The counterintelligence/human intelligence capabilities of the MAGTF are exceptionally useful in the surveillance of indigenous peoples and identification and targeting of the hostile segments of the population.

COUNTERRECONNAISSANCE

At the same time a force conducts its reconnaissance operations, the opposition will conduct similar operations to determine the disposition of those reconnaissance forces. For example, a force under indirect fire will increase its counterreconnaissance operations to locate and destroy the reconnaissance elements controlling the fire. Counterreconnaissance prevents the opposition from collecting sufficient information about friendly activities.

Counterreconnaissance consists of all measures taken to prevent hostile observation of a force or area. It focuses on denying the enemy access to essential elements of friendly information, information about the MAGTF in the security area, the flanks, and the rear that would further enemy objectives.

Counterreconnaissance consists of active and passive measures. Active measures detect, fix, and destroy enemy reconnaissance elements. Passive measures conceal friendly units and capabilities and deceive and confuse the enemy.

There are two components of counterreconnaissance—the detection of enemy reconnaissance forces and the targeting, destruction, or suppression of those reconnaissance forces so they cannot report friendly unit positions or activities. Counterreconnaissance consists of—

- Developing named areas of interest and target areas of interest for likely enemy reconnaissance forces.
- Conducting continuous surveillance of designated named areas of interest and target areas of interest.
- Executing a targeting plan against enemy reconnaissance forces.
- Recovering forward security elements.

Reconnaissance operations support counterreconnaissance by collecting information on enemy reconnaissance forces, assets, and activities. Counterreconnaissance supports security operations by protecting the MAGTF from enemy collection.

SECURITY OPERATIONS

Security is the measures taken by a military unit, activity, or installation to protect itself against all acts designed to, or which may, impair its effectiveness. Local security is an inherent responsibility of command at every echelon. Additionally, Marine Corps forces may conduct specific security operations designed to aggressively and continuously seek the enemy and reconnoiter key terrain. The forces assigned to conduct security operations are generically referred to as a "security force." Security forces conduct active reconnaissance to detect enemy movement or preparations for action and to learn as much as possible about the terrain. The ultimate goal is to determine the enemy's COA and assist the main body in countering it. Security forces may employ a combination of ground patrols, observation posts, electronic warfare, and aviation assets.

Note

"Security forces" in this context should not be confused with those Marine Corps units that perform security duties as a primary mission in support of fleet commanders and Department of State, as identified in chapter 1. Similarly, it should not be confused with the broader Department of Defense definiton of security forces being composed of the duly constituted military, paramilitary, police, and constabulary forces of a state.

Security in offensive operations employs security elements to protect the MAGTF from unexpected attack, long-range fires, and observation by the enemy. The MAGTF commander can employ a wide range of forces and capabilities to conduct security operations, which can include—

- Aviation forces to screen the main force from enemy interference.
- Ground forces to control, seize, or retain terrain to prevent enemy observation.
- Detection devices, such as unmanned aircraft systems, radar, and seismic sensors, to discover the enemy or his long-range fires.

There are three types of security missions—screen, guard, and cover. Each varies in the degree of security provided, the forces and capabilities required, and the degree of engagement with the enemy the commander desires. The forces conducting these security missions are called a screening, a guarding, or a covering force. These forces may be further identified by the establishing headquarters and the location of the security force, such as a MEF covering force, division advance guard, or regimental flank screen. Security forces may consist of existing units, reinforced units, or task-organized forces.

Screening Force

A screening force observes, identifies, and reports information. It only fights in self-protection. A screening force—

- Provides early warning of enemy approach.
- Gains and maintains enemy contact and reports enemy activity.
- Conducts counterreconnaissance within capabilities.
- Impedes and harasses the enemy within capabilities.

A screening force provides surveillance and early warning of enemy action, not physical protection. It can employ as an economy of force measure in a low-risk area because it provides security on a broad frontage with limited assets. A screening force provides the least amount of protection of any security mission, lacking the combat power to develop the situation. Aviation combat forces may be used to screen large, open areas. Terrain, weather, and the duration of the screen are critical considerations when assigning screening missions to aviation forces. The screening force may operate within range of friendly artillery positioned with the ground forces because of its immediate availability. The ACE can also provide this fire support capability, but the cost in resources versus time

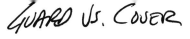

is a factor. For example, one on-station of F/A-18s may require an entire squadron for 24-hour coverage.

Guarding Force

A guarding force protects the main force from attack, direct fire, and ground observation by fighting to gain time, while also observing and reporting information. A guarding force—

- Provides early warning of enemy approach.
- Provides maneuver space to the front, flanks, and rear of the force.
- Screens, attacks, defends, or delays within its capabilities to protect the force.

A guarding force differs from a screening force in that a guarding force contains sufficient combat power to defeat, repel, or fix the lead elements of an enemy ground force before they can engage the main body with direct fire.

Covering Force

A covering force operates apart from the main force to intercept, engage, delay, disorganize, and deceive the enemy before he can attack the main body. It prevents surprise during the advance. A covering force—

- Gains and maintains contact with the enemy.
- Denies the enemy information about the size, strength, composition, and intention of the main force.
- Conducts counterreconnaissance and destroys enemy security forces.
- Develops the situation to determine enemy dispositions, strengths, and weaknesses.

A covering force is a self-contained maneuver force that screens, guards, attacks, defends, and delays. In order to operate independently, a covering force may task-organize to include aviation, artillery, tank reconnaissance, and combat service support. The covering mission may operate in terms of time or friendly and enemy disposition. One example of a covering mssion is engaging enemy forces until our main body deploys for attack.

CHAPTER 12

Stability Operations

"In virtually every province, city, and village it was the same. Corrupt governing councils and courts, the former regime's local means of control and repression, were replaced by the most honorable men and women that commanders could locate and convince to serve. . . .The citizens also looked to the commanders, and the civil affairs soldiers attached from our Army to every battalion headquarters, for the lessons on how to govern democratically."

—Brigadier General John F. Kelly,
Marine Corps Gazette

Stability operations encompass various military missions, tasks, and activities conducted outside the United States. In coordination with other instruments of national power, stability operations seek to maintain or re-establish a safe and secure environment and provide essential governmental services, emergency infrastructure reconstruction, and humanitarian relief.

To achieve conditions that ensure a stable and lasting peace, stability operations capitalize on coordination, cooperation, integration, and synchronization among military and nonmilitary organizations. These complementary civil-military efforts aim to strengthen legitimate governance, restore or maintain rule of law, support economic and infrastructure development, and foster a sense of national unity that enable the host nation government to assume responsibility for civil administration.

Civil-military operations are a primary military instrument to integrate military and nonmilitary instruments of national power, particularly in support of stability operations. These operations are the activities of a commander that establish collaborative relationships among military forces, governmental and nongovernmental civilian organizations and authorities, and the civilian populace in a friendly, neutral, or hostile operational area in order to facilitate military operations that are nested in support of the overall US objectives.

In 2005, Department of Defense Directive 3000.05, *Military Support for Stability, Security, Transition, and Reconstruction (SSTR) Operations*, established stability operations as a core US military mission and directed the Armed Forces to prepare to conduct these types of operations with a level of proficiency equivalent to combat operations. In 2009, the directive was revised and re-issued as Department of Defense Instruction 3000.05, *Stability Operations*. The Department of Defense must be prepared to—

- Conduct stability operations activities throughout all phases of conflict and across the range of military operations. The magnitude of stability operations missions may range from small scale, short duration to large scale, long duration.
- Support stability operations activities conducted by other US Government departments or agencies (hereafter referred to collectively as "US Government agencies"), foreign governments and security forces, international governmental organizations, or when otherwise directed.
- Lead stability operations activities to establish civil security and civil control, restore essential services, repair and protect critical infrastructure, and deliver humanitarian assistance until such time as it is feasible to transition lead responsibility to other US Government agencies, foreign governments and security forces, or international governmental organizations.

While stability operations are often considered largely in terms of actions ashore, they have a maritime application as well. The maritime domain, which includes both landward and seaward portions of the littorals, connects the nations of the world by carrying 90 percent of the world's trade and two thirds of its petroleum. The maritime domain is the lifeline of the modern global economy, which relies on free transit through increasingly urbanized littoral regions. Marine Corps forces have an important and enduring role in the conduct of stability operations in the littorals. Often task-organized with Navy and Coast Guard forces, Marine Corps forces perform a variety of tasks associated with stability operations in both landward and seaward portions of the maritime domain. Examples include, but are not limited to, nation assistance, maritime security operations, combating terrorism, sanctions enforcement/maritime interception operations, protection of shipping, freedom of navigation and overflight, exclusion zone enforcement, Department of Defense support to counterdrug operations, consequence management, foreign humanitarian assistance, and peace operations.

Stability operations have occurred with increasing frequency during the past twenty years in such places as Bosnia, Kosovo, Iraq, Somalia, the Philippines, Haiti, and Afghanistan, as well as on the high seas in places like the Gulf of Aden, the Arabian Sea, Adriatic Sea, and Caribbean Sea. As these examples illustrate, stability operations are not limited to post-conflict applications and may occur across the range of military operations. Conceptually, actions associated with stability operations reside within three broad categories—the initial response, transformation, and fostering sustainability.

INITIAL RESPONSE

Initial response encompasses those tasks to stabilize the operational environment in a crisis. During this phase, which normally occurs during or directly after a conflict or crisis, the MAGTF performs tasks aimed at providing a safe, secure environment and attending to the immediate essential service needs of the local population. The duration of the first phase can vary. It may be relatively brief following a natural disaster or conventional combat. When conducted within the context of counterinsurgency, the initial response may last for years. Due to the expeditionary nature of the MAGTF, it is very likely that naval forces will be the first responders and responsible for setting conditions for the successful accomplishment of national stability campaign objectives and goals.

TRANSFORMATION

Transformation represents a broad range of post-conflict reconstruction, stabilization, and capacity-building activities. The transformation phase may occur in either crisis or vulnerable states. The desire in this stage is to develop and build enduring capability and capacity in the host nation government and security forces. As civil security improves, focus expands to include the development of legitimate governance, provision of essential services, and stimulation of economic development. Concurrently and as a result of the expanded focus, stability force relationships develop and strengthen with host nation counterparts and with the local populace.

FOSTERING STABILITY

The third phase encompasses long-term efforts that capitalize on capacity-building and reconstruction activities to establish conditions enabling sustainable development. This phase emphasizes capacity building with the goal of transitioning responsibility to host nation leadership and security forces.

FUNCTIONS

The primary stability operations functions align with the five end states—safe and secure environment, rule of law, stable governance, social well-being, and sustainable economy—adopted in the *Guiding Principles for Stabilization and*

Reconstruction published by the Department of State. The document provides a framework for stabilization efforts that stems from the policies, doctrine, and training of civilian agencies across the US Government and internationally. These guiding principles present a series of end states in stabilization, conditions describing those end states, and approaches to achieving those end states. These functions are—

- Security.
- Foreign humanitarian assistance.
- Economic stabilization and infrastructure.
- Rule of law.
- Governance and participation.

Together, they provide a framework for integration of the instruments of national power.

Security

Security activities seek to protect and control civil populations and territory—friendly, hostile, or neutral. They may be performed as part of a military occupation during or after combat, to help defeat an insurgency, or in response to a humanitarian disaster. Security activities seek ultimately to reassure rather than compel. They conclude successfully when civil violence is reduced to a level manageable by host nation law enforcement authorities. A safe and secure environment is one in which the population has the freedom to pursue daily activities without fear of politically motivated, persistent, or large-scale violence. Such an environment is characterized by an end to large-scale fighting; an adequate level of public order; the subordination of security forces accountable to legitimate state authority; the protection of key individuals, communities, sites, and infrastructure; and the freedom for people and goods to move about the country and across borders without fear of undue harm.

Foreign Humanitarian Assistance

Foreign humanitarian assistance includes programs conducted to meet basic human needs in order to ensure the social well-being of the population. Social well-being is characterized by equal access to and delivery of basic needs, such as water, food, shelter, sanitation, and health services; the provision of primary and secondary education; the return or voluntary resettlement of those displaced by violent conflict; and the restoration of a social fabric and community life. Some foreign humanitarian assistance activities are not conducted within the overall context of stability operations. Delivery of foreign humanitarian assistance in these cases may be of short duration, with no intention to intrude on society and culture.

Economic Stabilization and Infrastructure

The function of economic stabilization and infrastructure includes programs conducted to ensure an economy exists in which people can pursue opportunities for livelihoods within the local system of economic governance. A sustainable economy is characterized by market-based macroeconomic stability, control over the illicit economy and economic-based threats to the peace, development of a market economy, and employment generation. Meeting the needs of human security—both in terms of the provision of physical security and foreign humanitarian assistance—lays the foundation for the stabilization of fragile states. Economic stabilization and development help to consolidate gains made in human security and enable political solutions. Although security and governance reform remain priorities, early attention to economic growth improves the likelihood of success. Accordingly, while economic measures and reconstruction are not the panacea for stability, they should constitute a significant component of the solution. Priorities for international agencies and forces include measures designed to stabilize the economy, protect, and reconstruct critical economic infrastructure, generate employment, and address any underlying economic drivers of conflict.

Rule of Law

The rule of law function refers to programs conducted to ensure all individuals and institutions, public and private, and the state itself are held accountable to the law. The rule of law in a country is characterized by just legal frameworks, public order, accountability to the law, access to justice, and a culture of lawfulness. Rule of law requires laws that are publicly promulgated, equally enforced, and independently adjudicated and that are consistent with international human rights principles. It also requires measures to ensure adherence to the principles of supremacy of law, equality before the law, accountability to the law, fairness in applying the law, separation of powers, participation in decisionmaking, and legal certainty. Such measures also help to avoid arbitrariness as well as promote procedural and legal transparency.

Governance and Participation

Programs that support governance and participation help people to share, access, or compete for power through nonviolent political processes and to enjoy the collective benefits and services of the state. Stable governance involves a government that provides essential services and serves as a responsible steward of public resources; government officials who are held accountable through political and legal processes; and a population that can participate in governance through civil society organizations, an independent media, and political parties. Stable governance is the mechanism through which basic human needs of the population are largely met, respect for minority rights is assured, conflicts are managed peacefully through inclusive political processes, and competition for power occurs nonviolently.

CHAPTER 13

Sustainment Operations

> *"Strategy and Tactics will indicate the extent of operations that are proposed, and Logistics will provide the means therefor [sic]. . . ."*
>
> —Pure Logistics: The Science of War Preparation

The terms sustainment, logistics, and combat service support are often used interchangeably, but there are differences among them. Sustainment is the ability to ensure combat forces are provided the support required until the mission is completed. Logistics is the science of planning and executing the movement and support of forces and is a fundamental element of MAGTF expeditionary operations. Combat service support is the tactical activity that actually provides essential services and supplies to operating forces in theater.

United States Code, Title 10 assigns each Service responsibility for organizing, training, and equipping forces for employment in the national interest. The Commandant is responsible for Marine Corps logistics, ensuring Marine Corps forces under the combatant command of a combatant commander or the operational control of a unified, subunified, or joint task force commander are trained, equipped, and prepared logistically to undertake assigned missions.

The principal logistic responsibilities of the Marine Corps include—

- Preparing forces and establishing reserves of equipment and supplies for the effective prosecution of war.
- Planning and executing the expansion and reduction of forces to meet the needs of war.
- Preparing budgets for submission through the Department of the Navy based on input from Marine Corps operating forces.
- Conducting research and development and recommending procurement of weapons, equipment, and supplies essential to the fulfillment of the combat mission assigned to the Marine Corps.
- Developing, garrisoning, supplying, equipping, and maintaining bases and other installations.

- Providing administrative and logistic support for all Marine Corps forces and bases.
- Ensuring supported unified commanders are advised of significant changes in Marine Corps logistic support, including base adjustments that would impact plans and programs.

The Commandant, as a member of the Joint Chiefs of Staff, ensures the Marine Corps—

- Prepares integrated logistic plans, which include assignment of logistic responsibilities.
- Prepares integrated plans for military mobilization.
- Reviews major personnel, materiel, and logistic requirements in relation to strategic and logistic plans.
- Reviews the plans and programs of commanders of unified and specified commands to determine their adequacy, feasibility, and suitability for the performance of assigned missions.

The Commandant tasks Marine Corps commanders with the responsibility and authority to ensure their commands are logistically ready for employment and logistic operations are efficient and effective. This authority is exercised through administrative command channels for routine matters of logistic readiness and service planning. Marine Corps component commanders, MAGTF commanders, and their subordinate commanders exercise the appropriate logistic responsibilities and authorities. Operational assignments do not preclude Service administrative command responsibilities and obligations.

LEVELS OF LOGISTIC PLANNING

Although the Marine Corps generally focuses on the tactical level of logistics, it is imperative Marines understand the interaction of all three logistic levels. These levels interconnect like sections of a pipeline, tying together logistics at the strategic, operational, and tactical levels.

Strategic Logistics

Strategic logistics supports organizing, training, and equipping the force. It applies the national economic base—people, resources, and industry—toward fielding the desired operational capabilities. These capabilities include Department of Defense; the Military Services; functional component commands, such as the United States Transportation Command or other government agencies, as necessary or appropriate; and the private sector.

The Marine Corps supporting establishment and Headquarters, Marine Corps plan and conduct Marine Corps strategic logistics—with the exception of aviation-peculiar support, which is planned and conducted by the Chief of Naval Operations, the Navy supporting establishment, and the Navy Reserve. At the strategic level, the Marine Corps—

- Procures weapons and equipment, except aircraft and aviation ordnance.
- Recruits, trains, and assembles forces.
- Establishes bases, stations, and facilities, to include ranges and airspace, to stockpile resources and house, train, and maintain forces.
- Mobilizes forces.
- Oversees and coordinates employment of strategic-level transportation assets.
- Regenerates forces.
- Provides command and control to manage the flow of resources from the strategic, to the operational/theater, to the tactical levels, using nodes controlled by organizations, such as the Defense Distribution Center under the Defense Logistics Agency and the United States Transportation Command.

Operational Logistics

Operational logistics involves the preparation, movement, and positioning of forces and resources in the sequence, timeliness, and readiness-level necessary to accomplish established operational goals and objectives. It includes the support required to sustain campaigns and major operations. Marine Corps operational logistics orients on force closure, sustainment, reconstitution, and redeployment of Marine Corps forces in theater. Operational logisticians coordinate with logisticians at the tactical level to identify and communicate theater shortfalls to the strategic source. The focus of operational logistics is to balance the MAGTF deployment, employment, and support requirements to maximize the overall effectiveness of the force. Marine Corps operating forces, assisted by Headquarters, Marine Corps and the supporting establishment, are responsible for operational logistics. The Marine Corps component commander conducts operational logistics. In large operations, the Marine Corps component commander may establish a logistic support organization to perform operational logistic functions to support tactical logistics in the area of operations. During joint operations, the US Army will establish and control the theater/operational distribution nodes.

Tactical Logistics

Tactical logistics includes organic unit capabilities and the combat service support activities conducted in support of military operations. The goal of tactical-level logistics is to support maneuver forces in the battlespace.

The MAGTF task-organizes combat service support capabilities to accomplish assigned missions. Although no single MAGTF element has all of the logistic capabilities to operate independently for extended periods, each element can accomplish at least some basic self-support tasks.

The LCE provides general ground logistics to all MAGTF elements, while the ACE possesses logistic capabilities essential for aircraft operations. The MAGTF is able to deploy with accompanying supplies that enable it to conduct operations for 15 to 60 days, but resupply channels and the flow of supplies to support the MAGTF begin prior to the consumption of the MAGTF's organic supplies. An in-depth discussion on the levels of logistics is found in MCDP 4, and MCWP 4-1.

LOGISTIC FUNCTIONS

Seven core logistic capabilities are identified in JP 4-0, *Joint Logistics*—supply, maintenance operations, deployment and distribution, health service support, engineering, logistic services, and operational contract support. The Marine Corps views contract support as an operational/strategic function. Accordingly, the Marine Corps categorizes the above core capabilities into six functional areas—supply, maintenance, distribution/transportation, general engineering, health services, and other services. Operational contract support falls under other services.

LOGISTICS IN JOINT AND MULTINATIONAL OPERATIONS

In joint operations, the Services are normally responsible for providing their own logistics; however, the combatant commander, acting through the commanders of the component forces, is responsible for overall logistic coordination. The combatant commander has the directive authority for logistics for forces in his area of operations; JP 4-0 explains how the combatant commander is specifically responsible for developing and sustaining military effectiveness by establishing a logistic structure.

The combatant commander has the authority to coordinate the logistics of the Service components and to control distribution of support when shortages occur. The most common type of support is single Service logistic support; however, plans may require or direct the use of other types of support, such as common servicing, cross-servicing, or joint servicing, at the force, theater, Military Department, or Department of Defense level.

In multinational operations, logistics is a national responsibility; however, agreements may establish the framework for mutual support. The exchange of logistical support between US forces and multinational participants can lead to significant economies of effort and cost savings. If no appropriate international agreements exist, combatant commanders cannot provide for or accept logistic support from allies or coalition forces without direction from the Secretary of Defense.

STRATEGIC LOGISTIC SUPPORT

Organizations enabling the strategic logistic support effort include the United States Transportation Command, Department of Transportation, and Defense Logistics Agency.

Strategic Mobility

Strategic mobility includes the ability of the US Armed Forces to deploy expeditionary forces to any region in the world and sustain them for activities across the range of military operations. The strategic mobility triad is the combination of sealift, airlift, and prepositioning. Table 13-1 highlights the strengths of each component of the strategic lift triad.

The sea dominates the surface of the globe; hence, for any global power, sea power is essential. Lack of modern or developed infrastructure can pose significant problems for military action in the developing world. Many ports cannot accommodate deep-draft ships and many airfields in the developing world cannot handle large military transport aircraft. The MEF, as the premier

Table 13-1. Strategic Mobility Strengths.

	Closure Speed	Flexibility	Capability
Sealift		X	X
Prepositioning	X		X
Airlift	X	X	

expeditionary force in readiness, is capable of rapid response by sealift, prepositioning, and airlift.

United States Transportation Command

The United States Transportation Command is the single manager of the Defense Transportation System. It is also the Secretary of Defense-designated distribution process owner charged with "coordination and synchronization" of people and sustainment cargo throughout the Joint Deployment and Distribution Enterprise, providing air, land, and sea transportation and common-user port management at airports and seaports of debarkation as well as airports and seaports of embarkation for Department of Defense across the range of military operations. Deployment and distribution operation at the joint level is defined in JP 4-09, *Distribution Operations*.

Department of Transportation

Executive Order 12656, *Assignment of Emergency Preparedness Responsibilities*, established the Secretary of Transportation as the federal government lead for the transportation community. During national defense emergencies, the Secretary of Transportation has a wide range of delegated responsibilities, including executive management of the Nation's transportation resources. A more detailed account of Department of Transportation responsibilities appears in JP 4-01, *Joint Doctrine for the Defense Transportation System*.

Defense Logistics Agency

The Defense Logistics Agency is a strategic- and operational-level logistic agency of the Department of Defense. It provides worldwide logistic support to the Military Departments and the combatant commands across the range of military operations as well as to other Department of Defense components, federal agencies, foreign governments, or international organizations. It provides materiel and supplies to the Military Services and supports their acquisition of weapons and other equipment. Such Defense Logistics Agency-level support begins with joint planning with the Services regarding parts for new weapon systems, extends through production, and concludes with the disposal of materiel either obsolete or at the end of its service life. The Defense Logistics Agency provides supply, support, technical, and logistic services to all branches of the military.

OPERATIONAL LOGISTIC SUPPORT

The Marine Corps component commander takes on several additional responsibilities when providing operational logistic support.

Marine Corps Component

Assigned or attached Marine Corps forces provide their support requirements and priorities to the Marine Corps component commander, who then determines what resources will fulfill the requirements. The Marine Corps component commander develops agreements with other component commanders and participates in component command-level working groups. In some instances, Marine Corps forces may provide logistical support to other US forces, US Government agencies, multinational forces, or groups supported by the United States. During employment, the Marine Corps component commander concentrates on—

- Sustainment sourcing.
- Intratheater transportation asset allocation.
- Facility and base development.
- Host nation support.
- Health services management.

During redeployment, the Marine Corps component commander's focus is the reconstitution of Marine Corps forces. The identification of accurate mission costs and material losses is also important to the Marine Corps component commander.

Organization of MAGTF Logistics

The Marine Corps component commander may employ a short duration operational logistic organization when the commander believes an operational logistic capability is needed to ensure effective support for deploying MAGTFs and the following operational conditions occur:

- Expeditious force closure of a MEF-sized MAGTF and early linkage into operational logistic capabilities are required.
- Sequential MPF offloads or backloads are planned or required.

- Common item or user support will be in place by D+60 or later.
- The combatant commander or joint force commander has identified shortages in planned theater logistic support that will impact the MAGTF mission and operations.

Two key planning factors the Marine Corps component commander should consider prior to any decision regarding the formation and deployment of any operational logistic organization are—

- Maximizing reliance on the MAGTF construct and levying requirements on theater and common-user logistic support providers (United States Code, Title 10).
- Minimizing the size, scope, and number of Marine component operational logistic organizations.

Reconstitution

Reconstitution refers to those actions required to restore a unit to a desired level of combat effectiveness to meet future mission requirements. Reconstitution of Marine Corps forces is the responsibility of the Marine Corps component commander. Besides normal support actions, reconstitution may also include removing the unit from combat, assessing the unit with external assets, re-establishing the chain of command, training the unit for future operations, and re-establishing unit cohesion.

There are two methods for conducting reconstitution—reorganization and regeneration.

Reorganization is action taken to shift internal resources within a degraded unit to increase its level of combat effectiveness. Reorganization is normally done at the unit level and does not require extensive external support.

Regeneration reconstitutes a unit through significant replacement of personnel, equipment, and supplies in an attempt to restore a unit to full operational capability as rapidly as possible. When established, the operational logistic organization—augmented by the supporting establishment—is responsible for executing regeneration operations. When an operational logistic organization is not established, the Marine Corps component commander will plan movement of replacement personnel and equipment from outside the theater.

COMMAND AND CONTROL

Logistic command and control is the means to ensure the effective employment of resources. Effective logistics must match resources to warfighting requirements. Since requirements may be unlimited and resources are always limited, logistic commanders must allocate resources consistent with the MAGTF commander's intent and overall concept of operations.

Command and control of logistics must provide visibility of both capabilities and requirements, allowing the commander to make decisions regarding the effective allocation of scarce, high-demand resources. Additionally, command and control facilitates the integration of logistic activities with other warfighting functions in order to optimize the commander's time for planning, decisionmaking, execution, and assessment. An effective flow of information and directives enables the Marine Corps to manage materiel readiness, mobilization and deployment support, and materiel replenishment. At the strategic level, the principal agents for dissemination of logistic policy, directives, and information are the Deputy Commandant for Installations and Logistics and the Deputy Commandant for Aviation. The Commander, Marine Corps Logistics Command (MARCORLOGCOM) and Commander, Marine Corps Systems Command (MARCORSYSCOM) are principally responsible for executing Marine Corps strategic-level ground logistics, while Commander, Naval Air Systems Command executes strategic-level aviation support. At the operational level, the logistic effort enables force closure; establishes and maintains arrival and assembly areas; and coordinates intratheater airlift, sustainment needs, and force reconstitution and redeployment requirements.

Marine Corps component G-4s coordinate ground logistic issues with the subordinate MAGTF G-4/S-4. The Commander, Naval Air Force, Pacific and Commander, Naval Air Force, Atlantic deal directly with the MAGTF ACE logistic department to assist in resolving aviation logistic requirements. In joint operations, the principal logistic agent is the J-4.

LOGISTIC SUPPORT TO MAGTF OPERATIONS

Initially, logistics come from internal Marine Corps/Navy resources located within the operating forces, Marine Corps Forces Reserve, and the supporting establishment. Specific operational requirements dictate the extent to which additional logistic support comes from other Services, Defense Logistics Agency, non-Department of Defense resources, and multinational resources. The logistic mission of the Marine Corps is to ensure MAGTFs are deployable, self-reliant, self-sustaining, flexible, and capable of rapid reconstitution. In coordination and cooperation with the Navy, the Marine Corps has made logistical self-sufficiency a central element of MAGTF expeditionary warfighting capabilities.

Maritime Prepositioning Forces

The MPFs provide an added dimension to strategic mobility, readiness, and global responsiveness. By prepositioning the bulk of equipment and 30 days of supplies for a notional 17,600-troop force aboard specially-designed ships, the MPF program reduces MAGTF response time from weeks to days. Included in each MPSRON is organizational-level common aviation support equipment and limited intermediate-level support equipment. The ACE deploys with a fly-in support package that, when combined with prepositioned assets on the MPSRON, provides critical aviation support for 30 days of combat operations. While normally associated with MEB employment, supplies and equipment aboard MPSRONs can support other contingencies. Although normally offloaded pierside, the maritime prepositioning ships have a limited in-stream offload capability.

Aviation Logistics Support Ship

The two aviation logistics support ships—one located on the west coast and one on the east coast—are under the administrative control of the Military Sealift Command. They provide dedicated sealift for movement of the Marine aviation logistics squadron's supplies and equipment and an afloat intermediate maintenance activity capability. This task-organized intermediate maintenance activity repairs aircraft parts and equipment.

Norway Geoprepositioning Program

The Norway Geoprepositioning Program is a capability similar in scope to that of an MPSRON. The program, established with the Government of Norway, permits the prepositioning and maintenance of a MEB's worth of equipment in underground storage facilities in Norway.

War Reserve Materiel Support

War reserve materiel includes mission-essential principal end items, secondary items, and munitions required to attain operational objectives in the scenarios authorized for sustainability planning and other stockage objectives approved for programming in the *Defense Planning Guidance*. The Department of Defense acquires war reserve materiel inventories during peacetime. These inventories are flexible and provide an expansion capability that can respond to a range of regional contingencies while minimizing investment in resources. Authority to approve the release of war reserve materiel stocks is limited to specified commanders.

OTHER SUPPORT TO MAGTF OPERATIONS

The supporting establishment and separate field commands are inextricably linked to the operational forces, as they furnish logistics vital to the overall combat readiness and sustainment of the Marine Corps. Although not part of the Marine Corps, the Navy's supporting establishment also provides essential logistics to Marine Corps aviation.

Marine Corps Combat Development Command

Logistics is a significant focus of the Marine Corps Combat Development Command and is the principal responsibility of the Logistics Integration Division within the Combat Development Directorate.

Marine Corps Systems Command

Marine Corps Systems Command is responsible for the research, development, acquisition, and lifecycle management of Marine Corps-funded materiel and information systems. It directs Marine Corps-sponsored programs and represents the Marine Corps in the development of other Service-sponsored programs in which the Marine Corps participates. Marine Corps Systems Command coordinates program interface internally within the Marine Corps and externally with the Department of the Navy, Department of Defense, other Services, Congress, and industry.

Marine Corps Systems Command, in the execution of strategic level ground logistics duties, is primarily focused on equipping the Force. In coordination with Marine Corps Combat Development Command and MARCORLOGCOM, MARCORSYSCOM maintains a focus on product support management, also referred to as system sustainment. To that end, MARCORSYSCOM is actively engaged in the following activities:

- Assess and refine requirements for both urgent and deliberate needs.
- Develop lifecycle management plans for ground equipment.
- Report enterprise-level readiness.
- Analyze ongoing lifecycle of Marine Corps ground equipment to enable systems operational effectiveness and sustainment.

Marine Corps Systems Command is the instrument of the Marine Corps that shapes desired ground equipment capabilities through the national economic base to enable and sustain Marine Corps operations.

Marine Corps Logistics Command

Marine Corps Logistics Command's principal responsibilities include Service-level and assigned operational-level supply, maintenance, and distribution support to maximize Service readiness and increase the combat effectiveness of the operating forces. Marine Corps Logistics Command supports operational-level logistic operations through the following activities:

- Equipment sourcing, including principal end item inventory management, maintenance planning and execution, and storage and distribution.
- Prepositioning support, including MPF operations, planning and execution, and other planned prepositioned stocks and inventories.
- Logistic services, including planned logistic capabilities developed in response to a specified operating forces operational requirement.

Assistant Secretary of the Navy, Research, Development, and Acquisition provides policy, governance, and oversight to Marine Corps acquisition of ground equipment.

In order to ensure operational value to the Marine Corps forces, MARCORLOGCOM sources capabilities from a wide range of organizations, to include military, government, and commercial elements.

At the request of the Marine Corps forces, MARCORLOGCOM is capable of providing a forward-deployed command detachment, which is an organizational option available to the Marine Corps forces. This option is scalable and complementary to other operational logistic support providers. During operations, MARCORLOGCOM (Forward) attaches to the Marine Corps component; has direct liaison with supported MAGTFs; and leverages its parent organization, MARCORLOGCOM, for continental United States-coordinated support.

Maintenance centers in Albany, GA, and Barstow, CA, are capable of conducting depot-level repairs, rebuilds, and modifications to all Marine Corps ground combat equipment, combat support equipment, and combat service support equipment. The flexibility of the centers also allows for task-organized teams to provide rapid responses for equipment modification solutions and forward positioned maintenance teams.

In contrast to the maintenance centers, the Blount Island Command is responsible for inventory management, equipment maintenance, and replacement support for the MPF and the Norway Geoprepositioning Program. Upon request from the Marine Corps forces, Blount Island Command is also prepared to deploy a technical assistance advisory team for MPF regeneration operations and in support of MPF offload and backload operations.

Marine Corps Installations Command

Marine Corps Installations Command, planned for initial operational capability in 2011 and final operational capability in 2012, will consist of a headquarters with three subordinate components—Marine Corps Installations East, Marine Corps Installations West, and Marine Corps Installations Pacific. The mission of Marine Corps Installations Command is to exercise command and control of Marine Corps installations regional commanders, establish policies, exercise oversight, and prioritize resources in order to optimize installation support to the operating forces and tenant commands.

Marine Corps bases, stations, and reserve support centers provide the infrastructure and facilities that support the operating forces and allow training as a MAGTF. They support force deployments on routine and contingency response operations and provide critical logistics to deploying units from predeployment preparation through deployment and reconstitution.

In support of the total force, selected bases and stations are designated stations of initial assignment for Marine Corps Reserve mobilization. These designated stations are responsible for assisting the operating forces with the throughput of Marine Corps Reserve personnel and materiel in support of MAGTF deployments.

Department of the Navy Agencies

Selected Department of the Navy agencies support both the Navy and the Marine Corps. In logistics, the most visible functions are naval aviation materiel support and health service support.

The Navy's logistic effort is divided among the following commands—

- Naval Supply Systems Command provides materiel support as well as logistic support without aviation logistic support.
- Naval Air Systems Command provides aviation logistic support to include oversight of fleet readiness centers.

- Naval Sea Systems Command oversees the five depot maintenance shipyards.
- Naval Medical Logistics Command provides the Navy and Marine Corps with subject matter expertise for medical materiel and procures all medical and dental equipment, services, and supplies for naval forces.
- Naval Facilities Engineering Command provides initial outfitting of chemical, biological, and radiological defense material and equipment to overseas shore installations, naval construction force, and naval beach group units.
- Space and Naval Warfare Systems Command provides software support for the fleet logistic programs to automate supply, inventory control, maintenance, and financial management.

Naval Logistics Integration

The Secretary of the Navy Instruction 4000.37, *Naval Logistics Integration (NLI)*, is the ongoing effort to improve logistic support to both the Navy and the Marine Corps. The goal of naval logistic integration is to establish an integrated naval logistic capability to operate seamlessly, whether afloat or ashore, successfully supporting and sustaining naval operation units in a joint environment. Naval logistic integration initiatives currently support afloat MEUs. The MEU's use of Navy supply and cargo routing procedures has become an integral part of their deployed logistic support.

APPENDIX A

Principles of Joint Operations

The Marine Corps warfighting philosophy of maneuver warfare is rooted in the long-standing principles of war. These original nine principles: mass, objective, offensive, security, economy of force, maneuver, unity of command, surprise, and simplicity—known by the memory aid "MOOSEMUSS"—are part of the twelve principles of joint operations, which includes three principles specifically related to irregular warfare (perseverence, legitimacy, and restraint).

The principles of joint operations are useful aids to a commander as he considers how to accomplish his mission. They assist the commander in organizing his thinking about his mission, the enemy, the battlespace, and his forces. They should not be considered as prescriptive steps or actions that must be accomplished, but as tools to plan, execute, and assess operations. Successful application of the principles requires a commander's judgment, skill, and experience to adapt to constantly changing conditions and situations. The principles are explained in the following subparagraphs.

MASS

Mass refers to the concentration of friendly capabilities at the decisive place and time to achieve decisive results. Commanders mass capabilities to overwhelm the enemy and gain control of the situation. Mass applies to fires, combat support, combat service support, and numbers of forces. Proper use of the principle of mass, together with the other principles of war, may achieve decisive local superiority by a numerically inferior force. The decision to concentrate requires strict economy and the acceptance of risk elsewhere, particularly in view of the lethality of modern weapons that mandate the rapid assembly and speedy dispersal of forces.

OBJECTIVE

This principle advises the direction of every military operation toward a clearly defined, decisive, and attainable objective. The ultimate military objective of war is to defeat the enemy's forces or destroy his will to fight. The objective of each operation must contribute quickly and economically to the ultimate objective or purpose of the operation. The selection of an objective is based on consideration of the ultimate goal, forces available, the level of threat, and the area of operations. Every commander must clearly understand the overall mission of the higher command, his own mission, the tasks he must perform, and the reasons for them. He considers every contemplated action in light of its direct contribution to the objective. He must clearly communicate the overall objective of the operation to his subordinates.

Offensive

This principle refers to seizing, retaining, and exploiting the initiative. Offensive action is the decisive form of combat. It is necessary to seize, retain, and exploit the initiative and to maintain freedom of action. It allows the commander to exploit enemy weaknesses, impose his will upon the enemy, and determine the course of the battle. A defensive posture should only be a temporary expedient until the means are available to resume the offensive. Even in the conduct of a defense, the commander seeks every opportunity to seize the initiative by offensive action.

Security

The goal of security is never to permit the enemy to acquire an unexpected advantage. Security is those measures taken by a military unit, activity, or installation to protect itself against all acts designed to, or which may, impair its effectiveness. Security measures are designed to prevent surprise, ensure freedom of action, and deny the enemy information about friendly forces, capabilities, and plans. Security is essential to the preservation of combat power across the range of military operations, even in benign environments. However, since risk is an inherent condition of war, security does not imply overcautiousness or the avoidance of calculated risk. In fact, security can often be enhanced by bold maneuver and offensive action, which deny the enemy the chance to interfere. Adequate security requires an accurate appreciation of enemy capabilities, sufficient security measures, effective reconnaissance, and continuous readiness for action.

Economy of Force

The reciprocal of the principle of mass, economy of force allocates minimum essential combat power to secondary efforts. The commander allocates the minimum essential combat power to secondary efforts, requiring the acceptance of prudent risks in selected areas to achieve superiority at the decisive time and location with the main effort. Devoting means to unnecessary efforts or excessive means to necessary secondary efforts violates the principles of mass and objective. Economy of force measures are achieved through limited attacks, defense, deceptions, or delaying actions.

Maneuver

Maneuver is Department of Defense-defined as the employment of forces in the operational area through movement in combination with fires to achieve a position of advantage with respect to the enemy in order to accomplish the mission. Maneuver allows for the distribution or concentration of capabilities in support of the commander's concept of operations. The Marine Corps maneuver warfare philosophy expands the concept of maneuver to include taking action in *any* dimension, whether temporal, psychological, or technological, to gain an advantage.

Unity of Command

Unity of command requires that, for every objective, there is unity of effort ensured under one responsible commander. Unity of command is based on the designation of a single commander with the authority to direct and coordinate the efforts of all assigned forces in pursuit of a common objective. The goal of unity of command is unity of effort. In joint, multinational, and interagency operations where the commander may not control all elements in his area of operations, he seeks cooperation and builds consensus to achieve unity of effort.

Surprise

Striking the enemy at a time or place or in a manner for which he is unprepared is the element of surprise. It is not essential that the enemy be taken unaware, but only that he become aware too late to react effectively. Factors contributing to surprise include speed, the use of unexpected forces, operating at night, effective and timely intelligence, deception, security, variation in tactics and techniques, and the use of unfavorable terrain. Surprise can decisively affect the outcome of a battle and may compensate for numerical inferiority.

Simplicity

Preparing clear, uncomplicated plans and clear, concise orders to ensure thorough understanding follow the principle of simplicity. Plans should be as simple and direct as the situation and mission dictate. Direct, simple plans and clear, concise orders reduce the chance for misunderstanding and confusion and promote effective execution. In combat, even the simplest plan is usually difficult to execute, though usually the simplest plan is preferred. Multinational operations place great importance on simplicity, since language, doctrine, and cultural differences complicate military operations. Simple plans and orders minimize the confusion inherent in joint, multinational, and interagency operations.

PERSERVERANCE

Ensuring the commitment necessary to attain the national strategic end state requires perseverance. Commanders prepare for measured, protracted military operations in pursuit of the desired national strategic end state, which even some joint operations may require years to reach. The underlying causes of the crisis may be elusive, making resolving it and achieving conditions supporting the end state difficult. The patient, resolute, and persistent pursuit of national goals and objectives often is a requirement for success, frequently involving diplomatic, informational, and economic measures to supplement military efforts. In the end, the will of the American public, as expressed through their elected officials and advised by expert military judgment, determines the duration and size of any military commitment.

United States military forces' endurance and commanders' perseverance are necessary to accomplish long-term missions. A decisive offensive operation may swiftly create conditions for short-term success; however, protracted stability operations, executed simultaneously with defensive and offensive tasks, may be needed to achieve the strategic end state.

LEGITIMACY

A legitimate operation develops and maintains the will necessary to attain the national strategic end state. For US military forces, legitimacy comes from three important factors—

- First, the operation or campaign must be conducted under US law.
- Second, the operation must be conducted according to international laws and treaties recognized by the United States, particularly the law of war.
- Third, the campaign or operation should develop or reinforce the authority and acceptance for the host nation government by both the governed and the international community. This factor is frequently the decisive element.

Legitimacy is also based on the will of the American people to support the mission. The American people's perception of legitimacy is strengthened if obvious national or humanitarian interests are at stake. Their perception also depends on their assurance that American lives are not being placed at risk needlessly or carelessly.

Other interested audiences may include foreign nations, civil populations in and near the operational area, and participating multinational forces. Committed forces must sustain the legitimacy of the operation and of the host nation government, where applicable. Security actions must balance with the need to maintain legitimacy. Commanders must consider all actions potentially competing for strategic and tactical requirements. All actions must exhibit fairness in dealing with competing factions where appropriate. Legitimacy depends on the level of consent to the force and to the host nation government, the people's expectations, and the force's credibility.

RESTRAINT

In an effort to limit collateral damage and prevent the unnecessary use of force, restraint requires careful and disciplined balancing of security, the conduct of military operations, and the desired strategic end state. Excessive force antagonizes those friendly and neutral parties involved; hence, it damages the legitimacy of the organization that uses it while potentially enhancing the legitimacy of any opposing party. The rules of engagement must be carefully matched to the strategic end state and the situation. Commanders at all levels ensure their personnel are properly trained in rules of engagement and quickly informed of any changes. Rules of engagement may vary according to national policy concerns, but unit commanders always retain the inherent right and obligation to exercise unit self-defense in response to a hostile act or demonstrated hostile intent.

Restraint is best achieved when rules of engagement issued at the beginning of an operation address a range of plausible situations. Commanders should consistently review and revise rules of engagement as necessary. Additionally, commanders should carefully examine them to ensure that the lives and health of Marines are not needlessly endangered. National concerns may lead to different rules of engagement for multinational participants; commanders must be aware of national restrictions imposed on force participants.

APPENDIX B

Warfighting Functions

The warfighting functions encompass all military activities performed in the battlespace. Warfighting functions are a grouping of like activities into major functional areas that aid in planning and execution of operations. The six functional areas are command and control, maneuver, fires, intelligence, logistics, and force protection. The key advantage of using warfighting functions is they allow the commander and his planners to look at all aspects of the battlespace and not leave anything to chance if it is within their capability to coordinate, control, influence, and synchronize. By integrating the warfighting functions, the commander can increase the force's combat power, mass capabilities on the enemy, and aid in the assessment of the operation's success. As discussed in MCDP 1-2, the synchronization of all warfighting functions gives them their maximum impact on accomplishing the desired objective within the shortest time possible and with minimum casualties.

Planners consider and integrate the warfighting functions when analyzing how to accomplish the mission, because integrating the warfighting functions helps to achieve focus and unity of effort. Planners think in terms of how each function supports the accomplishment of the mission; moreover, they consider the coordination of activities not only within each warfighting function, but also among all the warfighting functions. By using warfighting functions as the integration elements, planners ensure all functions are focused toward a single purpose. The warfighting functions apply equally to conventional and other types of operations, such as information operations, counterinsurgency, or other forms of irregular warfare.

COMMAND AND CONTROL

Command and control is the exercise of authority and direction by a properly designated commander over assigned and attached forces to accomplish a mission. Command and control involves arranging personnel, equipment, and facilities to allow a commander to extend his influence over the force during the planning and conduct of military operations. Command and control is the overarching warfighting function that enables all of the other warfighting functions.

Command remains a very personal function—professional competence, personality, and the will of strong commanders represent a significant part of any unit's combat power. The commander goes where he can best influence the action; where his moral and physical presence can be felt; and where his will to achieve a decision can best be expressed, understood, and acted upon. The focus of command and control is on the commander—his intent, guidance, decisions, and how he receives feedback on the results of his actions. Commanders command while staffs coordinate and make necessary adjustments consistent with the commander's intent.

Control allows the commander to adjust and modify command action as needed based on feedback. Feedback is the basic mechanism of control. It is the continuous flow of information about the unfolding situation returning to the commander. This information indicates the difference between the goals and the situation as it exists. Feedback may come from any direction and in any form—intelligence about how the enemy is reacting, information about the status of subordinate or adjacent units, or revised guidance from above based on developments. Accordingly, feedback allows commanders to adapt to changing circumstances—to exploit fleeting opportunities, respond to developing problems, modify schemes, or redirect efforts. In this way, feedback "controls" subsequent command action. Control is not strictly something that seniors impose on subordinates; rather, the entire system comes "under control" based on feedback about the changing situation. Command and control is an interactive process involving all the parts of the system and working in all directions. The result is a mutually supporting system in which complementary commanding and controlling forces interact to ensure the force as a whole can adapt continuously to changing requirements.

MANEUVER

Maneuver is the employment of forces in the operational area through movement in combination with fires to achieve a position of advantage in respect to the enemy in order to accomplish the mission. (JP 1-02) Maneuver allows for the distribution or concentration of capabilities in support of a commander's concept of operations. The Marine Corps maneuver warfare philosophy expands the concept of maneuver to include taking action in *any* dimension, whether temporal, psychological, or technological, to gain an advantage.

FIRES

Fires use weapon systems to create a specific lethal or nonlethal effect on a target. Fires harass, suppress, neutralize, or destroy in order to accomplish the targeting objective—whether to disrupt, delay, limit, persuade, or influence. Fires include the collective and coordinated use of target acquisition systems, direct and indirect fire weapons, armed aircraft of all types, and other lethal and nonlethal means. Fires are normally used with maneuver and help shape the battlespace, setting conditions for decisive action.

INTELLIGENCE

Intelligence provides the commander with an understanding of the enemy and the battlespace and identifies the enemy's centers of gravity and critical vulnerabilities. It assists the commander in understanding the situation, alerts him to new opportunities, and helps him assess the effects of actions upon the enemy. Intelligence drives operations, is focused on the enemy, and supports the formulation and subsequent modification of the commander's estimate of the situation by providing as accurate an image of the battlespace and the enemy as possible. It is a dynamic process used to assess the current situation and confirm or deny the adoption of specific COAs by the enemy. It helps refine the commander's understanding of the battlespace and reduces uncertainty and risk.

LOGISTICS

Logistics encompasses all activities required to move and sustain military forces. At the tactical level, logistics is combat service support and involves arming, fueling, maintenance, transportation, supply, general engineering, and health services.

FORCE PROTECTION

Force protection is the measures taken to preserve the force's potential so that it can be applied at the appropriate time and place. It includes those measures the force takes to remain viable by protecting itself from the effects of adversary activities and natural occurrences. Force protection safeguards friendly centers of gravity and protects, conceals, reduces, or eliminates friendly critical vulnerabilities.

APPENDIX C

Tactical Tasks

The MAGTF tactical tasks may be specified, implied, or essential. They define actions commanders may take to accomplish their missions. In special circumstances, commanders may modify tasks to meet METT-T requirements. They must clearly state that they are departing from the standard meaning of these tasks. One way this can be done is by prefacing the modified task with the statement, "What I mean by [modified task] is . . . ."

Tactical tasks (see table C-1) are assigned based on capabilities. The GCE can execute all of the MAGTF's tactical tasks. The LCE can execute those tactical tasks essential for it to provide sustainment to the MAGTF. The ACE can execute many of the MAGTF's tactical tasks, but it cannot secure, seize, retain, or occupy terrain without augmentation by the GCE. Weather and task duration may significantly affect the ACE's ability to execute assigned tactical tasks.

The descriptions of tactical tasks that follow are for guided discussion only and are not official definitions of the terms in most cases. For the definitions, as applicable, see JP 1-02 and MCRP 1-10.2, *Marine Corps Supplement to the Department of Defense Dictionary of Military and Associated Terms*.

ENEMY-ORIENTED TACTICAL TASKS

The following tactical tasks focus friendly efforts on generating effects against enemy forces.

AMBUSH

A surprise attack by fire from concealed positions on a moving or temporarily halted enemy.

Note

An ambush is fundamentally a type of attack, enemy-oriented, and is planned and executed accordingly.

Table C-1. Tactical Tasks.

Enemy-Oriented Tactical Tasks	Terrain-Oriented Tactical Tasks	Friendly-Oriented Tactical Tasks
ambush	breach*	cover
attack by fire	clear	disengage
block	control*	displace
breach*	cordon*	exfiltrate
bypass	occupy*	follow and assume
canalize	reconnoiter*	follow and support
contain*	retain	guard
corrupt	secure*	protect
deceive	seize	screen
defeat		
degrade	**Population-Oriented Tactical Task**	
deny	advise	enable civil authorities
destroy	assess the population	exclude
disrupt	assist	influence*
exploit	build/restore infrastructure	occupy*
feint	contain*	reconnoiter*
fix	control*	secure*
influence*	coordinate with civil authorities	train
interdict	cordon*	transition to civil control
isolate		
neutralize		
penetrate		
reconnoiter*		
support by fire		
suppress		

*Tactical tasks with multiple classifications and applications.

ATTACK BY FIRE

Fires (direct and indirect) in the physical domains and/or through the information environment to engage the enemy from a distance to destroy, fix, neutralize, or suppress.

Note

Within the physical domains, an attack by fire closely resembles the task of support by fire. The chief difference is that one unit conducts the support by fire task to support another unit so it can maneuver against the enemy.

BLOCK

As a tactical task, to deny the enemy access to an area or prevent his advance in a direction or along an avenue of approach. It may be for a specified time. As an obstacle effect, to integrate fire planning and obstacle effort to stop an attacker along a specific avenue of approach or to prevent him from passing through an engagement area.

> Note
>
> Block differs from the tactical task fix because a blocked enemy force can still move in another direction, it just cannot advance. A fixed enemy force cannot move.

BREACH

To break through or secure a passage through an obstacle. *See also terrain-oriented tactical tasks.*

BYPASS

To maneuver around an obstacle, position, or enemy force to maintain the momentum of the operation while deliberately avoiding combat with an enemy force.

CANALIZE

To restrict enemy movement to a narrow zone by the use of existing or reinforcing obstacles, fires, or friendly maneuver.

CONTAIN

To stop, hold, or surround enemy forces or cause the enemy to center activity on a given front and prevent the withdrawal of any part of the enemy's forces for use elsewhere. *See also population-oriented tactical tasks.*

> Note
>
> Whereas the tactical task fix prevents enemy movement, the tactical task contain allows for some enemy movement within the designated area.

CORRUPT

To change, debase, or otherwise alter information from its original or correct form or version by intentionally introducing errors or alterations, thereby rendering it useless.

DECEIVE

To manipulate an enemy into believing and acting upon something that is not true for a selected period of time and/or at a particular location to create a friendly advantage.

DEFEAT

To disrupt or nullify the enemy commander's plan and overcome his will to fight, thus making the enemy commander unwilling or unable to pursue his adopted course of action and yield to the friendly commander's will.

DEGRADE

To diminish the effectiveness or efficiency of an enemy's C2 systems, communications systems, and/or information collection efforts or means; lower the morale of an enemy unit; reduce a target's worth or value; and/or impair an enemy's decision-making capability.

DENY

To hinder or prevent the enemy from using terrain, space, personnel, supplies, facilities, and/or specific capabilities.

DESTROY

To physically render an enemy force combat ineffective unless it can be reconstituted or render a target or capability so damaged that it can neither function as intended nor be restored to a useable condition.

Note

Defeat and destroy are not the same. Destruction of the enemy force normally leads to their defeat, but defeat does not necessarily require destruction.

DISRUPT

As a tactical task or effect, to employ or integrate fires and obstacles in order to break apart an enemy's formation and tempo, interrupt his timetable, or cause premature commitment or the piecemealing of his forces. In information warfare, to prevent efficient interaction of enemy combat and combat support systems by inflicting damage over the short term to specific facets of the system's operation.

EXPLOIT

To employ, to the greatest possible advantage, the success achieved in a military operation or enemy information that has come into friendly hands.

> Note
>
> Exploitation is an offensive operation following a successful attack that is designed to disorganize the enemy in depth. It extends the initial success of the attack by preventing the enemy from disengaging, withdrawing, and reestablishing an effective defense.

FEINT

Contact with the enemy to deceive him about the location or time of the actual main offensive action.

> Note
>
> Feint is the counterpart to the type of attack.

FIX

As a tactical task, to prevent the enemy from moving any part of his forces, either from a specific location or for a specific period of time, by holding or surrounding them to prevent their withdrawal for use elsewhere. As a tactical obstacle effect, to integrate fire planning and obstacle effort to slow an attacker within a specified area—normally an engagement area.

> Note
>
> Fixing an enemy force does not mean destroying it. However, the friendly force has to prevent the enemy from moving in any direction, which can be resource intensive.

INFLUENCE

To cause the enemy to behave in a manner favorable to friendly forces. *See also population-oriented tactical tasks.*

INTERDICT

To divert, disrupt, delay, or destroy the enemy's surface military potential before it can be used effectively against friendly forces.

ISOLATE

To seal off—both physically and psychologically—an enemy from sources of support, deny the enemy freedom of movement, and prevent that enemy force from having contact with other enemy forces.

NEUTRALIZE

As a tactical task, to render the enemy or his resources ineffective or unusable. As an effect of fires delivered, to render a target ineffective or unusable thereby degrading the enemy's capability of accomplishing its mission.

PENETRATE

To break through the enemy's defense and disrupt his defensive system.

> Note
>
> The tactical task penetrate is the counterpart to the form of offensive maneuver that is known as penetrate.

RECONNOITER

To obtain, by visual observation or other methods, information about the activities and resources of an enemy or adversary. *See also terrain- and population-oriented tactical tasks.*

SUPPORT BY FIRE

Movement to a position where the maneuver force can engage the enemy by direct fire in support of another maneuvering force.

> Note
>
> Support by fire closely resembles the task of attack by fire. The difference is a unit conducting attack by fire only uses direct and indirect fires. A unit conducting support by fire uses direct and indirect fires to support the maneuver of another friendly force.

SUPPRESS

The transient or temporary degradation of an opposing force or the performance of a weapons system below the level needed to fulfill its mission objectives.

TERRAIN-ORIENTED TACTICAL TASKS

The following tactical tasks focus friendly efforts on achieving some sort of condition as it relates to terrain.

BREACH

To break through or secure a passage through an obstacle. *See also enemy-oriented tactical tasks.*

CLEAR

To remove enemy forces and eliminate organized resistance in an assigned zone, area, or location by destroying, capturing, or forcing the withdrawal of enemy forces that could interfere with the unit's ability to accomplish its mission.

CONTROL

To maintain physical influence by occupation or range of weapon systems over the activities or access in a defined area. *See also population-oriented tactical tasks.*

> Note
>
> Control differs from the tactical task secure in that control prevents the movement of enemy ground forces through an area, but does not require the complete clearance of enemy forces or the prevention of enemy fires into the specified area.

CORDON

To prevent an enemy unit's withdrawal from or reinforcement to a position. *See also population-oriented tactical tasks.*

OCCUPY

To move onto an objective, key terrain, or other manmade or natural area without opposition and control the entire area. *See also population-oriented tactical tasks.*

RECONNOITER

To secure data, by visual observation or other methods, about the meteorological, hydrographic, or geographic characteristics of a particular area. *See also enemy- and population-oriented tactical tasks.*

Retain

To occupy and hold a terrain feature to ensure it is free of enemy occupation or use.

Secure

To gain possession of a position, terrain feature, piece of infrastructure, or civil asset, with or without force, and prevent its destruction or loss by enemy action. The attacking force may or may not have to physically occupy the area. *See also population-oriented tactical tasks*.

Seize

To clear a designated area and gain control of it.

> Note
>
> The tactical task seize differs from occupy in that seizure occurs in the face of enemy opposition.

FRIENDLY-ORIENTED TACTICAL TASKS

The following tactical tasks focus friendly efforts on supporting the actions of other friendly forces.

Cover

To conduct offensive and defensive actions independent of the main body to protect the covered force and develop the situation.

> Note
>
> It is the tactical task associated with the security operation cover.

Disengage

To break contact with the enemy and move to a point where the enemy cannot observe nor engage friendly forces by direct fire.

DISPLACE

To leave one position to take another while remaining in contact with the enemy.

> Note
>
> Displace differs from the tactical task disengage in that units disengage to break contact with the enemy, while units displace to continue the mission or execute alternate missions.

EXFILTRATE

To remove personnel or units from areas under enemy control by stealth.

FOLLOW AND ASSUME

A second committed force follows a force conducting an offensive operation and is prepared to continue the mission if the lead force is fixed, attrited, or unable to continue.

> Note
>
> The follow-and-assume force is not a reserve but is prepared to execute all missions of the followed unit.

FOLLOW AND SUPPORT

A committed force follows and supports a lead force conducting an offensive operation.

> Note
>
> The follow-and-support force is not a reserve but is a force committed to supporting the followed unit. The difference between follow and assume and follow and support: the follow and assume force is prepared to take over the lead element's mission; whereas, the follow and support force acts to create the conditions necessary to allow the lead element to continue its success (such as destroying bypassed elements, blocking enemy movement of reinforcements, clearing obstacles, or controlling dislocated civilians).

GUARD

To protect the main force by fighting to gain time while also observing and reporting information.

> Note
>
> It is the tactical task associated with the security operation guard.

PROTECT

To prevent observation by engagement with or interference from an adversarial or enemy force, system, capability, or location.

SCREEN

To observe, identify, and report information, and only fight in self-protection.

> Note
>
> It is the tactical task associated with the security operation screen.

POPULATION-ORIENTED TACTICAL TASKS

The following tactical tasks focus friendly efforts on achieving some sort of condition as it relates to the population within the area of operations.

ADVISE

To improve the individual and unit capabilities and capacities of host nation security forces through the development of personal and professional relationships between United States and host nation forces.

ASSESS THE POPULATION

To evaluate the nature, situation, and attitudes of a designated population or elements of a population inhabiting the area of operations.

ASSIST

To provide designated support or sustainment capabilities to host nation security forces to enable them to accomplish their objectives.

Build/Restore Infrastructure

To construct, rebuild, or repair local infrastructure to support the host nation and gain or maintain the cooperation of the local population.

Contain

To prevent or halt elements of a population or designated party from departing or projecting physical influence beyond a defined area. *See also enemy-oriented tactical tasks.*

Control

To use physical control measures and information-related capabilities to influence elements of a population or designated actors to respond as desired. *See also terrain-oriented tactical tasks.*

Coordinate With Civil Authorities

To interact with, maintain communication, and harmonize friendly military activities with those of other interorganizational agencies and coalition partners to achieve unity of effort.

Cordon

To temporarily prevent movement to or from a prescribed area such as a neighborhood, city block, series of buildings, or other feature. *See also terrain-oriented tactical tasks.*

Enable Civil Authorities

To support or assist the host nation government and designated interorganizational agencies in providing effective governance.

Exclude

To prevent or halt elements of a population or designated party from entering or projecting physical influence into a defined area.

Influence

To persuade the local population, including potential and known adversaries, within the operational area to support, cooperate with, or at least accept the friendly force presence, and to dissuade the local population from interfering with operations. *See also enemy-oriented tactical tasks.*

OCCUPY

To move onto an objective, key terrain, or other manmade or natural area without opposition and control the entire area. *See also terrain-oriented tactical tasks.*

RECONNOITER

To obtain, by visual observation or other methods, information about civil considerations. *See also enemy- and terrain-oriented tactical tasks.*

SECURE

To gain possession of a position, terrain feature, piece of infrastructure, or civil asset, with or without force, and prevent its destruction or loss by enemy action. *See also terrain-oriented tactical tasks.*

TRAIN

To teach designated skills or behaviors to improve the individual and unit capabilities and capacities of host nation security forces.

TRANSITION TO CIVIL CONTROL

To handover civil government and security responsibilities from friendly force military authorities to legitimate civil authorities.

Glossary

Section I: Acronyms

ACE . . . . aviation combat element
ARG . . . . .amphibious ready group

CBIRF . . . . chemical and biological incident response force
CCIR . . . . commander's critical information requirement
COA . . . . course of action

G-4 . . . . logistics staff officer
GCE . . . . ground combat element

J-4 . . . . logistics directorate of a joint staff
JP . . . . .joint publication

LCE . . . . logistics combat element

MAGTF . . . . Marine air-ground task force
MARCORLOGCOM . . . . Marine Corps Logistics Command
MARCORSYSCOM . . . . Marine Corps Systems Command
MARDIV . . . . Marine division
MARFORCOM . . . . United States Marine Corps Forces Command
MARFORCYBER . . . . United States Marine Corps Forces, Cyber Command
MARFORPAC . . . . United States Marine Corps Forces, Pacific
MARSOC . . . . United States Marine Corps Forces, Special Operations Command
MAW . . . . Marine aircraft wing
MCDP . . . . .Marine Corps doctrinal publication
MCPP . . . . .Marine Corps Planning Process
MCRP . . . . Marine Corps reference publication
MCWP . . . . .Marine Corps warfighting publication
MEB . . . . Marine expeditionary brigade
MEF . . . . Marine expeditionary force
MEF (Fwd) . . . . Marine expeditionary force (Forward)
METT-T . . . . .mission, enemy, terrain and weather,
                                                                 troops and support available-time available
MEU . . . . Marine expeditionary unit
MLG . . . . .Marine logistics group
MPSRON . . . . maritime prepositioning ships squadron

S-4 .... logistics officer
SPMAGTF .... special purpose Marine air-ground task force

US .... United States
USCYBERCOM .... United States Cyber Command
USSOCOM .... United States Special Operations Command

Section II: Definitions

action phase—In amphibious operations, the period of time between the arrival of the landing forces of the amphibious force in the operational area and the accomplishment of their mission. (JP 1-02)

administrative control—Direction or exercise of authority over subordinate or other organizations in respect to administration and support, including organization of Service forces, control of resources and equipment, personnel management, unit logistics, individual and unit training, readiness, mobilization, demobilization, discipline, and other matters not included in the operational missions of the subordinate or other organizations. Also called **ADCON**. (JP 1-02)

adversary—A party acknowledged as potentially hostile to a friendly party and against which the use of force may be envisaged. (JP 1-02)

alliance—The relationship that results from a formal agreement (e.g., treaty) between two or more nations for broad, long-term objectives that further the common interests of the members. (JP 1-02)

amphibious assault—The principal type of amphibious operation that involves establishing a force on a hostile or potentially hostile shore. (JP 1-02)

amphibious demonstration—A type of amphibious operation conducted for the purpose of deceiving the enemy by a show of force with the expectation of deluding the enemy into a course of action unfavorable to him. (JP 1-02)

amphibious force—An amphibious task force and a landing force together with other forces that are trained, organized, and equipped for amphibious operations. Also called **AF**. (JP 1-02)

amphibious operation—A military operation launched from the sea by an amphibious force, embarked in ships or craft with the primary purpose of introducing a landing force ashore to accomplish the assigned mission. (JP 1-02)

amphibious raid—A type of amphibious operation involving swift incursion into or temporary occupation of an objective followed by a planned withdrawal. (JP 1-02)

amphibious support to other operations—A type of amphibious operation that contributes to conflict prevention or crisis mitigation. These may include operations such as security cooperation, foreign humanitarian assistance, civil support, noncombatant evacuations, peace operations, recovery operations, or disaster relief. (Proposed for inclusion in the next edition of MCRP 5-12C.)

amphibious task force—A Navy task organization formed to conduct amphibious operations. The amphibious task force, together with the landing force and other forces, constitutes the amphibious force. Also called **ATF**. (JP 1-02)

amphibious withdrawal—A type of amphibious operation involving the extraction of forces by sea in ships or craft from a hostile or potentially hostile shore. (JP 1-02)

antiair warfare—That action required to destroy or reduce to an acceptable level the enemy air and missile threat. Antiair warfare integrates all offensive and defensive actions against enemy aircraft, surface-to-air weapons, and theater missiles into a singular, indivisible set of operations. Antiair warfare is one of the six functions of Marine aviation. (MCRP 5-12C)

antiterrorism—Defensive measures used to reduce the vulnerability of individuals and property to terrorist acts, to include rapid containment by local military and civilian forces. Also called **AT**. (JP 1-02)

area defense—A type of defense in which the bulk of the defending force is disposed in selected tactical localities where the decisive battle is to be fought. Principal reliance is placed on the ability of the forces in the defended localities to maintain their positions and to control the terrain between them. The reserve is used to add depth, to block, or restore the battle position by counterattack. (Proposed for inclusion in the next edition of MCRP 5-12C.)

area of influence—A geographical area wherein a commander is directly capable of influencing operations by maneuver or fire support systems normally under the commander's command or control. (JP 1-02)

area of interest—That area of concern to the commander, including the area of influence, areas adjacent thereto, and extending into enemy territory to the objectives of current or planned operations. This area also includes areas occupied by enemy forces who could jeopardize the accomplishment of the mission. Also called **AOI**. (JP 1-02)

area of operations—An operational area defined by the joint force commander for land and maritime forces. Areas of operations do not typically encompass the entire operational area of the joint force commander, but should be large enough for component commanders to accomplish their missions and protect their forces. Also called **AO**. (JP 1-02)

area of responsibility—The geographical area associated with a combatant command within which a geographic combatant commander has authority to plan and conduct operations. Also called **AOR**. (JP 1-02)

area reconnaissance—A directed effort to obtain detailed information concerning the terrain or enemy activity within a prescribed area such as a town, ridge line, woods, or other features critical to operations. Air reconnaissance is one of the six functions of Marine aviation. (MCRP 5-12C)

asymmetry—Unconventional, unexpected, innovative, or disproportional means used to gain advantage over an adversary. (MCRP 5-12C)

attack—An offensive action characterized by coordinated movement, supported by fire, conducted to defeat, destroy, or capture the enemy or seize and/or secure key terrain. (Proposed for the next edition of. (MCRP 5-12C)

avenue of approach—An air or ground route of an attacking force of a given size leading to its objective or to key terrain in its path. Also called **AA**. (JP 1-02)

aviation combat element—The core element of a Marine air-ground task force (MAGTF) that is task-organized to conduct aviation operations. The aviation combat element (ACE) provides all or a portion of the six functions of Marine aviation necessary to accomplish the MAGTF's mission. These functions are antiair warfare, offensive air support, assault support, electronic warfare, air reconnaissance, and control of aircraft and missiles. The ACE is usually composed of an aviation unit headquarters and various other aviation units or their detachments. It can vary in size from a small aviation detachment of specifically required aircraft to one or more Marine aircraft wings. In a joint or multinational environment, the ACE may contain other Service or multinational forces assigned or attached to the MAGTF. The ACE itself is not a formal command. Also called **ACE**. (MCRP 5-12C)

axis of advance—A line of advance assigned for purposes of control; often a road or a group of roads, or a designated series of locations, extending in the direction of the enemy. (JP 1-02)

barrier—A coordinated series of obstacles designed or employed to channel, direct, restrict, delay, or stop the movement of an opposing force and to impose additional losses in personnel, time, and equipment on the opposing force. Barriers can exist naturally, be man-made, or a combination of both. (JP 1-02)

battle drill—A critical collective action or task performed by a platoon or smaller element without the application of a deliberate decisionmaking process, initiated on cue, accomplished with minimal leader orders, and performed to standard throughout like units. (Proposed for inclusion in the next edition of MCRP 5-12C.)

battle position—1. In ground operations, a defensive location oriented on an enemy avenue of approach from which a unit may defend. 2. In air operations, an airspace coordination area containing firing points for attack helicopters. Also called **BP**. (MCRP 5-12C)

battle rhythm—A deliberate daily cycle of command, staff, and unit activities intended to synchronize current and future operations. (JP 1-02)

battlespace—The environment, factors, and conditions that must be understood to successfully apply combat power, protect the force, or complete the mission. This includes the air, land, sea, space, and the included enemy and friendly forces; facilities; weather; terrain; the electromagnetic spectrum; and the information environment within the operational areas, areas of interest, and areas of influence. (MCRP 5-12C)

battlespace dominance—The degree of control over the dimensions of the battlespace that enhances friendly freedom of action and denies enemy freedom of action. It permits force sustainment and application of power projection to accomplish the full range of potential operational and tactical missions. It includes all actions conducted against enemy capabilities to influence future operations. (MCRP 5-12C)

boundary—A line that delineates surface areas for the purpose of facilitating coordination and deconfliction of operations between adjacent units, formations, or areas. (JP 1-02)

breakout—An operation conducted by an encircled force to regain freedom of movement or contact with friendly units. It differs from other attacks only in that a simultaneous defense in other areas of the perimeter must be maintained. (Proposed for inclusion in the next edition of MCRP 5-12C)

campaign—A series of related major operations aimed at achieving strategic and operational objectives within a given time and space. (JP 1-02)

center of gravity—The source of power that provides moral or physical strength, freedom of action, or will to act. Also called **COG**. (JP 1-02)

close air support—Air action by fixed- and rotary-wing aircraft against hostile targets that are in close proximity to friendly forces and that require detailed integration of each air mission with the fire and movement of those forces. Also called **CAS**. (JP 1-02)

close operations—Military actions conducted to project power decisively against enemy forces that pose an immediate or near term threat to the success of current battles or engagements. These military actions are conducted by committed forces and their readily available tactical reserves, using maneuver and combined arms. (MCRP 5-12C)

close reconnaissance—Ground reconnaissance and surveillance conducted in the area extending forward of the forward edge of the battle area. It is directed toward determining the location, composition, disposition, capabilities, and activities of enemy committed forces and is primarily conducted by elements of combat units. (MCRP 5-12C)

close support—That action of the supporting force against targets or objectives which are sufficiently near the supported force as to require detailed integration or coordination of the supporting action with the fire, movement, or other actions of the supported force. (JP 1-02)

coalition—An ad hoc arrangement between two or more nations for common action. (JP 1-02)

combat air patrol—An aircraft patrol provided over an objective area, the force protected, the critical area of a combat zone, or in an air defense area, for the purpose of intercepting and destroying hostile aircraft before they reach their targets. Also called **CAP**. (JP 1-02)

combatant command (command authority)—Nontransferable command authority established by Title 10 (Armed Forces), United States Code, Section 164, exercised only by commanders of unified or specified combatant commands unless otherwise directed by the President or the Secretary of Defense. Combatant command (command authority) cannot be delegated and is the authority of a combatant commander to perform those functions of command over assigned forces involving organizing and employing commands and forces, assigning tasks, designating objectives, and giving authoritative direction over all aspects of military operations, joint training, and logistics necessary to accomplish the missions assigned to the command. Combatant command (command authority) should be exercised through the commanders of subordinate organizations. Normally this authority is exercised through subordinate joint force commanders and Service and/or functional component commanders. Combatant command (command authority) provides full authority to organize and employ commands and forces as the combatant commander considers necessary to accomplish assigned missions. Operational control is inherent in combatant command (command authority). Also called **COCOM**. (JP 1-02)

combatant commander—A commander of one of the unified or specified combatant commands established by the President. Also called **CCDR**. (JP 1-02)

combating terrorism—Actions, including antiterrorism and counterterrorism, taken to oppose terrorism throughout the entire threat spectrum. Also called **CbT**. (JP 1-02)

combat power—The total means of destructive and/or disruptive force which a military unit/formation can apply against the opponent at a given time. (JP 1-02)

combat service support—The essential capabilities, functions, activities, and tasks necessary to sustain all elements of operating forces in theater at all levels of war. Within the national and theater logistic systems, it includes but is not limited to that support rendered by service forces in ensuring the aspects of supply, maintenance, transportation, health services, and other services required by aviation and ground combat troops to permit those units to accomplish their missions in combat. Combat service support encompasses those activities at all levels of war that produce sustainment to all operating forces on the battlefield. Also called **CSS**. (JP 1-02)

combined—Between two or more forces or agencies of two or more allies. (When all allies or services are not involved, the participating nations and services shall be identified, e.g., combined navies.) (JP 1-02)

combined arms—1. The full integration of combat arms in such a way that to counteract one, the enemy must become more vulnerable to another. 2. The tactics, techniques, and procedures employed by a force to integrate firepower and mobility to produce a desired effect upon the enemy. (MCRP 5-12C)

combined force—A military force composed of elements of two or more allied nations. (JP 1-02)

command and control—The exercise of authority and direction by a properly designated commander over assigned and attached forces in the accomplishment of the mission. Command and control functions are performed through an arrangement of personnel, equipment, communications, facilities, and procedures employed by a commander in planning, directing, coordinating, and controlling forces and operations in the accomplishment of the mission. Also called C2. (JP 1-02) The means by which a commander recognizes what needs to be done and sees to it that appropriate actions are taken. (MCRP 5-12C)

command element—The core element of a Marine air-ground task force (MAGTF) that is the headquarters. The command element is composed of the commander, general or executive and special staff sections, headquarters section, and requisite communications support, intelligence, and reconnaissance forces necessary to accomplish the MAGTF's mission. The command element provides command and control, intelligence, and other support essential for effective planning and execution of operations by the other elements of the MAGTF. The command element varies in size and composition; and, in a joint or multinational environment, it may contain other Service or multinational forces assigned or attached to the MAGTF. Also called **CE**. (MCRP 5-12C)

commander, amphibious task force—The Navy officer designated in the initiating directive as the commander of the amphibious task force. Also called **CATF**. (JP 1-02)

commander, landing force—The officer designated in the initiating directive as the commander of the landing force for an amphibious operation. Also called **CLF**. (JP 1-02)

commander's critical information requirement—An information requirement identified by the commander as being critical to facilitating timely decisionmaking. The two key elements are friendly force information requirements and priority intelligence requirements. (JP 1-02) Information regarding the enemy and friendly activities and the environment identified by the commander as critical to maintaining situational awareness, planning future activities, and facilitating timely decisionmaking. The two subcategories are priority intelligence requirements and friendly force information requirements. Also called **CCIR**. (MCRP 5-12C)

commander's intent—A commander's clear, concise articulation of the purpose(s) behind one or more tasks assigned to a subordinate. It is one of two parts of every mission statement which guides the exercise of initiative in the absence of instructions. (MCRP 5-12C)

component—1. One of the subordinate organizations that constitute a joint force. Normally a joint force is organized with a combination of Service and functional components. (JP 1-02, part 1 of a 2 part definition)

concept of operations—A verbal or graphic statement that clearly and concisely expresses what the joint force commander intends to accomplish and how it will be done using available resources. The concept is designed to give an overall picture of the operation. Also called **commander's concept** or **CONOPS**. (JP 1-02)

contiguous area of operations—An area of operations where all of a commander's subordinate forces' areas of operation share one or more common boundaries. (MCRP 5-12A)

conventional forces—1. Those forces capable of conducting operations using nonnuclear weapons. 2. Those forces other than designated special operations forces. Also called **CF**. (JP 1-02)

counterattack—Attack by part or all of a defending force against an enemy attacking force, for such specific purposes as regaining ground lost or cutting off or destroying enemy advance units, and with the general objective of denying to the enemy the attainment of the enemy's purpose in attacking. In sustained defensive operations, it is undertaken to restore the battle position and is directed at limited objectives. (JP 1-02)

counterfire—Fire intended to destroy or neutralize enemy weapons. Includes counterbattery and countermortar fire. (JP 1-02)

counterinsurgency—Comprehensive civilian and military efforts taken to defeat an insurgency and to address any core grievances. Also called **COIN**. (JP 1-02)

counterintelligence—Information gathered and activities conducted to identify, deceive, exploit, disrupt, or protect against espionage, other intelligence activities, sabotage, or assassinations conducted for or on behalf of foreign powers, organizations or persons or their agents, or international terrorist activities. Also called **CI**. (JP 1-02)

counterreconnaissance—All measures taken to prevent hostile observation of a force, area, or place. (JP 1-02)

counterterrorism—Actions taken directly against terrorist networks and indirectly to influence and render global and regional environments inhospitable to terrorist networks. Also called **CT**. (JP 1-02)

cover—1. A type of security operation that protects the force from surprise, develops the situation, and gives commanders time and space in which to respond to the enemy's actions. 2. A form of security operation whose primary task is to protect the main body by fighting to gain time while also observing and reporting information and preventing enemy ground observation of and direct fire against the main body. 3. Offensive or defensive actions to protect the force. 4. Protection from the effects of direct and indirect fire. It can be provided by ditches, caves, river banks, folds in the ground, shell craters, buildings, walls, and embankments. (MCRP 5-12C)

covering force—1. A force operating apart from the main force for the purpose of intercepting, engaging, delaying, disorganizing, and deceiving the enemy before the enemy can attack the force covered. 2. Any body or detachment of troops which provides security for a larger force by observation, reconnaissance, attack, or defense, or by any combination of these methods. (JP 1-02)

crisis action planning—One of the two types of joint operation planning. The Joint Operation Planning and Execution System process involving the time-sensitive development of joint operation plans and operation orders for the deployment, employment, and sustainment of assigned and allocated forces and resources in response to an imminent crisis. Crisis action planning is based on the actual circumstances that exist at the time planning occurs. Also called **CAP**. (JP 1-02)

critical vulnerability—An aspect of a center of gravity that, if exploited, will do the most significant damage to an adversary's ability to resist. A vulnerability cannot be critical unless it undermines a key strength. Also called **CV**. (MCRP 5-12C)

cross-cultural competence—The ability to quickly and accurately comprehend, then appropriately and effectively act, to create the desired effect in a culturally complex environment. (Proposed for inclusion in the next edition of MCRP 5-12C.)

culminating point—The point at which a force no longer has the capability to continue its form of operations, offense or defense. a. In the offense, the point at which effectively continuing the attack is no longer possible and the force must consider reverting to a defensive posture or attempting an operational pause. b. In the defense, the point at which effective counteroffensive action is no longer possible. (JP 1-02)

decentralized execution—Delegation of execution authority to subordinate commanders. (JP 1-02)

deception operation—A military operation conducted to mislead the enemy. A unit conducting a deception operation may or may not make contact with the enemy. (MCRP 5-12C)

deep operations—Military actions conducted against enemy capabilities that pose a potential threat to friendly forces. These military actions are designed to isolate, shape, and dominate the battlespace and influence future operations. (MCRP 5-12C)

deep reconnaissance—Ground reconnaissance and surveillance conducted in the commander, landing force's area of interest. It is directed toward determining the location, composition, disposition, and movement of enemy reinforcement. (MCRP 5-12C)

defense—A coordinated effort by a force to defeat an attack by an opposing force and prevent it from achieving its objectives. (MCRP 5-12C)

defense in depth—The siting of mutually supporting defense positions designed to absorb and progressively weaken attack, prevent initial observations of the whole position by the enemy, and to allow the commander to maneuver the reserve. (JP 1-02)

defensive operations—Operations conducted to defeat an enemy attack, gain time, economize forces, and develop conditions favorable to offensive and stability operations. The three types of defensive operations are area, mobile, and retrograde. (MCRP 5-12C)

defensive sector—A section assigned to a subordinate commander in which he is provided the maximum latitude to accomplish assigned tasks in order to conduct defensive operations. (Proposed for inclusion in the next edition of MCRP 5-12C.)

delay—A form of retrograde in which a force under pressure trades space for time by slowing the enemy's momentum and inflicting maximum damage on the enemy without, in principle, becoming decisively engaged. (MCRP 5-12C)

deliberate attack—A fully coordinated operation that is conducted when preparation time is available for lengthy reconnaissance, precise planning, and rehearsals. Deliberate attacks normally include large volumes of supporting fires, main and supporting attacks, and deception measures. (MCRP 5-12C)

deliberate breach—1. The creation of a lane through a minefield or a clear route through a barrier or fortification that is systematically planned and carried out. (MCRP 5-12C, part 1 of a 2 part definition)

deliberate defense—A defense normally organized when out of contact with the enemy or when contact with the enemy is not imminent and time for organization is available. (Proposed for inclusion in the next edition of MCRP 5-12C.)

deny—To hinder or prevent the enemy from using terrain, space, personnel, supplies, or facilities. (MCRP 5-12C)

demonstration—1. An attack or show of force on a front where a decision is not sought, made with the aim of deceiving the enemy. 2. In military deception, a show of force in an area where a decision is not sought, made to deceive an adversary. It is similar to a feint, but no actual contact with the adversary is intended. (JP 1-02)

deployment—4. The relocation of forces and materiel to desired operational areas. (Excerpt of JP 1-02, part 4 of a 4-part definition.)

deterrence—The prevention from action by fear of the consequences. Deterrence is a state of mind brought about by the existence of a credible threat of unacceptable counteraction. (JP 1-02)

direct support—A mission requiring a force to support another specific force and authorizing it to answer directly to the supported force's request for assistance. Also called **DS**. (JP 1-02)

double envelopment—An offensive maneuver designed to force the enemy to fight in two or more directions simultaneously to meet the converging axis of the attack. (Proposed for inclusion in the next edition of MCRP 5-12C.)

economy of force—The allocation of minimum essential combat capability to supporting efforts, with attendant degree of risk, so that combat power may be concentrated on the main effort. Economy of force is used to describe a principle of war and a condition of tactical operations; it is not used to describe a mission. (MCRP 5-12C)

embarkation phase—In amphibious operations, the phase that encompasses the orderly assembly of personnel and materiel and their subsequent loading aboard ships and/or aircraft in a sequence designed to meet the requirements of the landing force concept of operations ashore. (JP 1-02)

encircling force—In pursuit operations, the force that maneuvers to the rear or flank of the enemy to block its escape so that it can be destroyed between the direct pressure force and encircling force. This force advances or flies along routes parallel to paralleling the enemy's line of retreat. If the encircling force cannot out distance the enemy to cut him off, the encircling force may attack the enemy's flank. (MCRP 5-12C)

end state—The set of required conditions that defines achievement of the commander's objectives. (JP 1-02)

envelopment—An offensive maneuver in which the main attacking force passes around or over the enemy's principal defensive positions to secure objectives to the enemy's rear. (Proposed for inclusion in the next edition of MCRP 5-12C.)

exclusion zone—A zone established by a sanctioning body to prohibit specific activities in a specific geographic area. The purpose may be to persuade nations or groups to modify their behavior to meet the desires of the sanctioning body or face continued imposition of sanctions, or use or threat of force. (JP 1-02)

expedition—A military operation conducted by an armed force to accomplish a specific objective in a foreign country. (JP 1-02)

expeditionary force—An armed force organized to accomplish a specific objective in a foreign country. (JP 1-02)

exploitation—An offensive operation following a successful attack that is designed to disorganize the enemy in depth. It extends the initial success of the attack by preventing the enemy from disengaging, withdrawing, and reestablishing an effective defense. (Proposed for inclusion in the next edition of MCRP 5-12C.)

fires—The use of weapon systems to create a specific lethal or nonlethal effect on a target. (JP 1-02)

fire support coordination measure—A measure employed by land or amphibious commanders to facilitate the rapid engagement of targets and simultaneously provide safeguards for friendly forces. Also called **FSCM**. (JP 1-02)

flanking attack—An offensive maneuver directed at the flank of an enemy. (Proposed for inclusion in the next edition of MCRP 5-12C.)

fly-in echelon—Airlifted forces and equipment of the Marine air-ground task force and Navy support element plus aircraft and personnel arriving in the flight ferry of the aviation combat element. (MCRP 5-12C)

follow-on forces—All enemy ground forces not committed during their offensive operations to the contact battle, their command and control installations, and their logistic and other support provided for sustained operations. (MCRP 5-12C)

force continuum—The wide range of possible actions ranging from voice commands to application of deadly force that may be used to gain and maintain control of a potentially dangerous situation. (MCRP 5-12C)

force-oriented reconnaissance—A directed effort to find a specific enemy force quickly and stay with it wherever it moves on the battlefield. (MCRP 5-12C)

force protection—Preventive measures taken to mitigate hostile actions against Department of Defense personnel (to include family members), resources, facilities, and critical information. Force protection does not include actions to defeat the enemy or protect against accidents, weather, or disease. (JP 1-02) Actions or efforts used to safeguard own centers of gravity while protecting, concealing, reducing, or eliminating friendly critical vulnerabilities. Force protection is one of the six warfighting functions. (MCRP 5-12C)

forcible entry—Seizing and holding of a military lodgment in the face of armed opposition. (JP 1-02)

foreign humanitarian assistance—Department of Defense activities, normally in support of the United States Agency for International Development or Department of State, conducted outside the United States, its territories, and possessions to relieve or reduce human suffering, disease, hunger, or privation. Also called **FHA**. (JP 1-02)

forward edge of the battle area—The foremost limits of a series of areas in which ground combat units are deployed, excluding the areas in which the covering or screening forces are operating, designed to coordinate fire support, the positioning of forces, or the maneuver of units. Also called **FEBA**. (JP 1-02)

frontal attack—An offensive maneuver in which the main action is directed against the front of the enemy forces. (MCRP 5-12C.)

function—The specific responsibilities assigned by the President and Secretary of Defense to enable Services to fulfill legally established roles. (MCRP 5-12C)

functional component command—A command normally, but not necessarily, composed of forces of two or more Military Departments which may be established across the range of military operations to perform particular operational missions that may be of short duration or may extend over a period of time. (JP 1-02)

general engineering—Those engineering capabilities and activities, other than combat engineering, that modify, maintain, or protect the physical environment. Examples include: the construction, repair, maintenance, and operation of infrastructure, facilities, lines of communications, and bases; terrain modification and repair; and selected explosive hazard activities. Also called **GE**. (JP 1-02)

general support—1. That support which is given to the supported force as a whole and not to any particular subdivision thereof. 2. A tactical artillery mission. Also called **GS**. (JP 1-02)

governance—The process, systems, institutions, and actors that enable a state to function. (Proposed for inclusion in the next edition of MCRP 5-12C.)

ground combat element—The core element of a Marine air-ground task force (MAGTF) that is task-organized to conduct ground operations. It is usually constructed around an infantry organization but can vary in size from a small ground unit of any type, to one or more Marine divisions that can be independently maneuvered under the direction of the MAGTF commander. It includes appropriate ground combat and combat support forces, and in a joint or multinational environment, it may also contain other Service or multinational forces assigned or attached to the MAGTF. The ground combat element itself is not a formal command. Also called **GCE**. (MCRP 5-12C)

guard—1. A form of security operation whose primary task is to protect the main force by fighting to gain time while also observing and reporting information, and to prevent enemy ground observation of and direct fire against the main body by reconnoitering, attacking, defending, and delaying. A guard force normally operates within the range of the main body's indirect fire weapons. (JP 1-02, part 1 of a 3 part definition.)

hasty attack—Offensive action conducted when preparation time must be traded for speed. Forces readily available are committed immediately to the attack. (Proposed for inclusion in the next edition of MCRP 5-12C.)

hasty breach—The rapid creation of a route through a minefield, barrier, or fortification by any expedient method. (Proposed for inclusion in the next edition of MCRP 5-12C.)

hasty crossing—The crossing of an inland water obstacle using crossing means at hand or those readily available and made without pausing for elaborate preparations. Preferably, a hasty crossing is conducted by seizing an intact crossing site. (Proposed for inclusion in the next edition of MCRP 5-12C.)

hasty defense—A defense normally organized while in contact with the enemy or when contact with the enemy is imminent and time for organization is limited. (Proposed for inclusion in the next edition of MCRP 5-12C.)

health service support—All services performed, provided, or arranged to promote, improve, conserve, or restore the mental or physical well-being of personnel. These services include, but are not limited to, the management of health services resources, such as manpower, monies, and facilities; preventive and curative health measures; evacuation of the wounded, injured, or sick; selection of the medically fit and disposition of the medically unfit; blood management; medical supply, equipment, and maintenance thereof; combat stress control; and medical, dental, veterinary, laboratory, optometric, nutrition therapy, and medical intelligence services. Also called **HSS**. (JP 1-02)

hostile environment—Operational environment in which hostile forces have control as well as the intent and capability to effectively oppose or react to the operations a unit intends to conduct. (JP 1-02)

host nation—A nation which receives the forces and/or supplies of allied nations and/or NATO organizations to be located on, to operate in, or to transit through its territory. Also called **HN**. (JP 1-02)

infiltration—A form of maneuver in which friendly forces move through or into an area or territory occupied by either friendly or enemy troops or organizations. The movement is made, either by small groups or by individuals, at extended or irregular intervals. When used in connection with the enemy, it implies that contact is to be avoided. (Proposed for inclusion in the next edition of MCRP 5-12C.)

information operations—The integrated employment, during military operations, of information-related capabilities in concert with other lines of operations to influence, disrupt, corrupt, or usurp the decision-making of adversaries and potential adversaries while protecting our own. Also called **IO**. (JP 1-02)

initiating directive—An order to a subordinate commander to conduct military operations as directed. It is issued by the unified commander, subunified commander, Service component commander, or joint force commander delegated overall responsibility for the operation. (JP 1-02)

instruments of national power—All of the means available to the government in its pursuit of national objectives. They are expressed as diplomatic, economic, informational and military. (JP 1-02)

insurgency—The organized use of subversion and violence by a group or movement that seeks to overthrow or force change of a governing authority. Insurgency can also refer to the group itself. (JP 1-02)

intelligence preparation of the battlespace—The analytical methodologies employed by the Services or joint force component commands to reduce uncertainties concerning the enemy, environment, time, and terrain. Intelligence preparation of the battlespace supports the individual operations of the joint force component commands. Also called **IPB**. (JP 1-02)

interdiction—1. An action to divert, disrupt, delay, or destroy the enemy's military surface capability before it can be used effectively against friendly forces, or to otherwise achieve objectives. 2. In support of law enforcement, activities conducted to divert, disrupt, delay, intercept, board, detain, or destroy, as appropriate, vessels, vehicles, aircraft, people, and cargo. (JP 1-02)

irregular warfare—A violent struggle among state and non-state actors for legitimacy and influence over the relevant population(s). Irregular warfare favors indirect and asymmetric approaches, though it may employ the full range of military and other capacities, in order to erode an adversary's power, influence, and will. Also called **IW**. (JP 1-02)

joint force air component commander—The commander within a unified command, subordinate unified command, or joint task force responsible to the establishing commander for making recommendations on the proper employment of assigned, attached, and/or made available for tasking air forces; planning and coordinating air operations; or accomplishing such operational missions as may be assigned. The joint force air component commander is given the authority necessary to accomplish missions and tasks assigned by the establishing commander. Also called **JFACC**. (JP 1-02)

joint force commander—A general term applied to a combatant commander, subunified commander, or joint task force commander authorized to exercise combatant command (command authority) or operational control over a joint force. Also called **JFC**. (JP 1-02)

joint force land component commander—The commander within a unified command, subordinate unified command, or joint task force responsible to the establishing commander for making recommendations on the proper employment of assigned, attached, and/or made available for tasking land forces;, planning and coordinating land operations; or accomplishing such operational missions as may be assigned. The joint force land component commander is given the authority necessary to accomplish missions and tasks assigned by the establishing commander. Also called **JFLCC**. (JP 1-02)

joint force maritime component commander—The commander within a unified command, subordinate unified command, or joint task force responsible to the establishing commander for making recommendations on the proper employment of assigned, attached, and/or made available for tasking maritime forces and assets; planning and coordinating maritime operations, or accomplishing such operational missions as may be assigned. The joint force maritime component commander is given the authority necessary to accomplish missions and tasks assigned by the establishing commander. Also called **JFMCC**. (JP 1-02)

joint force special operations component commander—The commander within a unified command, subordinate unified command, or joint task force responsible to the establishing commander for making recommendations on the proper employment of assigned, attached, and/or made available for tasking special operations forces and assets; planning and coordinating special operations; or accomplishing such operational missions as may be assigned. The joint force special operations component commander is given the authority necessary to accomplish missions and tasks assigned by the establishing commander. Also called **JFSOCC**. (JP 1-02)

joint task force—A joint force that is constituted and so designated by the Secretary of Defense, a combatant commander, a subunified commander, or an existing joint task force commander. Also called **JTF**. (JP 1-02)

kill zone—That part of an ambush site where fire is concentrated to isolate, fix, and destroy the enemy. (MCRP 5-12C)

landing force—A Marine Corps or Army task organization formed to conduct amphibious operations. The landing force, together with the amphibious task force and other forces, constitute the amphibious force. Also called **LF**. (JP 102)

landing zone—Any specified zone used for the landing of aircraft. Also called **LZ**. (JP 1-02)

law of war—That part of international law that regulates the conduct of armed hostilities. Also called the *law of armed conflict*. (JP 1-02)

line of communications—A route, either land, water, and/or air, that connects an operating military force with a base of operations and along which supplies and military forces move. Also called **LOC**. (JP 1-02)

line of operations—1. A logical line that connects actions on nodes and/or decisive points related in time and purpose with an objective(s). 2. A physical line that defines the interior or exterior orientation of the force in relation to the enemy or that connects actions on nodes and/or decisive points related in time and space to an objective(s). Also called **LOO**. (JP 1-02)

linkup—An operation wherein two friendly ground forces join together in a hostile area. (MCRP 5-12C)

littoral—A zone of military operations along a coastline, consisting of the seaward approaches from the open ocean to the shore, which must be controlled to support operations ashore, as well as the landward approaches to the shore that can be supported and defended directly from the sea. (MCRP 5-12C)

logistics—1. The science of planning and executing the movement and support of forces. 2. All activities required to move and sustain military forces. Logistics is one of the six warfighting functions. (Proposed for inclusion in the next edition of MCRP 5-12C.)

logistics combat element—The core element of a Marine air-ground task force (MAGTF) that is task-organized to provide the combat service support necessary to accomplish the MAGTF's mission. The logistics combat element varies in size from a small detachment to one or more Marine logistics groups. It provides supply, maintenance, transportation, general engineering, health services, and a variety of other services to the MAGTF. In a joint or multinational environment, it may also contain other Service or multinational forces assigned or attached to the MAGTF. The logistics combat element itself is not a formal command. Also called **LCE**. (MCRP 5-12C)

main battle area—That portion of the battlespace in which the commander conducts close operations to defeat the enemy. Normally, the main battle area extends rearward from the forward edge of the battle area to the rear boundary of the command's subordinate units. (Proposed for inclusion in the next edition of MCRP 5-12C.)

main body—The principal part of a tactical command or formation. It does not include detached elements of the command such as advance guards, flank guards, and covering forces. (MCRP 5-12C)

main effort—The designated subordinate unit whose mission at a given point in time is most critical to overall mission success. It is usually weighted with the preponderance of combat power and is directed against a center of gravity through a critical vulnerability. (MCRP 5-12C)

major operation—A series of tactical actions (battles, engagements, strikes) conducted by combat forces of a single or several Services, coordinated in time and place, to achieve strategic or operational objectives in an operational area. These actions are conducted simultaneously or sequentially in accordance with a common plan and are controlled by a single commander. For noncombat operations, a reference to the relative size and scope of a military operation. (JP 1-02)

maneuver—4. Employment of forces in the operational area through movement in combination with fires to achieve a position of advantage in respect to the enemy in order to accomplish the mission. (JP 1-02, part 4 of a 4 part definition) The movement of forces for the purpose of gaining an advantage over the enemy. Maneuver is one of the six warfighting functions. (MCRP 5-12C)

maneuver warfare—A warfighting philosophy that seeks to shatter the enemy's cohesion through a variety of rapid, focused, and unexpected actions that create a turbulent and rapidly deteriorating situation with which the enemy cannot cope. (MCRP 5-12C)

Marine air-ground task force—The Marine Corps' principal organization for missions across a range of military operations, composed of forces task-organized under a single commander capable of responding rapidly to a contingency anywhere in the world. The types of forces in the Marine air-ground task force (MAGTF) are functionally grouped into four core elements: a command element, an aviation combat element, a ground combat element, and a logistics combat element. The four core elements are categories of forces, not formal commands. The basic structure of the MAGTF never varies, though the number, size, and type of Marine Corps units comprising each of its four elements will always be mission dependent. The flexibility of the organizational structure allows for one or more subordinate MAGTFs to be assigned. In a joint or multinational environment, other Service or multinational forces may be assigned or attached. Also called **MAGTF**. (MCRP 5-12C)

Marine Corps forces—All Marine Corps combat, combat support, and combat service support units. These forces are normally task-organized as Marine air-ground task forces or as a Service component under joint force command. Also called **MARFOR**. Note: The Marine Corps forces are formally identified as Fleet Marine Forces in Title 10. (Proposed for inclusion in the next edition of MCRP 5-12C.)

Marine Corps operating forces—The Marine Corps forces (formally identified as Fleet Marine Forces in Title 10), the Marine Corps Reserve, Marine Corps security forces at Navy shore activities, Marine Corps special activity forces, and Marine Corps combat forces not otherwise assigned. (Proposed for inclusion in the next edition of MCRP 5-12C.)

Marine expeditionary brigade—A Marine air-ground task force (MAGTF) that is constructed around ana reinforced infantry regiment reinforced, a composite Marine aircraft group, and a combat logistics regiment. The Marine expeditionary brigade (MEB), commanded by a general officer, is task-organized to meet the requirements of a specific situation. It can function as part of a joint task force, or as the lead echelon of the Marine expeditionary force (MEF), or alone. It varies in size and composition, and is larger than a Marine expeditionary unit but smaller than a MEF. The MEB is capable of conducting missions across a range of military operations. In a joint or multinational environment, it may also contain other Service or multinational forces assigned or attached to the MAGTF. Also called **MEB**. (MCRP 5-12C)

Marine expeditionary force—The largest Marine air-ground task force (MAGTF) and the Marine Corps' principal warfighting organization, particularly for larger crises or contingencies. It is task-organized around a permanent command element and normally contains one or more Marine divisions, Marine aircraft wings, and Marine logistics groups. The Marine expeditionary force is capable of missions across a range of military operations, including amphibious assault and sustained operations ashore in any environment. It can operate from a sea base, a land base, or both. In a joint or multinational environment, it may also contain other Service or multinational forces assigned or attached to the MAGTF. Also called **MEF**. (MCRP 5-12C)

Marine expeditionary force (Forward)—A designated lead echelon of a Marine expeditionary force (MEF), task-organized to meet the requirements of a specific situation. A Marine expeditionary force (Forward) varies in size and composition, and it may be commanded by the MEF commander personally or by another designated commander. It may be tasked with preparing for the subsequent arrival of the rest of the MEF/joint/multinational forces, and/or the conduct of other specified tasks, at the discretion of the MEF commander. A Marine expeditionary force (Forward) may also be a stand-alone Marine air-ground task force (MAGTF), task-organized for a mission in which a MEF is not required. In a joint or multinational environment, it may also contain other Service or multinational forces assigned or attached to the MAGTF. Also called **MEF** (Fwd).

Marine expeditionary unit—A Marine air-ground task force (MAGTF) that is constructed around an infantry battalion reinforced, a composite squadron reinforced, and a task-organized logistics combat element. It normally fulfills Marine Corps' forward sea-based deployment requirements. The Marine expeditionary unit provides an immediate reaction capability for crisis response and is capable of limited combat operations. In a joint or multinational environment, it may contain other Service or multinational forces assigned or attached to the MAGTF. Also called **MEU**. (MCRP 5-12C)

Marine logistics group—The logistics combat element (LCE) of the Marine expeditionary force (MEF). It is a permanently organized command tasked with providing combat service support beyond the organic capabilities of supported units of the MEF. The Marine logistics group (MLG) is normally structured with direct and general support units, which are organized to support a MEF possessing one Marine division and one Marine aircraft wing. The MLG may also provide smaller task-organized LCEs to support Marine air-ground task forces smaller than a MEF. Also called **MLG**. (MCRP 5-12C)

maritime interception operations—Efforts to monitor, query, and board merchant vessels in international waters to enforce sanctions against other nations such as those in support of United Nations Security Council Resolutions and/or prevent the transport of restricted goods. Also called **MIO**. (JP 1-02)

maritime prepositioning force—A task organization of units under one commander formed for the purpose of introducing a Marine air-ground task force (MAGTF) and its associated equipment and supplies into a secure area. The maritime prepositioning force is composed of a command element, a maritime prepositioning ships squadron, a MAGTF, and a Navy support element. Also called **MPF**. (MCRP 5-12C)

maritime prepositioning ships squadron—A group of civilian-owned and civilian-crewed ships chartered by Military Sealift Command loaded with prepositioned equipment and 30 days of supplies to support up to a maritime prepositioning force Marine air-ground task force. Also called **MPSRON**. (MCRP 5-12C)

measure of effectiveness—A criterion used to assess changes in system behavior, capability, or operational environment that is tied to measuring the attainment of an end state, achievement of an objective, or creation of an effect. Also called **MOE**. (JP 1-02)

measure of performance—A criterion used to assess friendly actions that is tied to measuring task accomplishment. Also called **MOP**. (JP 1-02)

military engagement—Routine contact and interaction between individuals or elements of the Armed Forces of the United States and those of another nation's armed forces, or foreign and domestic civilian authorities or agencies to build trust and confidence, share information, coordinate mutual activities, and maintain influence. (JP 1-02)

mission—1. The task, together with the purpose, that clearly indicates the action to be taken and the reason therefore. 2. In common usage, especially when applied to lower military units, a duty assigned to an individual or unit; a task. 3. The dispatching of one or more aircraft to accomplish one particular task. (JP 1-02) Tasks assigned by the President to the combatant commanders in the Unified Command Plan. (MCRP 5-12C)

mission type order—1. An order issued to a lower unit that includes the accomplishment of the total mission assigned to the higher headquarters. 2. An order to a unit to perform a mission without specifying how it is to be accomplished. (JP 1-02)

mobile defense—Defense of an area or position in which maneuver is used with organization of fire and utilization of terrain to seize the initiative from the enemy. (Proposed for inclusion in the next edition of MCRP 5-12C.)

movement phase—In amphibious operations, the period during which various elements of the amphibious force move from points of embarkation to the operational area. This move may be via rehearsal, staging, or rendezvous areas. The movement phase is completed when the various elements of the amphibious force arrive at their assigned positions in the operational area. (JP 1-02)

movement to contact—A form of the offense designed to develop the situation and to establish or regain contact. (JP 1-02)

multinational operations—A collective term to describe military actions conducted by forces of two or more nations, usually undertaken within the structure of a coalition or alliance. (JP 1-02)

mutual support—That support which units render each other against an enemy, because of their assigned tasks, their position relative to each other and to the enemy, and their inherent capabilities. (JP 1-02)

noncombatant—1. An individual in an area of combat operations who is not armed and is not participating in any activity in support of any of the factions or forces involved in combat. 2. An individual, such as chaplain or medical personnel, whose duties do not involve combat. (MCRP 5-12C)

noncombatant evacuation operations—Operations directed by the Department of State or other appropriate authority, in conjunction with the Department of Defense, whereby noncombatants are evacuated from foreign countries when their lives are endangered by war, civil unrest, or natural disaster to safe havens as designated by the Department of State. Also called **NEOs**. (JP 1-02)

noncontiguous area of operations—An area of operations where one or more of the commander's subordinate forces' area of operations do not share a common boundary. (MCRP 5-12A)

objective area—A defined geographical area within which is located an objective to be captured or reached by the military forces. This area is defined by competent authority for purposes of command and control. Also called **OA**. (JP 1-02)

obstacle—Any obstruction designed or employed to disrupt, fix, turn, or block the movement of an opposing force, and to impose additional losses in personnel, time, and equipment on the opposing force. Obstacles can exist naturally or can be man-made, or can be a combination of both. (JP 1-02)

offensive air support—Those air operations conducted against enemy installations, facilities, and personnel to directly assist the attainment of MAGTF objectives by the destruction of enemy resources or the isolation of the enemy's military forces. Offensive air support is one of the six functions of Marine aviation. (MCRP 5-12C)

offensive operations—Operations conducted to take the initiative from the enemy, gain freedom of action, and generate effects to achieve objectives. The four types of offensive operations are movement to contact, attack, exploitation, and pursuit. (MCRP 5-12C)

operational area—An overarching term encompassing more descriptive terms for geographic areas in which military operations are conducted. Operational areas include, but are not limited to, such descriptors as area of responsibility, theater of war, theater of operations, joint operations area, amphibious objective area, joint special operations area, and area of operations. Also called **OA**. (JP 1-02)

operational control—Command authority that may be exercised by commanders at any echelon at or below the level of combatant command. Operational control is inherent in combatant command (command authority) and may be delegated within the command. Operational control is the authority to perform those functions of command over subordinate forces involving organizing and employing commands and forces, assigning tasks, designating objectives, and giving authoritative direction necessary to accomplish the mission. Operational control includes authoritative direction necessary to accomplish the mission. Operational control includes authoritative direction over all aspects of military operations and joint training necessary to accomplish missions assigned to the command. Operational control should be exercised through the commanders of subordinate organizations. Normally this authority is exercised through subordinate joint force commanders and Service and/or functional component commanders. Operational control normally provides full authority to organize commands and forces and to employ those forces as the commander in operational control considers necessary to accomplish assigned missions; it does not, in and of itself, include authoritative direction for logistics or matters of administration, discipline, internal organization, or unit training. Also called **OPCON**. (JP 1-02)

operational environment—A composite of the conditions, circumstances, and influences that affect the employment of capabilities and bear on the decisions of the commander. Also called **OE**. (JP 1-02)

operational level of war—The level of war at which campaigns and major operations are planned, conducted, and sustained to achieve strategic objectives within theaters or other operational areas. Activities at this level link tactics and strategy by establishing operational objectives needed to achieve the strategic objectives, sequencing events to achieve the operational objectives, initiating actions, and applying resources to bring about and sustain these events. (JP 1-02)

operational logistics—The art of applying the military resources available to operating forces to achieve national military objectives in a theater or area of operations or to facilitate the accomplishment of assigned missions in a military region, theater, or campaign. At the operational level of war, logistics involves fundamental decisions concerning force deployment and sustainability functions in terms of identifying military requirements, establishing priorities, and determining allocations necessary to implement the commander's concept. (MCRP 5-12C)

operational reach—The distance and duration across which a unit can successfully employ military capabilities. (JP 1-02)

order of battle—The identification, strength, command structure, and disposition of the personnel, units, and equipment of any military force. Also called **OB; OOB**. (JP 1-02)

passage of lines—An operation in which a force moves forward or rearward through another force's combat positions with the intention of moving into or out of contact with the enemy. A passage may be designated as a forward or rearward passage of lines. (JP 1-02)

peace operations—A broad term that encompasses multiagency and multinational crisis response and limited contingency operations involving all instruments of national power with military missions to contain conflict, redress the peace, and shape the environment to support reconciliation and rebuilding and facilitate the transition to legitimate governance. Peace operations include peacekeeping, peace enforcement, peacemaking, peace building, and conflict prevention efforts. Also called **PO**. (JP 1-02)

penetration—A form of maneuver in which an attacking force seeks to rupture enemy defenses on a narrow front to disrupt the defensive system. (Proposed for inclusion in the next edition of MCRP 5-12C.)

permissive environment—Operational environment in which host country military and law enforcement agencies have control as well as the intent and capability to assist operations a unit intends to conduct. (JP 1-02)

planning phase—In amphibious operations, the phase normally denoted by the period extending from the issuance of the initiating directive up to the embarkation phase. The planning phase may occur during movement or at any other time upon receipt of a new mission or change in the operational situation. (JP 1-02)

power projection—The application of measured, precise offensive military force at a chosen time and place, using maneuver and combined arms against enemy forces. (MCRP 5-12C)

principles of war—The most important nonphysical factors that affect the conduct of operations at the strategic, operational, and tactical levels. The nine principles of war are mass, objective, offensive, security, economy of force, maneuver, unity of command, surprise, and simplicity (Proposed for inclusion in the next edition of MCRP 5-12C)

procedures—Standard, detailed steps that prescribe how to perform specific tasks. (JP 1-02)

pursuit—An offensive operation designed to catch or cut off a hostile force attempting to escape, with the aim of destroying it. (Proposed for inclusion in the next edition of MCRP 5-12C.)

raid—An attack, usually small scale, involving a penetration of hostile territory for a specific purpose other than seizing and holding terrain. It ends with a planned withdrawal upon completion of the assigned mission. (Proposed for inclusion in the next edition of MCRP 5-12C.)

rear area—That area extending forward from a command's rear boundary to the rear of the area assigned to the command's subordinate units. This area is provided primarily for the performance of combat service support functions. (Proposed for inclusion in the next edition of MCRP 5-12C.)

rear guard—1. The rearmost elements of an advancing or a withdrawing force. It has the following functions: to protect the rear of a column from hostile forces; during the withdrawal, to delay the enemy; during the advance, to keep supply routes open. 2. Security detachment that a moving ground force details to the rear to keep it informed and covered. (Proposed for inclusion in the next edition of MCRP 5-12C.)

rear operations—Military actions conducted to support and permit force sustainment and to provide security for such actions. (MCRP 5-12C)

reconnaissance—A mission undertaken to obtain, by visual observation or other detection methods, information about the activities and resources of an enemy or adversary, or to secure data concerning the meteorological, hydrographic, or geographic characteristics of a particular area. Also called **RECON**. (JP 1-02)

reconnaissance in force—A deliberate attack made to obtain information and to locate and test enemy dispositions, strengths, and reactions. It is used when knowledge of the enemy is vague and there is insufficient time or resources to develop the situation. (Proposed for inclusion in the next edition of MCRP 5-12C.)

reconstitution—1. Those actions that commanders plan and implement to restore units to a desired level of combat effectiveness commensurate with mission requirements and available resources. Reconstitution operations include regeneration and reorganization. 2. In maritime prepositioning force operations, the methodical approach to restore the maritime prepositioned equipment and supplies aboard the maritime prepositioning ships squadron to full mission capable status. (MCRP 5-12C)

redeployment—The transfer of forces and materiel to support another joint force commander's operational requirements, or to return personnel, equipment, and materiel to the home and/or demobilization stations for reintegration and/or out-processing. (JP 1-02)

regeneration—Significant replacement of personnel, equipment, and supplies in an attempt to restore a unit to full operational capability as rapidly as possible. (Proposed for inclusion in the next edition of MCRP 5-12C.)

rehearsal phase—In amphibious operations, the period during which the prospective operation is practiced for the purpose of: (1) testing adequacy of plans, the timing of detailed operations, and the combat readiness of participating forces; (2) ensuring that all echelons are familiar with plans; and (3) testing communications-information systems. (JP 1-02)

relief in place—An operation in which, by direction of higher authority, all or part of a unit is replaced in an area by the incoming unit. The responsibilities of the replaced elements for the mission and the assigned zone of operations are transferred to the incoming unit. The incoming unit continues the operation as ordered. (JP 1-02)

reorganization—Action taken to shift internal resources within a degraded unit to increase its level of combat effectiveness. (Proposed for inclusion in the next edition of MCRP 5-12C.)

reserve—1. Portion of a body of troops that is kept to the rear, or withheld from action at the beginning of an engagement, in order to be available for a decisive movement. 2. Members of the Military Services who are not in active service but who are subject to call to active duty. (JP 1-02, parts 1 and 2 of a 3-part definition)

retirement—An operation in which a force out of contact moves away from the enemy. (Proposed for inclusion in the next edition of MCRP 5-12C.)

retrograde—Any movement or maneuver of a command to the rear, or away from the enemy. (MCRP 5-12C)

river crossing—A type of gap crossing operation required before ground combat power can be projected and sustained across a water obstacle. It is a centrally planned and controlled offensive operation that requires the allocation of external crossing means and a force dedicated to the security of the bridgehead. (MCRP 5-12C)

role—The broad, enduring purposes for which the Services and the United States Special Operations Command were established forced by Congress in Title 10, United States Code. (MCRP 5-12C)

route reconnaissance—A directed effort to obtain detailed information of a specified route and all terrain from which the enemy could influence movement along that route. (MCRP 5-12C)

rules of engagement—Directives issued by competent military authority that delineate the circumstances and limitations under which United States forces will initiate and /or continue combat engagement with other forces encountered. Also called **ROE**. (JP 1-02)

scheme of maneuver—Description of how arrayed forces will accomplish the commander's intent. It is the central expression of the commander's concept for operations and governs the design of supporting plans or annexes. (JP 1-02)

screen—1. A security element whose primary task is to observe, identify, and report information, and only fight in self-protection. 2. A form of security operation that primarily provides early warning to the protected force. (Proposed for inclusion in the next edition of MCRP 5-12C.)

seabasing—The deployment, assembly, command projection, reconstitution, and reemployment of joint power from the sea without reliance on land bases within the operational area. (JP 1-02)

sector—An area designated by boundaries within which a unit operates, and for which it is responsible. (Proposed for inclusion in the next edition of MCRP 5-12C.)

security area—The area that begins at the forward edge of the battle area and extends as far to the front and flanks as security forces are deployed, normally to the forward boundary of the area of operations. Forces in the security area conduct reconnaissance to furnish information on the enemy and to delay, deceive, and disrupt the enemy. (Proposed for inclusion in the next edition of MCRP 5-12C.)

security cooperation—All Department of Defense interactions with foreign defense establishments to build defense relationships that promote specific US security interests, develop allied and friendly military capabilities for self-defense and multinational operations, and provide US forces with peacetime and contingency access to a host nation. Also called **SC**. (JP 1-02)

security force—The detachment deployed between the main body and the enemy (to the front, flanks, or rear of the main body) tasked with the protection of the main body. The security force may be assigned a screening, guarding, or covering mission. (MCRP 5-12C)

Service component command—A command consisting of the Service component commander and all those Service forces, such as individuals, units, detachments, organizations, and installations under that command, including the support forces that have been assigned to a combatant command or further assigned to a subordinate unified command or joint task force. (JP 1-02)

shaping—The use of lethal and nonlethal activities to influence events in a manner that changes the general condition of war to an advantage. (MCRP 5-12C)

show of force—An operation designed to demonstrate US resolve that involves increased visibility of US deployed forces in an attempt to defuse a specific situation that, if allowed to continue, may be detrimental to US interests or national objectives. (JP 1-02)

situational awareness—Knowledge and understanding of the current situation that promotes timely, relevant, and accurate assessment of friendly, enemy, and other operations within the battlespace in order to facilitate decisionmaking. An informational perspective and skill that foster an ability to determine quickly the context and relevance of events that are unfolding. (MCRP 5-12C)

situational understanding—The product of applying analysis and synthesis to relevant information to determine the relationship among the mission, enemy, terrain and weather, troops and support available—time available variables to facilitate decisionmaking. (Proposed for inclusion in the next edition of MCRP 5-12C.)

special operations forces—Those Active and Reserve Component forces of the Military Services designated by the Secretary of Defense and specifically organized, trained, and equipped to conduct and support special operations. Also called **SOF**. (JP 1-02)

special purpose Marine air-ground task force—A Marine air-ground task force (MAGTF) organized, trained, and equipped with narrowly focused capabilities. It is designed to accomplish a specific mission, often of limited scope and duration. It may be any size, but normally it is a relatively small force—the size of a Marine expeditionary unit or smaller. In a joint or multinational environment, it may contain other Service or multinational forces assigned or attached to the MAGTF. Also called **SPMAGTF**. (MCRP 5-12C)

spoiling attack—A tactical maneuver employed to seriously impair a hostile attack while the enemy is in the process of forming or assembling for an attack. Usually employed by armored units in defense by an attack on enemy assembly positions in front of a main line of resistance or battle position. (JP 1-02)

stability operations—An overarching term encompassing various military missions, tasks, and activities conducted outside the United States in coordination with other instruments of national power to maintain or reestablish a safe and secure environment, provide essential governmental services, emergency infrastructure reconstruction, and humanitarian relief. (JP 1-02)

standing operating procedure—A set of instructions covering those features of operations that lend themselves to a definite or standardized procedure without loss of effectiveness. The procedure is applicable unless ordered otherwise. (Proposed for inclusion in the next edition of MCRP 5-12C.)

strategic level of war—The level of war at which a nation, often as a member of a group of nations, determines national or multinational (alliance or coalition) strategic security objectives and guidance, and develops and uses national resources to achieve these objectives. Activities at this level establish national and multinational military objectives; sequence initiatives; define limits and assess risks for the use of military and other instruments of national power; develop global plans or theater war plans to achieve those objectives; and provide military forces and other capabilities in accordance with strategic plans. (JP 1-02)

strategic mobility—The capability to deploy and sustain military forces worldwide in support of national strategy. (JP 1-02)

strike—An attack to damage or destroy an objective or a capability. (JP 1-02)

strong point—A key point in a defensive position, usually strongly fortified and heavily armed with automatic weapons, around which other positions are grouped for its protection. (Proposed for inclusion in the next edition of MCRP 5-12C.)

support—1. The action of a force that aids, protects, complements, or sustains another force in accordance with a directive requiring such action. 2. A unit that helps another unit in battle. 3. An element of a command that assists, protects, or supplies other forces in combat. (JP 1-02)

supported commander—1. The commander having primary responsibility for all aspects of a task assigned by the Joint Strategic Capabilities Plan or other joint operation planning authority. In the context of joint operation planning, this term refers to the commander who prepares operation plans or operation orders in response to requirements of the Chairman of the Joint Chiefs of Staff. 2. In the context of a support command relationship, the commander who receives assistance from another commander's force or capabilities, and who is responsible for ensuring that the supporting commander understands the assistance required. (JP 1-02)

supporting commander—1. A commander who provides augmentation forces or other support to a supported commander or who develops a supporting plan. This includes the designated combatant commands and Department of Defense agencies as appropriate. 2. In the context of a support command relationship, the commander who aids, protects, complements, or sustains another commander's force, and who is responsible for providing the assistance required by the supported commander. (JP 1-02)

supporting effort—Designated subordinate unit(s) whose mission is designed to directly contribute to the success of the main effort. (MCRP 5-12C)

supporting establishment—Those personnel, bases, and activities that support the Marine Corps operating forces. (Proposed for inclusion in the next edition of MCRP 5-12C.)

surveillance—The systematic visual or aural observation of an enemy force or named area of interest or an area and the activities in it to collect intelligence required to confirm or deny adversary courses of action or identify adversary critical vulnerabilities and limitations. (Proposed for inclusion in the next edition of MCRP 5-12C)

sustained operations ashore—The employment of Marine Corps forces on land for an extended duration. It can occur with or without sustainment from the sea. Also called **SOA**. (MCRP 5-12C)

sustainment—The provision of logistics and personnel services required to maintain and prolong operations until successful mission accomplishment. (JP 1-02)

tactical combat force—A combat unit, with appropriate combat support and combat service support assets, that is assigned the mission of defeating Level III threats. Also called **TCF**. (JP 1-02)

tactical control—Command authority over assigned or attached forces or commands, or military capability or forces made available for tasking, that is limited to the detailed direction and control of movements or maneuvers within the operational area necessary to accomplish missions or tasks assigned. Tactical control is inherent in operational control. Tactical control may be delegated to, and exercised at any level at or below the level of combatant command. Tactical control provides sufficient authority for controlling and directing the application of force or tactical use of combat support assets within the assigned mission or task. Also called **TACON**. (JP 1-02)

tactical level of war—The level of war at which battles and engagements are planned and executed to achieve military objectives assigned to tactical units or task forces. Activities at this level focus on the ordered arrangement and maneuver of combat elements in relation to each other and to the enemy to achieve combat objectives. (JP 1-02)

tactical logistics—The art of sustaining forces in combat. At the tactical level of war, logistics involves the performance of supply, maintenance, transportation, health services, general engineering, and other services with resources immediately or imminently available. Tactical logistics draws upon resources made available at the operational level and focuses on the provision of support within the force. (Proposed for inclusion in the next edition of MCRP 5-12C.)

tactics—The employment and ordered arrangement of forces in relation to each other. (JP 1-02)

techniques—Non-prescriptive ways or methods used to perform missions, functions, or tasks. (JP 1-02)

tempo—The relative speed and rhythm of military operations over time with respect to the enemy. (MCRP 5-12C)

turning movement—A variation of the envelopment in which the attacking force passes around or over the enemy's principal defensive positions to secure objectives deep in the enemy's rear to force the enemy to abandon his position or divert major forces to meet the threat. (JP 1-02)

uncertain environment—Operational environment in which host government forces, whether opposed to or receptive to operations that a unit intends to conduct, do not have totally effective control of the territory and population in the intended operational area. (JP 1-02)

unified action—The synchronization, coordination, and/or integration of the activities of governmental and nongovernmental entities with military operations to achieve unity of effort. (JP 1-02)

unity of effort—Coordination and cooperation toward common objectives, even if the participants are not necessarily part of the same command or organization - the product of successful unified action. (JP 1-02)

unmanned aircraft system—That system whose components include the necessary equipment, network, and personnel to control an unmanned aircraft. Also called **UAS**. (JP 1-02)

vertical envelopment—A tactical maneuver in which troops, either air-dropped or air-landed, attack the rear and flanks of a force, in effect cutting off or encircling the force. (JP 1-02)

warfighting functions—The six mutually supporting military activities integrated in the conduct of all military operations (command and control, fires, force protection, intelligence, logistics, and maneuver. (MCRP 5-12C)

withdrawal operation—A planned retrograde operation in which a force in contact disengages from an enemy force and moves in a direction away from the enemy. (JP 1-02)

zone of action—A tactical subdivision of a larger area, the responsibility for which is assigned to a tactical unit; generally applied to offensive action. (JP 1-02)

zone reconnaissance—A directed effort to obtain detailed information concerning all routes, obstacles (to include chemical or radiological contamination), terrain, and enemy forces within a zone defined by boundaries. A zone reconnaissance normally is assigned when the enemy situation is vague or when information concerning cross-country trafficability is desired. (MCRP 5-12C)

References

Federal Statutory Laws

Executive Order 12656, *Assignment of Emergency Preparedness Responsibilities*

Public Law 82-416, *Douglas-Mansfield Act of 1952.*

Public Law 99-433, *Goldwater-Nichols, Department of Defense Reorganization Act of 1986*

United States Code, Title 10, *Armed Forces*

United States Code, Title 18, *Crimes and Criminal Procedure*

United States Code, Title 22, *Foreign Relations and Intercourse*

United States Code, Title 50, *War and National Defense*

Strategic Guidance and Policies

National Security Strategy

National Strategy for Homeland Security

Unified Command Plan

Secretary of Defense Publications

National Defense Strategy

<u>Secretary of Defense Memoranda</u>

Establishment of a Subordinate Unified U.S. Cyber Command Under U.S. Strategic Command for Military Cyberspace Operations

Global Force Management Implement Guidance (GFMIG)

Defense Planning and Programming Guidance (Publication is classified SECRET/NOFORN)

Guidance for Employment of the Force (GEF) (Publication is classified SECRET/LIMDIS)

Department of Defense Directive (DODD)

3000.05   *Military Support for Stability, Security, Transition, and Reconstruction (SSIR) Operations*

5100.1   *Functions of the Department of Defense and Its Major Components*

Department of Defense Instruction (DODI)

3000.05   *Stability Operations*

Chairman of the Joint Chiefs of Staff Publications

Joint Strategic Capabilities Plan

The National Military Strategy of the United States of America

Chairman of the Joint Chiefs of Staff Manual (CJCSM)

3122.01_   *Joint Operation Planning and Execution System, (JOPES)*, Volume I, (Planning Policies and Procedures)

Joint Publications (JPs)

1	*Doctrine for the Armed Forces of the United States*
1-02	*Department of Defense Dictionary of Military and Associated Terms*
3-0	*Joint Operations*
3-02	*Joint Doctrine for Amphibious Operations*
3-10	*Joint Security Operations in Theater*
3-60	*Joint Targeting*
4-0	*Joint Logistics*
4-01	*Joint Doctrine for the Defense Transportation System*
4-09	*Distribution Operations*
5-0	*Joint Operation Planning*

Marine Corps Publications

Marine Corps Doctrinal Publications (MCDPs)

1	*Warfighting*
1-1	*Strategy*
1-2	*Campaigning*
1-3	*Tactics*
2	*Intelligence*
3	*Expeditionary Operations*
4	*Logistics*
5	*Planning*
6	*Command and Control*

Marine Corps Warfighting Publications (MCWPs)

3-1	*Ground Combat Operations*
3-33.5	*Counterinsurgency*
3-40.8	*Componency*
3-43.3	*Marine Air-Ground Task Force Fires*
4-1	*Logistics Operations*
5-1	*Marine Corps Planning Process*

Marine Corps Reference (MCRPs)

5-12A	*Operational Terms and Graphics*
5-12C	*Marine Corps Supplement to the Department of Defense Dictionary of Military and Associated Terms*

Fleet Marine Force Reference Publications (FMFRP)

12-15	*Small Wars Manual*

Marine Corps Orders (MCOs)

3120.3	*The Organization of Marine Air-Ground Tasks Forces*

3120.9 _Policy for Marine Expeditionary Unit (Special Operations Capable) (MEU[SOC])_

4470.1 _Marine Air-Ground Task Force (MAGTF) Deployment and Distribution Policy (MDDP)_

Other Marine Corps Publications

Marine Corps Manual

Marine Corps Vision and Strategy 2025

Commandant's Planning Guidance

Navy Publications

Secretary of the Navy Instruction 4000.37, _Naval Logistics Integration (NLI)_

Naval Operations Concept 2010

Miscellaneous Publications and Citations

Charter of the United Nations

Clancy, Tom, Zinni, General Tony (Retired), and Koltz, Tony, _Battle Ready_ (New York, NY: G.P. Putnam's Sons, 2004)

Clausewitz, Carl Von, _On War_ (Princeton, NJ: Princeton University Press, 1976)

Congressional Testimony of General Colin Powell, US Army, 14 March 1990

Department of State. _Guiding Principles for Stabilization and Reconstruction_

Gallula, David, _Counterinsurgency Warfare_, (Westport, CT: Frederick A. Praeger, Inc., 1964)

Hart, Sir Basil H. Liddel, _Deterrent of Defense: A Fresh Look at the West's Military Position_ (New York: Frederick A. Praeger, 1960)

Heinl, Robert Debs, Jr., Col., USMC, Retired, _Dictionary of Military and Naval Quotations_ (Annapolis, MD: United States Naval Institute, 1966)

Heinl, Robert Debs, Jr., Col., USMC, Retired, _Soldiers of the Sea_ (Baltimore, MD: The Nautical & Aviation Publishing Company of America, 1991)

Kaplan, Robert D., _Imperial Grunts_, (New York, NY: Random House, 2005)

Kelly, Brigadier General John F., USMC, "Tikrit, South to Babylon," *Marine Corps Gazette*, March 2004

Smith, Holland M., USMC, Retired, and Finch, Percy, *Coral and Brass* (Nashville, TN: The Battery Press, 1989

Thorpe, George C., *Pure Logistics: The Science of War Preparation* (Newport, RI: Naval War College Press, 1997)

Tsouras, Peter G., *Warriors' Words: A Quotation Book: from Sesostris III to Schwarzkopf, 1871 BC to AD 1991* (London, England: Arms and Armour Press, 1992)

Made in the USA
Middletown, DE
13 August 2019